AF291579

HITLER'S WAR AGAINST THE FRENCH RESISTANCE 1940-1944

HITLER'S WAR AGAINST THE FRENCH RESISTANCE 1940-1944

DR. ANTONIO J. MUÑOZ

First published in Great Britain in 2026
by Frontline Books
An imprint of
Pen & Sword Books Ltd
Yorkshire - Philadelphia
Copyright © Dr. Antonio J. Muñoz
ISBN 9781036190132

Typeset by Lapiz Digital
Printed and bound in the UK by CPI Group (UK) Ltd,
Croydon, CR0 4YY.

Printed on paper from a sustainable source by
CPI Group (UK) Ltd, Croydon, CR0 4YY

Pen & Sword Books Limited incorporates the imprints of
Archaeology, Atlas, Aviation, Battleground, Digital, Discovery, Family History, Fiction, History, Local, Local History, Maritime, Military, Military Classics, Politics, Select, Transport, True Crime, Air World, Claymore Press, Frontline Publishing, Leo Cooper, Remember When, Seaforth Publishing, The Praetorian Press, Wharncliffe Books, Wharncliffe Local History, Wharncliffe Transport, Wharncliffe True Crime and White Owl.

For a complete list of Pen & Sword titles please contact
PEN & SWORD BOOKS LTD
47 Church Street, Barnsley, South Yorkshire, S70 2AS, England
E-mail: enquiries@pen-and-sword.co.uk
Website: www.pen-and-sword.co.uk
or
PEN & SWORD BOOKS
1950 Lawrence Rd, Havertown, PA 19083, USA
E-mail: uspen-and-sword@casematepublishers.com

DEDICATION

To the French people, brave in battle, brave in defeat

CONTENTS

LIST OF FIGURES, MAPS AND TABLES

Figures

Tables

AUTHOR'S NOTE

The history of the German occupation of France and the subsequent rise of the French Resistance has, I believe, been underrated by many historians as to its importance in helping to hurt the German war machine and to make the Allied invasion of France all the easier to launch. Compared to the other Nazi-occupied Western nations, the intensity of the partisan and anti-partisan struggle in France during the German occupation was significantly higher, and as a result, the number of French losses proved commensurate. During the German occupation, hostages were often taken and executed by the Nazis in retaliation for attacks or sabotage carried out by the Resistance. These hostages included French civilians, Jewish individuals, communists, freemasons, and foreign nationals, especially those from occupied or enemy nations – e.g., Spanish Republicans, Eastern Europeans, and many Jewish foreigners from all across Europe.

During the German occupation between 1940 and 1944, approximately 4,500 to 5,000 hostages were executed in France in reprisal killings instituted by the Germans. One of the most infamous examples is the Châteaubriant executions in 1941, where twenty-seven hostages (including the communist Guy Môquet) were shot.

The *Maquis* were rural guerrilla bands of Resistance fighters that were organised all over France. They became increasingly active, especially after the German occupation of the southern zone of France in November 1942 and leading up to the Normandy invasion on 6 June 1944. Historical estimates as to how many *Maquisards* were killed by German forces during the occupation varies somewhat, but most scholars agree that roughly 20,000 Resistance fighters were killed during the occupation. This figure includes those killed in combat, like German or Resistance ambushes and battles, assassination attempts, German raids on suspected Resistance hideouts, etc. It also includes those French Resistance fighters who were executed after capture. The number also takes into account those partisans who died under torture or were deported to concentration camps. For example, during the repression of the *Maquis du Vercors* in July 1944, hundreds of *Maquisards* were killed in what turned out to be the most brutal German anti-partisan operation on French soil during the war.

As far as German losses due to Resistance activity, the accepted figure is somewhere between 24,000–25,000 Germans killed. These deaths generally occurred through assassinations, ambushes, raids and sabotage operations carried out between 1940 and 1944. As far as assassinations are concerned, those specifically targeted included individual *Wehrmacht* officers, NCOs and enlisted men or collaborators – e.g., *Gestapo* agents, or members of the security services: the *Sicherheitsdienst, Sicherheitspolizei, Kriminalpolizei, Ordnungspolizei*, or SS. These assassinations numbered in the hundreds. As for ambushes and raids, many *Maquis* groups located in rural parts of France, like in the region of Vercors, Limousin, and Cévennes, ambushed small German patrols and convoys whenever they could. These ambushes weren't just to kill Germans, but to capture weapons and to disrupt German operations and control of the country. These actions intensified after 1943 and peaked in 1944 (especially after the Allied landings).[1] Attacks on railways, bridges, and communication lines sometimes caused train derailments or explosions. Some German casualties occurred in these acts, though often fewer than in direct attacks. The historical estimate of German deaths from these kinds of Resistance activities appears to have been just a few hundred. Taking the above figures into account, the ratio of French Resistance fighters killed versus German losses taken is around 4:1.

The Germans had realised from the start of their occupation of France that resistance to their rule would be inevitable. With this in mind, they went about establishing control of France not only with the German Army occupation forces, but with the entire Nazi security apparatus. The German Army employed dozens of *Geheime Feldpolizei* (GFP, Secret Field Police) groups to perform all manner of security and counter-intelligence operations against the Resistance. Similarly, the *Sicherheitspolizei, Sicherheitsdienst, Kriminalpolizei, Geheimstaatspolizei* and *Ordnungspolizei* forces established station posts throughout occupied France to better control the population and to act as a counter to anti-German activities. Liaisons were established between the German security forces and the security apparatus of the Vichy French government.

Beginning in 1941 the Germans began to encounter more and more acts of resistance, which required not only intelligence and counter-intelligence work, but the systematic terrorisation of the general population by decreeing that for every act perpetrated against German interests, ten civilian hostages would be shot. This ratio soon increased in the autumn of 1941, as assassinations of German personnel continued. This murder ratio increased even more in November 1942, following the Allied landings in North Africa and the collapse of the Vichy French government. As the *Maquis* increased their sabotage and resistance activities, so too did the German repression of the French populace.

The Holocaust in France is important to cover in order to document how the Nazis targeted the Jewish population. It is also central, given that this was a planned part of Nazi rule, which worked in tandem with the overall repression in France and indirectly, in the fight against the Resistance. The deportations of the Jewish population living in France was coordinated by Nazi authorities, but with active collaboration by the Vichy regime and French police (notably in the Vel' d'Hiv Round-up of July 1942, which led to 13,000 arrests in two days). Roughly 250,000 Jews were living in France before the war. About 75 per cent of these Jews survived the Nazi occupation. This turned out to be one of the highest survival rates in Nazi-occupied Western Europe during the war. This happened largely thanks to the proactive hiding of Jews in mostly rural areas of the country. Help in this effort to save French Jewry came from the Catholic clergy, resistance networks, and ordinary citizens, especially in places like Le Chambon-sur-Lignon. All of these efforts were ultimately effective in also helping to save many Jewish lives.

Starting in 1943 and continuing into 1944, the German army as well as the Nazi security services launched several medium to large-scale anti-partisan operations against specific French guerrilla forces. Prior to 1943 the German command had been content with attempting to infiltrate the French resistance and to launch relatively small operations against the *Maquis*. By 1944 the guerrilla threat had become so rampant and pervasive, that the German command felt it necessary to create a special air force wing to support German anti-partisan drives, *Luftwaffe Geschwader Bongart*. This fighter-bomber force (which contained two 'Staffeln' or squadrons) was established in February 1944. Between February and October 1944 this air unit performed reconnaissance and combat missions against the partisans. The culmination of the Nazi terror campaign against the French occurred on 10 June 1944, with massacre of 642 men, women and children at Oradour-sur-Glane. The massacre had been perpetrated because the Resistance had killed a *Waffen-SS* soldier belonging to the *2. SS Panzer-Division 'Das Reich'* near the village.

In writing *Hitler's War Against the French Resistance, 1940-1944* I have attempted to describe the growth of French resistance to the German occupation as well as the German response and repression that followed. It is a succinct, though surprisingly detailed account of the struggle in France between the *Maquisards* and the occupation forces of the Third Reich.

INTRODUCTION

Between 1 September 1939 and 9 May 1940, despite the formal declarations of war by France and the United Kingdom following the German invasion of Poland, there was no significant land combat along the Franco-German border. This period, often referred to as the 'Phoney War' (*la drôle de guerre* in French, or *Sitzkrieg* in German), was marked by a conspicuous absence of ground hostilities. While the Royal Navy and the *Kriegsmarine* engaged actively in maritime warfare from the outset, the armies remained entrenched in defensive postures behind the respective lines, with France relying heavily on its formidable Maginot Line fortifications and a fixed belief in the superiority of static defence. From the German perspective, this strategic lull was by design. Adolf Hitler initially directed the *Wehrmacht*'s focus eastward toward Poland, and subsequently toward Scandinavia, with the invasions of Denmark and Norway in April 1940. Along the Western Front, Hitler issued strict orders to maintain a posture of non-aggression. In fact, German soldiers were encouraged to engage in fraternisation with their French counterparts across the border, exchanging cigarettes, food, and even alcohol, in an effort to foster complacency and mask the Reich's true intentions. This approach was both psychological and tactical: it served to reinforce French assumptions of German inertia while affording the *Wehrmacht* time to prepare its Blitzkrieg campaign in the West.

By contrast, French military inertia was rooted not only in strategic miscalculation but also in a deep psychological aversion to renewed war. Scarred by the trauma of the First World War, the French political and military leadership were reticent to initiate offensive operations, relying instead on a strategy of containment. The British Expeditionary Force (BEF), which began arriving in France in September 1939 and eventually reached a strength of nearly 400,000 troops, was deployed in the north to guard against a repeat of the German flanking manoeuvre through Belgium that had occurred in 1914. The illusion of a static front was shattered on 10 May 1940, when German forces launched their rapid and devastating assault on France and the Low Countries. Employing a concentrated armoured thrust through the Ardennes – a region the French General Staff had considered impassable to tanks – German panzer divisions bypassed the Maginot Line and encircled the Allied forces. By 14 June, Paris had been declared an open city and was occupied by German troops without resistance. The psychological impact of the capital's fall was immense. On 17 June, Marshal Philippe Pétain, a revered hero of the First World War, announced that France would seek an armistice.

Just five days later, on 22 June 1940, the French government formally signed the Armistice at Rethondes, in the very railway carriage where Germany had capitulated in 1918 – a potent symbol of reversed fortunes.[1] Even as Pétain's government prepared to collaborate with the Third Reich, one dissident voice rose in opposition. On 18 June 1940, from London, General Charles de Gaulle delivered a radio address via the BBC, calling on French soldiers, citizens, and colonial subjects to resist the armistice and continue the struggle. Though largely ignored at the time, de Gaulle's *Appel du 18 juin* would become one of the founding moments of the French Resistance. His Free French movement would go on to serve as both a military and symbolic counterweight to the Vichy regime. In the wake of the military collapse, over 1.8 million French soldiers were taken as prisoners of war and transported to Germany. The scale and rapidity of the defeat forced France into a deep national introspection. Two competing visions for France's future emerged: one centred on accommodation and collaboration under Pétain's Vichy regime, the other on continued resistance under de Gaulle. The Vichy regime, headquartered in the unoccupied southern zone of France, quickly established itself as the legitimate government of France – at least in the eyes of many French citizens and foreign powers. While it did not initially include fascists in its leadership, it was nonetheless ideologically conservative, authoritarian, and increasingly aligned with Nazi Germany.

One of Pétain's first actions was to pressure the National Assembly into granting him full executive powers, effectively ending the Third Republic. He subsequently implemented policies aimed at national regeneration through labour, hierarchy, and discipline – a programme dubbed the *Révolution nationale*. Internationally, Vichy France began aligning itself with the Axis powers, a relationship that would deepen through acts of cooperation such as the transfer of gold reserves and concessions of military infrastructure. The already precarious Franco-British relationship deteriorated further following the Royal Navy's controversial attack on the French fleet at Mers el-Kébir on 3 July 1940.

Fearing that the French ships could fall into German hands, Winston Churchill ordered their neutralisation. The resulting bombardment killed 1,297 French sailors, inflamed public opinion, and pushed many undecided French military officers and citizens into the Vichy camp. The operation was a tactical success but a strategic and moral catastrophe, casting doubt on British intentions and diminishing support for de Gaulle's call to arms.

As France settled uneasily into occupation and collaboration, the country was divided into multiple administrative zones. The German-occupied zone encompassed Paris and the economically vital northern and western regions.[2] The so-called 'free zone' under Vichy rule comprised the south and southwest, although it remained subject to German influence and pressure. In addition, Alsace and Lorraine were annexed *de facto* into the Reich, their populations subjected to forced Germanisation, and young men conscripted into the *Wehrmacht* – as exemplified by the case of Guy Sajer, an ethnic-German French citizen whose autobiographical work offers insight into this coerced complicity.[3] Despite Vichy's efforts to assert national sovereignty within its limited sphere, the regime entered into ever-deeper cooperation with the occupiers. A telling episode occurred in May 1941, when Admiral François Darlan negotiated with the German Armistice Commission to provide logistical and military support for anti-British operations in Iraq. In exchange for concessions on occupation costs and the promise of prisoner releases, Vichy agreed to facilitate German access to airfields in Syria and deliver arms to Iraqi insurgents.

This collaboration went far beyond passive accommodation and reveals the geopolitical aspirations of segments within Vichy's leadership. Amidst this complex political terrain, the first embers of resistance began to glow. Initially, the Resistance in France was fragmented, diverse, and largely improvisational. Comprising former soldiers, communists, Gaullists, monarchists, and anarchists, these groups were united only by a shared hostility toward occupation and collaboration. Many early resisters acted out of personal conviction rather than ideological coherence, engaging in small-scale sabotage, propaganda distribution, and intelligence-gathering. Charles de Gaulle's efforts to centralise the resistance bore fruit in 1941 with the appointment of Jean Moulin, who had been tasked with forging unity among the disparate movements. Moulin's success culminated in the formation of the *Conseil National de la Résistance* (CNR), a body that brought together major factions under a common political and strategic umbrella. The inclusion of the French Communist Party – previously neutral on orders from Moscow until Germany's invasion of the Soviet Union in June 1941 – marked a turning point in the scale and organisation of the Resistance.

Women played a vital, if often underappreciated, role in the French Resistance. Acting as couriers, intelligence agents, medical aides, saboteurs, and leaders, women such as Lucie Aubrac, Germaine Tillion, and Violette Szabo helped to maintain communication networks and coordinate clandestine operations. Their participation challenged both German expectations and traditional gender roles in wartime France. Women endured the same dangers as men – arrest, torture, deportation, and execution – yet their contributions were often overlooked in post-war narratives. As the Resistance grew in both scope and effectiveness, so too did the ferocity of the German response. Beginning in earnest in the spring of 1942, Nazi counterinsurgency tactics in France were modelled on prior campaigns in Eastern Europe and the Balkans. These methods included mass arrests, torture, hostage executions, and the razing of entire villages in retaliation for Resistance activity. The massacre at Oradour-sur-Glane in June 1944 remains a harrowing example: 642 civilians were killed by the *Waffen-SS* in reprisal for the kidnapping of a German officer.

The *Gestapo*, the SS, and the *Abwehr*, often with the collaboration of French police and the Vichy paramilitary *Milice*, intensified their efforts to dismantle the Resistance. Informant networks, surveillance, and widespread use of torture became standard tools of repression. Yet this climate of terror, rather than quelling Resistance activity, often intensified popular support for the underground movement. The Allies contributed to the Resistance through covert operations by the British SOE and American OSS, who provided arms, training, and funding. By early 1944, the Resistance had evolved into a formidable force, culminating in the formation of the *Forces Françaises de l'Intérieur* (FFI). In anticipation of the Allied invasion, the FFI played a critical role in sabotaging railways, ambushing German convoys, and delaying troop movements. Hitler's war against the Resistance reached its apex in this period, marked by mass executions, collective reprisals, and scorched-earth tactics intended to terrorise civilian populations and annihilate Resistance infrastructure. German counterinsurgency measures reached a fever pitch in the summer of 1944, as *Wehrmacht* and SS units, often aided by collaborationist forces such as the *Milice*, attempted to crush the internal enemy even as the Western Front collapsed under Allied pressure.

The Nazis considered Resistance fighters not as lawful combatants but as criminals and terrorists, denying them the protections of the Geneva Convention. Captured fighters were tortured, summarily executed, or deported to concentration camps such as Buchenwald, Mauthausen, and Ravensbrück. Civilians suspected of aiding the Resistance suffered similar fates. Atrocities such as those committed in Tulle, Ascq, and Maillé underscored the brutality of the German response and illustrated the systematic nature of the repression. Yet, this repression did not succeed in extinguishing the Resistance. Rather, it galvanised broader support. As the Normandy landings commenced on 6 June 1944, FFI forces initiated coordinated uprisings, seizing towns, sabotaging communications infrastructure, and tying down German reinforcements. The Resistance, once disparate and uncertain, had become a strategic asset in the liberation of France – an evolution that came at an extraordinary human cost.

This book traces the trajectory of Hitler's war against the French Resistance from 1940 to 1944, focusing on the methods of repression employed by the Nazi regime, the evolution of the Resistance in response, and the complex moral terrain navigated by those who chose to resist – or collaborate. It is a study not only of military occupation and clandestine warfare but also of ideology, betrayal, courage, and survival. Central to this inquiry is the relationship between the occupiers and the occupied, between Vichy and the Third Reich, and between the Resistance and the broader French population. Through this lens, we can better understand the unique dynamics of occupation in France and the broader challenges faced by societies under totalitarian domination. While the French Resistance did not win the war by itself, its contributions were indispensable to the liberation of France and the restoration of its national sovereignty. More than that, the Resistance represents a moral and political legacy that continues to inform France's national identity – a legacy forged in the shadows of repression, in the face of overwhelming odds, and often at the cost of the resisters' own lives.

The Impact of Allied Support and the D-Day Invasion

The transformative role of Allied support marked a decisive crossroads in the operational effectiveness of the French Resistance. As the war progressed and Allied strategic planning for a European invasion accelerated, coordination between Allied command and Resistance networks deepened substantially. The United Kingdom's Special Operations Executive (SOE) and the United States' Office of Strategic Services (OSS) were instrumental in this endeavour. These clandestine organisations provided extensive logistical and tactical assistance to the Resistance, including the delivery of parachuted arms shipments, encrypted radios, demolition materials, and financial resources. Equally critical was the provision of training in sabotage, reconnaissance, and guerrilla warfare, which enabled Resistance cells to undertake increasingly complex and coordinated actions against the occupiers. The pivotal moment arrived with Operation Overlord, launched on 6 June 1944, when Allied forces landed on the beaches of Normandy. The Resistance had long anticipated this invasion, having received coded messages from the BBC and direct orders through Allied liaisons that activated pre-arranged plans of disruption. Across occupied France, Resistance fighters – now organised into the FFI – undertook a wide array of sabotage missions: cutting railway lines, blowing up bridges, ambushing German convoys, and severing communication links.

These operations sowed confusion, diverted enemy resources, and severely impeded German reinforcements from reaching the front lines in Normandy. In the days and weeks following D-Day, Resistance groups launched insurrections in key urban and rural areas, securing territory, collecting intelligence, and facilitating the rapid advance of Allied divisions. In regions such as Brittany, the Massif Central, and the Rhône valley, FFI units played a quasi-military role in direct engagements with German forces, often fighting pitched battles to liberate towns before Allied armies arrived. The contributions of the Resistance were not merely auxiliary but strategically indispensable to the success of the invasion and subsequent liberation. Their intimate knowledge of the terrain, ability to mobilise civilian populations, and capacity to disrupt the German rear made them a force multiplier for the Allies. General Dwight D. Eisenhower later acknowledged the Resistance's effectiveness, noting that their actions shortened the war in France by several weeks, thereby saving thousands of Allied and civilian lives.

L'horrible guerre: The Shadow War in Occupied France

The guerrilla conflict that unfolded between the French Resistance and the German occupation forces has often been described by survivors and historians alike as *L'horrible guerre* – the horrible war. Unlike conventional military campaigns, this was a war fought in the shadows, characterised by assassinations, reprisals, espionage, and brutal counterinsurgency measures. It blurred the lines between combatant and civilian, heroism and martyrdom, order and anarchy. The Resistance comprised a broad and often ideologically disparate coalition: Gaullists, communists, socialists, conservative nationalists, clergy, students, rural peasants, and urban intellectuals. What unified them was a shared resolve to expel the occupier and to reclaim the soul of a defeated France. Operating under conditions of immense peril, these individuals and groups endured isolation, betrayal, and often death. Acts of defiance – cutting a telegraph wire, derailing a train, sheltering a fugitive – could bring down the full machinery of Nazi and Vichy retribution. Towns were razed, hostages executed, and entire communities subjected to terror as a method of collective punishment.

Yet, out of this grim reality emerged acts of extraordinary courage and moral clarity. In a context where collaboration often promised safety, and resistance meant torture or death, thousands chose the latter. For many, resistance was not only a patriotic duty but a profound existential affirmation in the face of dehumanization. Their war was not waged in conventional military terms, but through acts of sabotage, clandestine publishing, the rescue of Jews, and the refusal to submit. The cost of this war was staggering. Thousands of resisters were captured, tortured, and executed. Many were deported to concentration camps from which they never returned. Yet, the sacrifices of the Resistance laid the moral and political foundation for the rebirth of republican France. Though marginalised in some post-war narratives – especially during the early Cold War years – the legacy of the Resistance has since been reclaimed as a symbol of national resilience, unity, and defiance in the face of tyranny. The *L'horrible guerre* within occupied France was thus not merely a prelude to liberation but a central and defining front in the broader struggle against Nazism. Its history compels us to remember that some of the most decisive battles of the Second World War were fought not with tanks and armies, but in forests, farmhouses, city basements, and mountain hideouts – by ordinary citizens who chose to resist Nazi oppression.

Chapter 1

ORGANISATION OF THE GERMAN MILITARY GOVERNMENT IN FRANCE

The German occupation of France during the Second World War was a complex and multifaceted process, involving not only the German Army but also various police and security forces that worked in tandem to maintain control over the country. The German administration of occupied France was divided into two main zones: the German Occupied Zone (north and west, including Paris) and the Vichy French Zone (the unoccupied southern part). Both zones were under different administrative and military controls, and the way they were managed varied based on the evolving strategic situation and Nazi policies. In France, the German SS and *Ordnungspolizei* found themselves in a particular situation unlike any that they had yet encountered in other occupied countries.

Because of the armistice, the southern part of France was controlled by the newly established Vichy government under Marshal Philippe Pétain. The problem was that the existing French police establishment was to be the main policing force in unoccupied France. Although the policies of the government of Vichy France were either neutral or pro-German, the mere fact that the lower part of the country was not directly under German rule meant that the Germans did not have absolute control of that region of France. Therefore, many persons who were sought by the *Gestapo* and *Ordnungspolizei* (*Orpo*, Order Police) evaded capture by going to unoccupied France. The Vichy police, military and civilian government were mostly pro-German, so it was not completely safe, but it was preferable than living under German rule.

In addition, because the German Army ruled in occupied France, the SS and Police Command found it difficult to establish itself as the sole policing apparatus for Germany there. This was because in France, the *Abwehr* (German Army Intelligence) and its immediate police in the field, the *Geheime Feldpolizei* (GFP, Secret Field Police), was the natural competitor to Himmler's SS and Police apparatus. Indeed, as we shall see, a conflict arose that was only resolved by the continued pressure of *Reichsführer-SS* Himmler, who was eventually able to give his security forces freedom of action. However, the employment of these units and organisations in France was significantly delayed by at least one and a half years. This proved beneficial to the French Resistance as well as the Jewish community which only began to feel the Nazi chokehold beginning in late 1941. In fact, the first real large-scale round-up of Jews did not occur until mid-1942 when the city of Paris was witness to the event.

The German Armistice Commission

The *Deutsche Waffenstillstandskommission* (DWStK, German Armistice Commission) was initially chaired by Carl-Heinrich von Stülpnagel, who would later become the military commander in France. From 14 February 1941 to 27 September 1944, *General der Artillerie* Oskar Vogl took over.[1] The commission was created under Article 22 of the Franco-German Armistice Agreement and had its main headquarters in Wiesbaden, with an operational office in Paris and several inspection units stationed throughout the French provinces. These provincial teams maintained direct contact with French liaison officers. The DWStK's main duties were to address unresolved matters from the armistice treaty and, after November 1942, to supervise the disarmament of Vichy France's military forces.

The Struggle to Return French POWs

Following the defeat of France in June 1940, approximately 1.8 million French soldiers were taken prisoner by the Germans.[2] These POWs were held in camps across Germany (*Stalags* and *Oflags*), and their prolonged detention had deep social implications, particularly for families and the French labour force. The initial efforts by the Vichy government to secure the return of French prisoners of war (POWs) from German captivity were a central concern in the early period of the regime, beginning in mid-1940. These efforts were shaped by political, social, and propaganda considerations, as well as by the practical constraints of the Franco-German armistice signed on 22 June 1940. The Franco-German Armistice (June 1940) did not mandate the return of POWs. Article 20 stated that POWs would be retained until a peace treaty was signed – effectively allowing Germany to use them as political and economic leverage. This omission was a major grievance for the Vichy regime and one it attempted to address diplomatically from the outset.

Pétain and his government hoped that a policy of collaboration with Nazi Germany would lead to favourable outcomes, including the gradual release of French POWs. Pétain's early rhetoric strongly emphasised the duty of the government to bring 'our prisoners' home, linking it to national renewal and moral recovery. The Vichy government pursued bilateral negotiations, appealing to humanitarian concerns and the burden on French families. From 1940–1, these efforts were largely unsuccessful. Germany, needing labour for its war economy, was unwilling to release large numbers of able-bodied Frenchmen.[3] However, German authorities recognised the propaganda and coercive value of the POWs. Their return was used as a bargaining tool in negotiations with the Vichy government. For instance, Germany floated the idea that releases could be tied to labour recruitment, setting the stage for the 1942 *Relève* system.

By the end of March 1942, approximately 140,000 to 150,000 labourers had been recruited from France, of whom more than one-third subsequently returned. This situation soon posed difficulties for the German Reich, particularly as the anticipated swift military campaign against the Soviet Union had failed to materialise, resulting in an escalating demand for foreign labour. In response, during the early summer of 1942, and continuing through the end of September, Fritz Sauckel, the General Plenipotentiary for Labor Deployment (*Generalbevollmächtigter für den Arbeitseinsatz*), issued a demand for 250,000 additional French workers, specifying that 150,000 of them should be skilled labourers.

Faced with the need to preserve both the legitimacy of the collaborationist regime and public sentiment in France, Prime Minister Pierre Laval could not acquiesce to these demands without resistance. He initiated negotiations with German authorities, ultimately resulting in a compromise agreement known as the *Relève*. Under this arrangement, France agreed to provide 150,000 skilled workers in exchange for the release of 50,000 French prisoners of war.[4] Furthermore, France retained responsibility for recruiting the remaining 250,000 labourers.[5] At the time, the Vichy government viewed this compromise as a significant political achievement. Eventually, the number of French POWs released by the Germans was only one POW for every seven French workers sent to the Reich.[6]

As far as public sentiment in France was concerned, the issue of POWs was used by the Vichy regime to justify collaboration. The government claimed that cooperation with Germany would ease the suffering of POWs and speed their return. The Vichy government organised correspondence programmes, relief initiatives, and official visits to camps to show concern for prisoners' welfare – though with limited practical effect. Some prisoners – especially older, sick, or wounded soldiers, and those with large families – were gradually released under German criteria. By 1942, only around 200,000–300,000 had been freed, often in small numbers. In sum, the Vichy regime's initial efforts to secure the return of POWs were a mixture of symbolic diplomacy, humanitarian appeals, and strategic collaboration, but they largely failed to produce significant results until the introduction of the *Relève* system in 1942. Even then, the exchange of prisoners for labourers revealed the limitations of Vichy's autonomy and the transactional nature of its collaboration with Nazi Germany.

Despite Prime Minister Pierre Laval's implementation of extensive propaganda campaigns – such as posters implying that French workers could secure the release of prisoners from German camps through their participation in labour deployment within the Reich – and his framing of voluntary labour service as a patriotic obligation, the recruitment targets were not met. This shortfall prompted the German authorities to intensify pressure on the Vichy regime to enact legislation replacing voluntary service with compulsory labour conscription.

The German recruitment of French workers for labour deployment in the Reich during the Second World War exemplifies the complexities of occupation policies characterised by coercion, negotiation, and propaganda. As stated earlier, despite extensive propaganda efforts only about 32,000 French workers had been recruited. This figure fell significantly short of German demands, which had escalated to a request for 250,000 French labourers, including 150,000 skilled workers, as the demands of the war economy intensified following the failure of Blitzkrieg in the Soviet Union. In response to this shortfall, the German authorities pressured the Vichy government to enact the Law of 4 September 1942 (*Loi* n°869), instituting compulsory labour service for French men aged 18 to 50 and single women aged 21 to 35. This legislation marked a decisive shift from voluntary recruitment to forced conscription, underscoring the limits of collaborationist policy in the face of German occupation objectives.[7]

The negotiations surrounding labour recruitment also illustrate the political constraints faced by the Vichy regime, which sought to balance cooperation with German demands against the need to maintain domestic legitimacy. The *Relève* agreement, which tied the deployment of 150,000 skilled French workers to the release of 50,000 French prisoners of war, initially appeared as a diplomatic success but ultimately failed to satisfy German requirements or alleviate French public discontent. By the war's later stages, estimates suggest that up to 600,000 French workers had been deported for forced labour in Germany, including both voluntary and conscripted labourers, a figure that attests to the extensive human cost of the occupation labour policies.[8] These developments reveal how German labour recruitment efforts were central not only to sustaining the wartime economy but also to the broader dynamics of coercion, resistance, and political negotiation within occupied France.

Transitioning German-French Relations

Even after the Germans occupied southern France in November 1942, the DWStK remained active. It was then assigned to oversee the demobilisation of the 100,000-strong Vichy-French army as well as the paramilitary groups, including the *Garde Mobile*, the *Milice*, and the *Chantiers de la Jeunesse*. When serious anti-partisan operations began in 1943, the DWStK was tasked with lending their expertise to these operations and also to act as liaison with the Vichy French government in operations involving Vichy troops. This soon caused friction between the SS and the Army. The SS complained (rightly) that the DWStK liaison officers were more concerned with mediation than using severe methods to fight the *Francs-tireurs*.[9] The DWStK was also used by the Vichy French government as a mouthpiece for complaints against the occupation regarding individual and general violations of international law by the Germans. This too, became an annoyance to the SS command in France. Even some higher-ranking German Army officers eventually began to see the DWStK as merely a conduit for problems brought by the French against the German occupation.

One last avenue which the French government could use to force the Germans to address their complaints was the *Deutsche Botschaft in Paris* (German embassy in Paris). The contact person for Vichy was none other than the German ambassador, Otto Abetz. Although Abetz passed on French complaints and requests, he had an agenda of his own. Abetz was working directly for the Reich Foreign Minister, Joachim von Ribbentrop. His mission, as assigned by Ribbentrop was (1) try to divide the various French political interests as much as possible and (2) to increase French collaboration as much as possible. With this in mind, funds were to be provided for right-wing political groups in France. The height of power and influence for ambassador

Otto Abetz, was the period 1940–3. He performed his duties to the best of his abilities until 1944. By then, the Germans had given up all pretence of caring about French sensibilities.

The German Military Administration in Occupied France

The German military administration in France was primarily managed by the *Wehrmacht* – the German Armed Forces. But beginning in the spring of 1942, it also included the Nazi internal security forces for police and security matters. The German military structure in occupied France was divided into multiple layers of command. First, there was the *Militärbefehlshaber Frankreich* (Military Commander France).[10] This was the highest German military authority in the Occupied Zone. This position was responsible for overseeing the German military's operations, the implementation of Nazi orders, and maintaining order in the occupied territories. Then there was the *Oberbefehlshaber West* (OB-West) – Supreme Commander Western Theatre Command. This command was responsible for the German military in France, Belgium, and the Low Countries. The commander until 1944 was *Generalfeldmarschall* Gerd von Rundstedt, followed by *Generalfeldmarschall* Erwin von Witzleben.

The headquarters of OB-West was in Paris. It operated under the direct supervision of the *Oberkommando der Wehrmacht* (OKW, the High Command of the Armed Forces), whose headquarters was in Berlin. Within the Occupied Zone, France was subdivided into military districts known as '*Militärbezirke*'. These districts were managed by the *Wehrmacht* as well as the internal security forces of the Third Reich. Paris was the French capital and most strategic area which was directly controlled by the *Militärbefehlshaber* in Paris. The rest of occupied France was divided into regional military commands. Each regional military command was responsible for a specific area. For example, *Militärbefehlshaber Nordfrankreich* (military commander for northern France) and *Militärbefehlshaber Südfrankreich* (military commander for southern France). There were subordinate military posts, which were located in major cities such as Lyon, Marseille, and Bordeaux, each with military commanders directly reporting to OB-West or *Militärbefehlshaber West* in Paris.

For organisational purposes, the German Military Administration in France was divided into three *Militär Verwaltungs Bezirk* (Military Administrative Districts) labelled 'A', 'B', and 'C'. *Militär Verwaltungs Bezirk 'A'* governed northwestern France; *Militär Verwaltungs Bezirk 'B'* administered southwestern France, while *Militär Verwaltungs Bezirk 'C'* controlled northeastern France.[11] In addition, the large capital city of

Paris had its own separate military government on the same level as the three *Bezirk* named above. The manner in which the rear area of the German forces was organised was through administrative commands.

The *Oberfeldkommandantur* (administrative area headquarters) was the highest military administrative body. This type of headquarters in all theatres of operation came under the control of the commander of an Army or Army Group Rear Area. In occupied territories outside the theatre of operations they came under the military commander in charge of the military administration for that country. Subordinate administrative headquarters were the *Feldkommandantur* (administrative sub-area headquarters), usually led by an *Oberst* (Colonel) or *Generalmajor* (Major-General). The *Ortskommandantur* (Town headquarters) was normally officered by a Major. The *Kreiskommandantur* (District headquarters) was a rural district also usually led by a Major. The *Stadtkommandantur* (City headquarters) were found in the major cities and were led by either a colonel or general.

The *Militärverwaltungsbezirk* (Military Administrative District) were subdivisions under the *Militärbefehlshaber in Frankreich* (MBF), corresponding to large geographic regions (like provinces).[12] These commands managed regional governance which included civil affairs, economy, censorship, etc. These headquarters were staffed by military officials and civil administrators. A *Militärverwaltungsbezirk* could encompass multiple *Feldkommandanturen*, so, this was a higher-level regional administrative body, not just tactical military.[13] As mentioned earlier, there was also the Military Commander in France – based in Paris. The *Oberfeldkommandantur* (OFK) was a military field headquarters which controlled several *Feldkommandanturen* (FK). The OFK oversaw local German military operations, including security, policing (sometimes with the use of *Geheime Feldpolizei* units), control of French civil authorities, and the requisitioning, conscription, and suppression of French resistance. The *Oberfeldkommandanturen* were more tactical and military-focused, while the *Militärverwaltungsbezirk* were more administrative and regional in nature.

Key Figures in the German Military Administration
Key German military figures in France included *Generaloberst* (Colonel-General) Hans von Kluge. He replaced Gerd von Rundstedt in 1944 as part of the reorganised command structure in the Western theatre. Von Kluge was responsible for military operations in France, especially after the Allies landed in Normandy. Then there was

General der Infanterie Otto von Stülpnagel. Von Stülpnagel was the German military governor of the Occupied Zone (France North) from 1940 until 1942. He served as the MBF and was initially responsible for overseeing military operations and the suppression of resistance in France. From February 1942 to June 1944, his cousin Carl Heinrich Rudolf von Stülpnagel assumed the post.

As far as the occupation policies implemented by Stülpnagel were concerned, they included taking hostages and threats against the French civilian population, General Stülpnagel publicised threats of mass executions to deter Resistance attacks. Notices were posted across towns warning that for every German soldier killed, multiple French hostages would be executed. This was part of a deliberate policy of terror and deterrence aimed at intimidating the civilian population into compliance. Stülpnagel closely targeted the *Francs-Tireurs et Partisans* (FTP), the armed wing of the French Communist Party, which was especially active from mid-1941 onward following the German invasion of the Soviet Union. He worked with the *Gestapo*, the SD, and the Vichy French police to arrest, torture, and deport suspected communist Resistance members. An example of his actions against the French Resistance was the following notice posted publicly:

> On the evening of October 21, 1941, cowardly murderers in the pay of England and Moscow treacherously shot a German military administration officer in Bordeaux. The assassins escaped. The perpetrators of the Nantes attack are also still at large. As a first reprisal for this new crime, I have once again ordered the execution of 50 hostages. If the murderers are not apprehended by midnight on October 26, 1941, an additional 50 hostages will be executed.
>
> I offer a total reward of 15 million francs to the inhabitants of France who contribute to the discovery of the culprits.
>
> Paris, 23 October 1941
>
> The Military Commander in France
>
> von Stülpnagel
>
> General of Infantry[14]

The next officer to head the MBF was Carl Heinrich Rudolf von Stülpnagel. Though sometimes he became frustrated with the Nazi security services, he coordinated with Vichy French authorities, especially the *Service d'ordre légionnaire* (SOL) and *Milice*, to hunt down

Resistance fighters. He encouraged the use of local collaborationist forces in tracking, denouncing, and interrogating suspected resisters. Von Stülpnagel supported the establishment of German military courts (*Feldgerichte*) in France, which often handed down death sentences to captured Resistance fighters. In many cases, summary executions occurred without trial, especially in rural areas where German units conducted reprisals after acts of sabotage. While more often attributed to the Vichy regime under the *Service du Travail Obligatoire* (STO, Compulsory Labour Service), Carl-Heinrich Rudolf von Stülpnagel also supported the round-up and deportation of Resistance suspects to concentration camps in Germany, particularly Compiègne, Buchenwald, and Mauthausen.

Table 1. *Höhere Verbindungs- und Verbindungsstäbe* **in France under the** *Kommandant Heeresgebiet Südfrankreich* **command.**[15]

Kommandant Heeresgebiet Südfrankreich – Generalleutnant Heinrich Niehoff, then:
General der Artillerie Theodor Geib (died of wounds 30 July 1944), then:
General der Infanterie Ernst Dehner (at the beginning of August 1944).

HVSt. 564	Toulouse	*Generalleutnant* Otto Schmidt-Hartung
VSt. 495	Cahors	*Oberst* Zenke
VSt. 496	Albi	*Oberst* Beigel
VSt. 626	Toulouse	*Generalmajor* Karl Bickel
VSt. 659	Tarbes	*Generalmajor* Leo Mayr[16]
VSt. 732	Pau	*Generalmajor* Johannes Hahn
VSt. 798	Agen	*Oberst* Eugen Lobach
VSt. 806	Foix	*Oberst* Krafft von Oelhafen
VSt. 993	Auch	*Oberst* Hans Leistikau
VSt. 996	Montauban	*Generalmajor* Eugen Bilharz
HVSt. 588	Clermont-Ferrand	*Generalleutnant* Fritz von Brodowski[17]
VSt. 494	Aurillac	*Oberstleutnant* Ulrich Borgmann[18]
VSt. 586	Limoges	*Generalmajor* Walter Gleininger[19]
VSt. 730	Périgueux	*Oberst* Paul Sternkopf
VSt. 739	Brive-la-Gaillarde	*Oberst* Walter Kalkowski
VSt. 785	Clermont-Ferrand	*Oberst* Erwin von Ilsemann
VSt. 786	Montluçon	*Oberst* Graf von Pückler

VSt. 896	Guéret	*Oberstleutnant* Reinhard Biebricher[20]
VSt. 990	Châteauroux	*Oberst* Hugo Wiest (replacing *Major* Müller)
VSt. 995	Le Puy	*Oberst* Enno Metger[21]
HVSt. 590	Lyon	*Generalleutnant* Otto Kohl
VSt. 493	Bourg-en-Bresse	*Oberst* Werner Heydrich
VSt. 502	Chambéry	*Oberst* Kurt Niezoldi
VSt. 577	Privas	*Oberst* Karl Benczek
VSt. 711	Lons-le-Saunier	*Oberst* Willhelmi
VSt. 735	Grenoble	*Oberst* Werner Kirsten[22]
VSt. 893	(Mâcon, Saônet-et -Liore)	*Oberstleutnant der Reserve* Wilhem Brückner
VSt. 987	Lyon (Rhône)	*Oberst* Joachim-Egmont von Versen
VSt. 988	Annecy (Haute-Savoie)	*Oberst* Friedrich Meyer
VSt. 992	St. Etienne (Loire)	*Oberst* Kurt Wittekind
VSt. 998	Valence (Drôme)	*Generalmajor* Johann Wolpert

These included reprisals not only for direct Resistance actions, but also sheltering Allied pilots or Jews. Interestingly, Stülpnagel became disillusioned with Hitler's policies, and later participated in the 20 July 1944 plot to assassinate Hitler. After the plot's failure, he attempted suicide and was later executed by the Nazi regime. After Stülpnagel's arrest for his role in the 20 July plot, he was replaced by *Generaloberst* Johannes Blaskowitz in July 1944. He oversaw the German retreat from France during the Allied liberation. Another notable figure was *General der Infanterie* Dietrich Hugo Hermann von Choltitz was the military governor of Paris in 1944, the man who oversaw the German defences during the liberation of Paris. He famously disobeyed orders to destroy the city during its liberation by the French Resistance and the advancing Allies.

The command structure of the German military administration was divided between various administrative sectors. These included *Befehlshaber Nordostfrankreich* (Commander Northeast France), *Befehlshaber Nordwestfrankreich* (Commander Northwest France), *Befehlshaber Südwestfrankreich* (Commander Southeast France), and *Kommandant Groß-Paris* (Commander of Greater Paris), which was an independent administrative sector all its own. When the Germans occupied southern France in November 1942, another sector was established, called *Befehlshaber Südfrankreich* (Commander Southern France). These various sectors were in turn directed by several *Militärverwaltungsbezirk* labeled 'A', 'B', and 'C'. Strangely, although one source lists these commands as 'liaison staffs', another document, dated August 1944, lists these army commands as *Feldkommandanturen* or *Oberfeldkommandanturen*.[23]

Adding to the confusion is the fact that many of these *Verbindungsstäbe* were originally referred to as *Kreiskommandanturen*. The staff of the *Kreiskommandantur* was a district-level military command authority below that of the *Ortskommandantur*. It served as a subordinate administrative unit within the larger occupation command structure. For example, *Kreiskommandantur 990* (KK 990), which was established on 8 December 1942 in the *Militärverwaltungsbezirk A* (Military Administrative District 'A') in France, was also referred to as *Verbindungsstab 990* (Liaison Staff 990) shortly after its formation. In the late summer of 1944, this command was disbanded. The explanation as to the confusion over unit designation probably has to do with downsizing, within the context of *Verbindungsstäbe* as substitutes for *Kreiskommandanturen*, *Ortskommandanturen*, or even *Feldkommandanturen*.

Early in the occupation (1940–2), the German military governed France through a dense network of *Feldkommandanturen* (FK) – field commands overseeing entire departments or regions. Below the FK were the *Ortskommandanturen* (OK) – local commands in cities and towns. Above the post of *Feldkommandantur* was the post of *Oberfeldkommandantur*. As the military situation deteriorated, especially after 1943, manpower and resources were stretched. German forces reorganised to focus more on security, anti-partisan warfare, and coordination with collaborators (e.g., Vichy officials, *Milice*). The function of the *Verbindungsstäbe*, was to act as liaison missions to French local administrations and Vichy and *Heer* military units. They were also tasked with continuing essential occupation duties without the full structure of a *Feldkommandantur*. In addition, they were to serve as the point of contact between local collaborators (e.g., Vichy police, GMR, the *Milice*) and the German military.

The duties of the *Verbindungsstab* were similar to the *Kreiskommandantur*, *Ortskommandantur*, or *Feldkommandantur*. They were in charge of security coordination (anti-Resistance operations), intelligence gathering, the oversight of labour in the region, requisitions, and transportation. They also coordinated with the German police forces (e.g., the *Gestapo*, the SD), and were tasked with maintaining public order. All of this was to be accomplished with fewer personnel. The *Verbindungsstäbe* in France operated in such a capacity, functioning effectively as a military governor or command post without bearing the formal title or staff size of a *Kreiskommandantur*, *Ortskommandantur*, or *Feldkommandantur*. For a list of the forces and headquarters under the German military commands in France in 1941, please refer to Appendix I of this work.

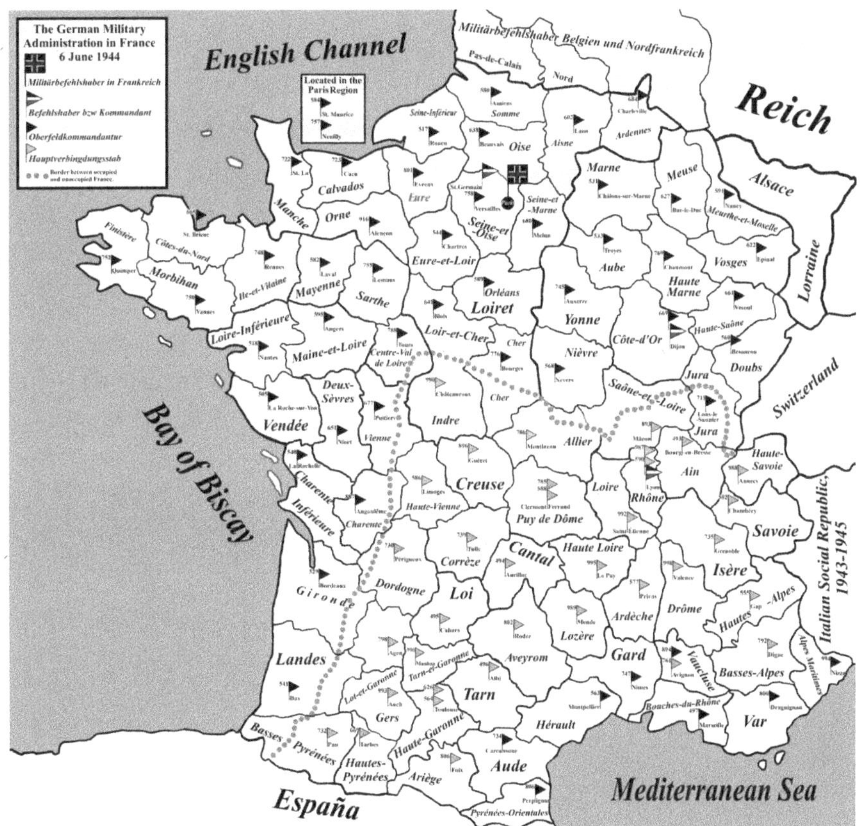

Figure 1. Smaller-sized map showing all of France on 6 June 1944.

Figure 2. Western half of occupied France, 6 June 1944.

Figure 3. Eastern half of occupied France, 6 June 1944.

The *Höherer Verbindungsstab* (HVSt.) operated above the *Verbindungsstäbe*, overseeing and coordinating their efforts. They often reported to the MBF or another high command like the OKW. The purpose of this headquarters was to provide strategic coordination between German military occupation structures, Vichy French authorities, German police and SS units, as well as local collaborationist organisations. Finally, they were to ensure unified policy enforcement and consistent communication between field commands and high-level occupation leadership. The functions also included supervising the lower *Verbindungsstäbe*, coordinate policy and operations across multiple departments or regions, act as military-political advisors, implement anti-resistance strategies on a regional or national scale, and facilitate diplomatic or military negotiations with Vichy or foreign units, like Italian forces of occupation. In addition to the various *Verbindungsstäbe* the German command also possessed *Oberfeldkommandantur* and *Feldkommandantur* headquarters located in the region of the *Kommandant Heeresgebiet Südfrankreich*. The following table lists the headquarters as they existed in August 1944:

**Table 2. *Oberfeldkommandantur* and *Feldkommandantur*
commands in Southern France, late summer 1944.**

Kommandant Heeresgebiet Südfrankreich – *Generalleutnant* Heinrich Niehoff, then: *General der Artillerie* Theodor Geib (died of wounds 30 July 1944), then: *General der Infanterie* Ernst Dehner (at the beginning of August 1944).[24]

OFK 564	Toulouse	*Generalleutnant* Otto Schmidt-Hartung[25]
FK 495	Cahors	*Oberst* Zenke
FK 496	Albi	*Oberst* Beigel
FK 626	Toulouse	*Generalmajor* Karl Bickel
FK 659	Tarbes	*Generalmajor* Leo Mayr[26]
FK 732	Pau	*Generalmajor* Johannes Hahn
FK 806	Foix	*Oberst* Krafft von Oelhafen
FK 993	Auch	*Oberst* Hans Leistikau (then *Oberst* Dr. Theodore Pripke)
FK 996	Montauban	*Generalmajor* Eugen Bilharz
OFK 894	Avignon	*Generalleutnant* Rudolf Hühnermann[27]
FK 761[28]		*Oberst* Irnfried freiherr von Wechmar

FK 497	Marseilles	*Generalmajor der Infanterie* Claus Boie
Platzkommandantur	Marseilles	*Major* Kurt Marshall
FK 800	Draguignan	*Generalmajor* Ludwig Bieringer
Platzkommandantur	Toulon	*Oberstleutnant* Nikolai
FK 994	Nizza	*Generalmajor* Hellmuth Nickelmann
FK 747	Nimes	*Generalmajor* Oskar Doepping[29]
FK 563	Montpellier	*Oberst* Friedrich-Wilhelm Dernen
Platzkommandantur	Montpellier	*Major* Neuse
FK 734	Carcassone	*Oberst* Ludwig Dischler[30]
OFK 590	Lyon	*Generalleutnant* Otto Kohl
FK 987	Lyon (Rhône)	*Oberst* Joachim-Egmont von Versen
FK 893	Macon (Saônet-et-Liore)	*Oberstleutnant der Reserve* Wilhelm Brückner
FK 493	Bourg-en-Bresse	*Oberst* Werner Heydrich
FK 711	Lons-le-Saunier	*Generalmajor* Hans Mönch
FK 988	Annecy (Haute-Savoie)	*Oberst* Friedrich Meyer
FK 502	Chambery	*Oberst* Kurt Niezoldi
FK 735	Grenoble	*Oberst* Wilhelm Stenz[31]
FK 998	Valence	*Generalmajor* Johann Wolpert[32]
FK 577	Privas	*Oberst* Dr. Theodore Pripke
FK 992	St. Etienne	*Oberst* Kurt Wittekind
OFK 588	Clermont-Ferrand	*Generalleutnant* Fritz von Brodowski[33]
FK 785	Clermont-Ferrand	*Oberst* Erwin von Ilsemann
FK 995	Le Puy	*Oberst* Enno Metger
FK 739	Tulle (Brive)	*Oberst* Karl Luyken
FK 730	Perigueux	*Oberst* Paul Sternkopf[34]
FK 586	Limoges	*Generalmajor* Walter Gleiniger[35]
FK 896	Gueret	*Oberst* Reinhard Biebricher
FK 990	Chateauroux	*Oberst* Hugo Wiest[36]
FK 786	Montlugon	*Oberstleutnant* Dr. Carl-Heinz Quetsch
FK 494	Aurillau	*Oberstleutnant* Ulrich Borgmann

The Italian Occupation of Southern France, 1940–1943: Forces and Deployment

Between 1940 and 1943, the Italian occupation of southern France – within the designated *zone d'occupation italienne* – was carried out by several distinct military formations. Chief among these was the Italian Fourth Army (*Quarta Armata*), whose headquarters was initially located in Turin. Following Italy's limited invasion of southeastern France in June 1940, the Fourth Army's command was transferred to Grenoble, reflecting its new operational responsibilities. The Fourth Army served as the primary occupation force within the Italian zone, which encompassed strategic areas of Savoy, Nice, and the Alpes-Maritimes. Of the original number of 850,000 troops which Italy employed in the invasion of southern France, 500,000 were later withdrawn back to Italy. Following Operation *Anton* in November 1942 – the Axis seizure of Vichy France – the area under Italian control expanded significantly to include additional parts of southeastern France and the entirety of Corsica. The Italian forces stationed in southern France and Corsica included a combination of regular army divisions, specialised mountain units, coastal defence formations, and internal security forces. The principal units were as follows:

a. *Divisione Cuneense* (4th Alpine Division)
    An *Alpini* (mountain infantry) division, the *Cuneense* was primarily tasked with operations in the Alpine sector along the Franco-Italian border. Renowned for its expertise in mountain warfare, the division played a key role in securing and patrolling rugged terrain within the occupation zone.

b. *Divisione Pusteria* (5th Alpine Division)
    Also, an *Alpini* formation, the *Pusteria* Division advanced into southern France on 21 June 1940 during the final days of the Battle of France. In November 1940, it was redeployed to Albania to reinforce Italian forces engaged in the Greco-Italian War. Repatriated in August 1942, the division underwent a brief period of rest before participating in Operation *Anton*, after which it was assigned garrison duties in key urban centres including Grenoble, Chambéry, Gap, and Digne-les-Bains.

c. *Divisione Lupi di Toscana* (7th Infantry Division)
    Initially involved in the June 1940 occupation of southern France, the *Lupi di Toscana* was withdrawn later that year. The division returned to southeastern France in November 1942 and participated in Operation *Anton* from 3 to 9 November. Following the operation, it remained in the region on garrison duty, first along the Menton–Nice corridor, then in Grasse and Cagnes-sur-Mer, and later in the Fuveau–Rousset–Bouches-du-Rhône–Châteauneuf-le-Rouge area. The division also

performed coastal defence operations near Ollioules until 3 September 1943, when it was ordered to redeploy to Rome.

    d.   *Divisione Rovigo* (105th Infantry Division)

In June 1942, the *Rovigo* Division was transferred to southern Piedmont, and in November of the same year, redeployed to Liguria. This shift followed the involvement of the XXII Army Corps, whose units – previously responsible for the defence of the Ligurian coast – had participated in 'Operation *Anton*' and subsequently remained in southern France to conduct garrison and occupation duties along the French Riviera.

The Occupation of Corsica

Following Operation *Anton*, Corsica was transferred to Italian control in late 1942. Responsibility for the island's occupation was assigned to the VIII Army Corps, with headquarters established in Bastia and Ajaccio. The primary garrison force on Corsica was the 44th Infantry Division *Cremona*, supported by the 225th Coastal Division, a static infantry formation tasked with coastal defence and the security of Corsican ports and shorelines.

Internal Security Forces

Throughout the occupation of both southern France and Corsica, internal security and administrative control were enforced by units of the Carabinieri, as well as elements of the *Milizia Volontaria per la Sicurezza Nazionale* (MVSN), also known as the Blackshirts. The MVSN operated in limited numbers, primarily during the later stages of the occupation, and were instrumental in maintaining order and supporting Italian military governance.

Italian-French Relations

The Italian occupation, like the German occupation, resulted in the establishment of Resistance groups in the regions occupied by the Italians. The *raison d'être* for resisting the Italian occupation wasn't just that Italy had declared war on France when France was fighting for its life – thus a type of betrayal. It wasn't just because Italy was occupying French territory. It was also because, as the Germans did with Alsace-Lorraine, the Italians were attempting to Italianise the occupied French territories. Therefore, while Germanisation was going on in only the two French provinces of Alsace-Lorraine, the Italians were attempting to do the same thing in all of the provinces occupied by the Italians, especially the provinces nearest to the pre-1940 Italian-French border.

The targets of the French Resistance in the Italian occupied zone were not just directed at the Italian military or police forces. These attacks extended to ethnic-Italian civilians living in the regions of the Italian occupied zone. When the Italian invasion began, the initial reaction of the French population was to pile abusive language and threats on people living in French territories of Italian extraction. Although the Italians made an effort to transplant Italian citizens into some of the border provinces, French people of Italian descent, many whom had lived in France for years, also became targets of the Resistance. It didn't matter how long these Italians had been living in France, or even if they had become French citizens. The fact is that, as in all wars, innocent people often pay alongside the guilty. After the occupation, this reproach against ethnic-Italians or Italian transplants who, in many cases, had been friends with their French neighbours for years, very quickly turned violent.[37]

Chapter 2

THE SECRET FIELD POLICE IN FRANCE

The German Secret Field Police

During the German occupation of France, the internal security situation presented the Third Reich with a distinct and unprecedented set of challenges. Following the Franco-German Armistice of 1940, France was divided into two zones: the northern and western regions were occupied by the German military, while the southern portion remained under the administration of the Vichy regime. Unlike in other occupied territories, the Germans did not exercise direct control over all of France, which complicated efforts to impose a unified system of internal surveillance and repression. In the unoccupied zone, the Vichy government retained its own police forces. Although the Vichy regime was ideologically aligned with and often cooperative toward the German occupiers, the absence of direct German authority created opportunities for political dissidents, members of the French Resistance, and especially Jews to seek refuge. Until early 1942, the unoccupied zone served as a relatively safer area for those fleeing German persecution, although it was not entirely free from danger, given the presence of collaborationist elements within the Vichy administration.

Initially, responsibility for countering Resistance activities in occupied France fell to the German Army, which included the *Abwehr* (military intelligence) and its associated policing body, the *Geheime Feldpolizei* (GFP, Secret Field Police). This structure delayed the full establishment of the SS and its subordinate agencies – the *Sicherheitsdienst* (SD), *Sicherheitspolizei* (*SiPo*), and *Gestapo* – as the dominant security forces within France. The GFP, along with the *Feldgendarmerie* (Military Field Police), played a leading role in security and counter-resistance operations from 1940 to 1942. The rivalry between these military security organs and Heinrich Himmler's SS empire reflected the broader struggle within the Nazi state for control over occupied territories. This military dominance in internal security significantly impeded Himmler's efforts to assert SS authority in France, delaying the *Gestapo*'s full operational control by approximately 18 months. As a result, both the Jewish population and Resistance groups experienced a brief window during which German repression, though present, was not yet at its most severe. The first major mass arrest of Jews in Paris, for instance, did not occur until the summer of 1942.

Structure and Role of the Secret Field Police in France

Until the SS successfully expanded its influence over occupied France, the GFP and the *Feldgendarmerie* served as the principal instruments of German security policy. Between 1940 and 1942, the GFP divided its jurisdiction in France and Belgium into five administrative districts (*Bezirke*): 'A', 'B', 'C', 'Paris', and '*Belgien-Nordfrankreich*' (Belgium-Northern France). Due to its political and strategic significance, Paris hosted between five and seven GFP groups at any given time. By March 1942, GFP forces in France numbered approximately 2,500 personnel, organised into sixteen companies, excluding those stationed in the *Militärverwaltungsbezirk Belgien-Nordfrankreich*. On average, each GFP company comprised roughly 147 members. These units were tasked with intelligence-gathering, counter-espionage, suppression of Resistance activities, and the enforcement of German military authority. Below is a list of the GFP units and where they were stationed:

> *Militärverwaltungsbezirk 'A'* with:
>   *Geheimfeldpolizei-Gruppe 633* – Orleans
>   *Geheimfeldpolizei-Gruppe 701* – Rouen
>   *Geheimfeldpolizei-Gruppe 731* – Maison Laffitte
>
> *Militärverwaltungsbezirk 'B'* with:
>   *Geheimfeldpolizei-Gruppe 2* – Rennes
>   *Geheimfeldpolizei-Gruppe 14* – Bordeaux
>   *Geheimfeldpolizei-Gruppe 632* – La Rochelle
>   *Geheimfeldpolizei-Gruppe 732* – Angers
>
> *Militärverwaltungsbezirk 'C'* with:
>   *Geheimfeldpolizei-Gruppe 7* – Dijon (led by Paul Boehm)

Geheimfeldpolizei-Gruppe 30 – Nancy
Geheimfeldpolizei-Gruppe 627 – Troyes
Geheimfeldpolizei-Gruppe 736 – Besancon

Militärverwaltungsbezirk 'Paris' with:
   Geheimfeldpolizei-Gruppe 11 – Paris
   Geheimfeldpolizei-Gruppe 550 – Paris
   Geheimfeldpolizei-Gruppe 603 – Paris
   Geheimfeldpolizei-Gruppe 649 – Paris
   Geheimfeldpolizei-Gruppe 733 – Paris

Militärverwaltungsbezirk 'Belgien-Nordfrankreich' with:[1]
   Geheimfeldpolizei-Gruppe 3 – Lille (led by Adam Guttman)
   Geheimfeldpolizei-Gruppe 8 – Bruges
   Geheimfeldpolizei-Gruppe 9 – Scheveningen
   Geheimfeldpolizei-Gruppe 611 – Nord-Pas-de-Calais

During the period of German occupation, the GFP operated under the authority of the German Army across several military administrative districts (*Militärverwaltungsbezirke*) in France and Belgium. Senior GFP officers were appointed to oversee security operations in each of these regions. In *Militärverwaltungsbezirk A*, headquartered in Saint-Germain-en-Laye, the GFP was led by Ernst Rassow. Hans Tesenfitz commanded the GFP in *Bezirk B* (Angers–Bordeaux), while Hermann Herold held the corresponding position in *Bezirk C*, based in Dijon. In Paris, Heinz Seyfriz served as the head of GFP operations within the *Militärverwaltungsbezirk Paris*. Even prior to the spring and summer of 1942, the *Reichssicherheitshauptamt* (RSHA, Reich Security Main Office) had begun encroaching upon what had previously been the exclusive domain of the German Army in matters of internal security within France and Belgium. Though the Army retained official control during the early occupation period, Reinhard Heydrich – chief of the RSHA – initiated efforts to insert SS intelligence services into the Western theatre. In 1940, a small SD detachment was dispatched to Paris, and another was sent to Belgium. Notably, the SD operatives deployed to Belgium arrived wearing GFP uniforms, effectively concealing their true affiliation.

This SD contingent, placed under the direction of *Kriminaldirektor* Franz Straub, began operating out of Brussels in July 1940. Although formally part of the RSHA, these men functioned under the auspices of *SS-Brigadeführer* Eggert Reeder's *Verwaltungstab*, and were tasked with intelligence-gathering activities focused on perceived enemies of the Nazi regime – namely Jews, Communists and Freemasons. Their use of GFP uniforms allowed the SD to circumvent *Wehrmacht* oversight and establish an early foothold in internal security operations in the West. This initial infiltration by RSHA operatives marked a significant turning point. By spring 1942, the SS had succeeded in establishing an official *Sicherheitspolizei* (*Gestapo* and *Kriminalpolizei*) and SD presence in Brussels. This expansion coincided with a restructuring of security forces in occupied France and Belgium, wherein numerous GFP units were formally disbanded and their personnel reassigned to *SiPo* and SD commands. This transition often involved men returning to the RSHA from which they had originally been seconded. In total, seventeen GFP units operating in France were dissolved in this initial phase of reorganisation.

The SS applied a similar structural model in Western Europe as it had in Poland and the Soviet Union, where RSHA death squads (*Einsatzgruppen*) were eventually broken up and their personnel redistributed to form permanent *SiPo* and SD station commands. In contrast, the Western campaign had not employed SS killing units at the same scale, and the consolidation of SS control was thus achieved largely through the absorption of GFP personnel and the dismantling of Army-led security formations. One further GFP formation – GFP-20 – was disbanded in 1942 in the region of northeastern Slovenia, an area annexed into the Reich that same year. Its personnel were used to strengthen newly established *SiPo*/SD commands in that region.

The disbanded GFP units in France during the autumn of 1942 included: GFP-2, GFP-7, GFP-11, GFP-14, GFP-30, GFP-550, GFP-603, GFP-627, GFP-632, GFP-633, GFP-649, GFP-701, GFP-731, GFP-732, GFP-733, GFP-734, and GFP-736. An additional wave of GFP disbandment occurred in 1944, comprising GFP-718 (February), GFP-711 and GFP-712 (April), GFP-730 (August), and GFP-722, GFP-724, GFP-739, and GFP-740 (September). These personnel transfers significantly augmented the strength of the *SiPo* and SD across France and the Western occupied territories. As a result, many of the new SD stations established throughout France in late 1942 were staffed in part by former GFP operatives. Following the war, a number of senior GFP officials were interrogated regarding their roles. Among them was *Feldpolizeidirektor* Philipp Greiner, who testified that the operational GFP units in France fell under the authority of *Feldpolizeidirektor* Erich Vogel, designated *Leitender Geheime Feldpolizei West* (Chief of the Secret Field Police, Western Command). Greiner also stated that the intelligence officer (*Ic*) attached to each German Army headquarters held direct operational control over the deployment and tasking of GFP units under their respective commands.

Feldpolizeidirektor Philipp Greiner, who served as *Leitender Feldpolizeidirektor beim Militärbefehlshaber Frankreich* (Chief Secret Field Police Director under the Military Commander in France), emphasised the division of authority within the GFP. According to his post-war testimony, GFP units assigned to the territorial military administrative zones (*Bezirke 'A', 'B', 'C',* and *'Paris'*) fell under his jurisdiction and were organisationally distinct from those GFP detachments directly subordinated to individual German field armies operating in France. The military district of *Belgien-Nordfrankreich* (Belgium-Northern France), by contrast, was assigned its own senior police official – *Leitender Feldpolizeidirektor beim Militärbefehlshaber Nord-Frankreich* – stationed in Brussels. This separate command structure had significant operational implications, notably that surveillance and policing along the Franco-Belgian border were overseen not by Paris but by GFP headquarters in Brussels. Greiner's own position was largely administrative in scope, with responsibilities designed to ensure cohesion, oversight, and liaison between various branches of the occupation administration. His specific duties as *Leitender Feldpolizeidirektor beim Militärbefehlshaber Frankreich* included:

Maintaining liaison between the MBF and the GFP territorial headquarters across the administrative districts;
Coordinating between the MBF and the GFP groups operating in Paris;
Acting as intermediary between his office and the *Stadtkommandantur* (city commandant's office) of Paris;
Facilitating communication and cooperation between the GFP and the Paris municipal police;
Representing GFP interests at military conferences held by the MBF and implementing relevant directives;
Supervising GFP units in France, ensuring adequate training and equipment, and submitting reports to both the MBF and the office of the *Leitender Geheime Feldpolizei West*;
Advising military authorities on criminal policing matters;
Inspecting and overseeing the operations of subordinate GFP directors in the various *Militärverwaltungsbezirk*;
Managing the overall organisation and administrative functioning of the GFP in occupied France.

Greiner was replaced in this role by *Feldpolizeidirektor* Karl Dräger in late 1941. Dräger remained in this position even after most GFP groups in Western Europe were absorbed into the *SiPo* and the SD) during the course of 1942. Following his removal, Greiner returned to the *Kriminalpolizei* in Nuremberg, where he was promoted to *Regierungs- und Kriminalrat* in early 1942.

Leitender Geheime Feldpolizei West

The position of *Leitender Geheime Feldpolizei West* (Senior Secret Field Police Superintendent for the Western Theatre) was held from 1941 by *Feldpolizeidirektor* Erich Vogel. This role included oversight of regional GFP leadership, such as that exercised in Paris by Greiner and later by *Feldpolizeidirektor* Friedrich Sowa. From 1940 to 1941, the GFP headquarters under the *Militärbefehlshaber Frankreich* operated out of the Hôtel Lutetia in Paris before relocating to Rue de la Faisanderie in 1941. The headquarters staff in Paris during this period included Greiner, *Feldpolizeikommissar* Hochgrabe and Retzeok, *Feldpolizeisekretär* Rudi Engel, as well as three non-commissioned officers, two orderlies, and one driver. Engel, notably, had prior experience serving with GFP units 603 and 610 in Paris and was responsible for managing the unit registry under the authority of the *Leitender Geheime Feldpolizei West*. Subordinate to the *Leitender Feldpolizeidirektor beim Militärbefehlshaber Frankreich* were a number of lower-tier GFP commands, each responsible for regional policing and counterintelligence operations in the occupied zones:

- *Leitender Feldpolizeidirektor beim Chef des Militärverwaltungsbezirk A* (Leading Field Police Director by the Chief of Military District 'A'), stationed in Saint Germain and led by *Feldpolizeidirektor* Ernst Rassow until May 1941,[2] then *Feldpolizeidirektor* Hans-Jochen Bartsch beginning in June.

- *Leitender Feldpolizeidirektor beim Chef des Militärverwaltungsbezirk B* (Leading Field Police Director by the Chief of Military District 'B'), stationed in Bordeaux and Angers and led by *Feldpolizeidirektor* Tesenfitz. Later *Feldpolizeidirektor* Zucklic assumed command. *Leitender Feldpolizeidirektor beim Chef des Militärverwaltungsbezirk C* (Leading Field Police Director by the Chief of Military District 'C'), stationed in in Dijon and led by *Feldpolizeidirektor* Dr. Hermann Herold.[3]

- *Leitender Feldpolizeidirektor beim Paris* (Leading Field Police Director in Paris).[4] According to Greiner's US Army interrogation report, the position of the Paris GFP command was to be left under the command of *Feldpolizeidirektor* Vogel. However, in the same report Greiner listed *SS-Sturmbannführer* Karl Dräger as the *Feldpolizeidirektor* for Paris. Karl Dräger was born on 21 June 1896. He was married and spoke fluent French. He had served in the Berlin *Kriminalpolizei* (*Kripo*, Criminal Police). He was said to have left Paris in the autumn of 1942.

- *Leitender Feldpolizeidirektor beim Militärbefehlshaber Nord-Frankreich* (Senior Field Superintendent for the Military Commander Northern France) stationed in Brussels and led by *Feldpolizeidirektor* Kurt Kletzke.

As France's capital and largest city, Paris held such strategic importance that it was heavily garrisoned by GFP units. Typically, between five and seven GFP formations were stationed there at any given time. Recognised as the symbolic heart of France and a hub for Resistance operations, the city warranted a strong German security presence. One of the primary responsibilities of the GFP in Paris, especially before 1942, was to identify and suppress the French Resistance. Between August 1941 and June 1942, 471 French hostages were executed due to their involvement in anti-German actions in the capital. In addition to counter-Resistance efforts, the GFP also oversaw the regulation of prostitution in Paris, particularly at the Sphinx – a high-end brothel located at 31 boulevard Edgar-Quinet. Established in 1931 and shut down in 1946, the Sphinx was a popular venue among senior German officers during the occupation. Several GFP units were assigned to this task, though the specific formations involved included multiple distinct groups.

Overview of GFP Units in Paris and Occupied France

In spring 1941, GFP units in France and Belgium stood at fifty-one units. During the German occupation of France, numerous GFP units were stationed throughout Paris and the wider French territory. These formations had diverse roles ranging from counter-resistance operations to administrative policing duties, and many were eventually absorbed into the SS or SD. They also sought German soldiers who had gone AWOL and black marketeers.

Paris-Based GFP Units

- GFP-11 was initially commanded by Dr. Bohlsen, headquartered at the Hotel Chatham and later at the Hotel Sport. Dr. Theodore Mommsen took over in May 1942. The unit included officials like Josef Sonka, Christian Hemmer, Hans Jessen, and others. GFP-11 was disbanded in June 1942, with personnel integrated into the *SiPo*/SD. Some members were reassigned to the Eastern Front.
- GFP-550 was led by Dr. Bernhard Niggemeyer and later Bernhard Hannig, was stationed at Avenue de la Grande Armée. Hannig, a former *Kriminalpolizei* officer from Hannover, exemplified the typical GFP officer of his generation. In 1942, after disbandment, he joined the security police command in Paris.
- GFP-603 was initially commanded by *Feldpolizeikommissar* Johann Alexander von Ostrowski[5], based at the Hotel Matignon. It was dissolved in late 1942.

- GFP-610 under Hargard and later Arthur Kallenborn, was headquartered at the Hotel Edward III on Avenue de l'Opéra. Dr. Theodore Mommsen served here before leading GFP-11. The unit moved to the Eastern and later Italian fronts.
- GFP-649 led by Jetzinger, was also dissolved in 1942 with personnel absorbed into the SD.
- GFP-625 (L) was an air force GFP unit led by Kühn and adjutant Jellositz, supported *Luftflotte III* headquartered in Paris. The unit operated across various French towns and remained active in the Paris region until July 1944.
- GFP-626 was deployed to Poland in 1941, later joining *Panzergruppe 1* on the Eastern Front, remaining active into 1945 in Slovakia.

A document dated 22 March 1942, listed six GFP units officially under Paris command: GFP-11, 550, 603, 649, 733, and 734.

GFP Units in Northwest France (Military District A)

Within *Militärverwaltungsbezirk A*, covering northwestern France, several GFP units played key roles in local security operations prior to their eventual dissolution:

- GFP-633, initially commanded by *Feldpolizeidirektor* Kollath and later by *Feldpolizeikommissar* Retzeck, was relocated from Château-des-Éspoir to Orléans before being disbanded in late 1942.
- GFP-644, under the command of Dr. Paulat, was based in Le Mans and maintained several satellite posts throughout the region.
- GFP-701 and GFP-731 were headquartered in Rouen and Maisons-Laffitte respectively; both units were disbanded in November 1942 as part of the broader SS-led reorganisation.

GFP Units in Southwest France (Military District B)

In the southwest, within *Militärverwaltungsbezirk B*, GFP formations were concentrated around Bordeaux, Angers, and La Rochelle:

- GFP-2, stationed in Rennes, was one of several units dissolved during the November 1942 reorganisation.
- GFP-14, commanded by SS officer Kurt Arlt, operated in Bordeaux before being reassigned to service in Russia and later attached to the OKH.

Additional units such as GFP-520, GFP-590, GFP-632, and GFP-732 were based in Bordeaux, La Rochelle, and Angers, and were likewise either disbanded or transferred out of France by late 1942.

GFP Units in Northeast France (Military District C)

In *Militärverwaltungsbezirk C*, covering northeastern France, GFP-7, based in Dijon, may have remained active until the German surrender in 1945, although some sources indicate its disbandment in 1942.

Units such as GFP-30, GFP-611, GFP-612, GFP-627, GFP-639, GFP-647, and GFP-736 were dispersed across key regional centres including Nancy, Neufchâteau, Troyes, and Besançon.

These formations were largely either disbanded or redeployed to the Balkans and Eastern Front. Younger personnel were typically assigned to front-line GFP units in the Soviet Union, while older officers were retained in France, often to support the expanding SS-run security apparatus under the RSHA.

GFP Units in Northern France and Belgium

In Northern France and occupied Belgium, the GFP was active across a wide swath of urban centres. Units including GFP-3, GFP-8, GFP-530, GFP-540, GFP-648, and GFP-716 operated in Lille, Ghent, Brussels, Laon, Liège, and Arras.

GFP-3 was later relocated to the Netherlands, indicative of the fluid nature of GFP deployments in the Western theatre.

Additional GFP Units and Strategic Redeployments

Several GFP units were not confined to specific territorial jurisdictions but were assigned to support German military headquarters and special security operations:

Units such as GFP-1 (which moved from Dijon to Trieste), GFP-590, GFP-639, GFP-560, GFP-644, GFP-580, and GFP-131 served in both Western Europe and on the Eastern Front.

Three units – GFP-312, GFP-540, and GFP-610 – were designated *Zur besonderen Verwendung* (Z.b.V., 'for special employment') and subordinated to the intelligence department of the OKW.

Beyond France and Belgium, GFP units were also deployed to Norway (GFP-629), Denmark (GFP-171), and Finland (GFP-735), underscoring the GFP's multinational operational footprint.

Reorganisation and Absorption of GFP Units (1940–1942)

Between 1940 and 1941, approximately thirty-five GFP units operated throughout France, Belgium, and the Netherlands. However, the structure of GFP command underwent substantial transformation beginning in 1941 and accelerating in 1942. With the launch of Operation *Barbarossa* in June 1941 and the subsequent intensification of German security efforts, many GFP units stationed in Western Europe were redeployed to the Eastern Front or disbanded outright. By late 1942, around seventeen GFP units in France and Belgium were dissolved. On 25 April 1942, a directive formally reassigned approximately 1,300 GFP personnel from the jurisdiction of the *Militärbefehlshaber Frankreich* to the *SiPo* and SD. Some sources suggest the total number of reassigned personnel may have reached 2,000, many of whom were former officers of the *Kripo*.

The discrepancy in reported figures likely reflects selection criteria employed by the SS, which prioritised younger, physically fit GFP officers for deployment to the Eastern Front. Roughly 700 such individuals were transferred east, where GFP units participated in operations alongside the *Einsatzgruppen*, engaging in mass executions of Jews, Soviet commissars, and suspected partisans. In contrast, older or less fit GFP personnel remained in France, where their experience in criminal investigations and policing made them valuable assets for the RSHA's domestic intelligence and repression network. These officers were frequently integrated into the SD or local *SiPo* detachments and helped staff newly established security stations throughout the western occupied territories. This reorganisation marked a decisive shift in German security policy in Western Europe, reducing the influence of the *Wehrmacht*'s military police structures in favour of SS-led political and racial policing. The absorption of GFP units by the RSHA also mirrored practices already in place in Eastern Europe, particularly in Poland and the Soviet Union, where the GFP had earlier supported or collaborated with SS extermination efforts.

The GFP in Belgium and Northern France

During the German occupation, seven GFP units operated within Belgium and northern France. Of these, four were directly subordinate to the *Leitender Feldpolizeidirektor beim Militärbefehlshaber Nord-Frankreich* (Senior Field Police Director for the Military Commander in Northern France). These units played key roles in both military security and political surveillance across a strategically significant region of the Western Front.

- GFP-3 was initially based in Brussels but was later relocated to Lille. It maintained branch offices in Valenciennes, Cassel, Arras, and Wimereux.
- GFP-8 operated from its headquarters in Ghent, with auxiliary offices in Bruges and Kortrijk.
- GFP-131, led by *Feldpolizeikommissar* Brosius, was stationed in Tourcoing (near the Belgian border) and oversaw posts in Aire and Antwerp.

- GFP-501 was originally located in Tourcoing but redeployed to East Prussia in the spring of 1941 alongside the *16. Armee*.
- GFP-530 began operations in Brussels before moving first to Lille and subsequently to Poland in 1941.
- GFP-621 was also based in Brussels until its transfer to the Balkans in March 1941 under *12. Armee*.
- GFP-637 (L) operated under *Luftflotte II*, with its primary station in Brussels and branch offices in Lille and Noailles.

Additional GFP formations included:

- GFP-712, initially in Antwerp with branches in Brussels and Hasselt, was later transferred to Namur.
- GFP-738, GFP-739, and GFP-740 were all established on 21 June 1941 and stationed respectively in Mons, Namur, and Brussels.

Command Structure and Administrative Integration of the GFP in Occupied France

The German occupation regime in France was structured around two principal bodies: the *Führungsstab* (Command Staff) and the *Militärverwaltungsstab* (Military Administrative Staff). Within this framework, the GFP operated under the oversight of Major Friedrich Dernbach, who served under the authority of the MBF.[6] Although the Command Staff occasionally intervened in GFP operations – particularly through regional defence battalions – the GFP remained, until 1942, largely subordinate to the Military Administrative Staff. This administrative organ was also responsible for involving GFP personnel in operations involving the systematic seizure of French cultural assets, particularly those destined for Hermann Göring's private art collection.

While Major Philipp Greiner, head of the Paris GFP, later claimed to oppose the looting of French art, archival evidence indicates that his unit nonetheless cooperated with both the German Embassy and occupation authorities when seizures were sanctioned by the military. In relation to Jewish property, a key development occurred on 4 October 1941, when a formal agreement between the *Wehrmacht* and the SS granted the GFP temporary exclusive authority over the confiscation of Jewish assets in occupied France. This agreement represented a tactical concession to the military, allowing it a measure of jurisdiction over internal security and Jewish affairs, at least briefly forestalling SS dominance. However, this temporary ascendancy was undermined beginning in early 1942, when the RSHA expanded its operational reach through the integration of former GFP personnel into the SD and *SiPo*. As a result, the SS gradually supplanted the *Wehrmacht*'s role in overseeing Jewish deportations and counter-resistance operations, signalling a decisive victory in the ongoing bureaucratic struggle for internal control of occupied France.

Collaboration with the Vichy Regime and the Role of the French Police

In unoccupied Vichy France, GFP units worked in close coordination with French intelligence and security services, particularly the *Brigades spéciales des Renseignements généraux* (Special Brigades of the General Intelligence Service). These units, created under the auspices of the Vichy government, were tasked with identifying and apprehending both communist and non-communist resistance members. They also collaborated in anti-Jewish actions, including the rounding up of individuals for deportation to extermination camps in the East. Among these collaborators, the *Deuxième Brigade spéciale* (2nd Special Service Brigade) proved especially zealous and reliable from the German perspective.

The GFP regularly relied on this unit to assist in security operations, benefiting from its aggressive pursuit of partisans and its ideological alignment with Axis goals. From the outset of the occupation, the GFP recognised the impracticality of maintaining internal order in France without French collaboration. The sheer scale of surveillance and repression required to suppress resistance and control the civilian population necessitated a working relationship with French police forces. In this capacity, the GFP functioned in a manner closely resembling the *Gestapo*, particularly in its early efforts to dismantle underground networks, monitor political dissidents, and enforce anti-Semitic policies. However, without the assistance of the French police, the work of the GFP would prove more difficult:

> From a numerical point of view, it is obvious that a couple of hundred men of the GFP could not conduct any large-scale operations. Its limited strength forced the GFP to collaborate very closely with the French police and led to the creation of a so-called *Kommission auf Kapitalverbrechen Bekämpfung* ('Commission to Combat Capital Crimes'), which consisted of GFP and French criminal police. Up to 1942, that is, up to the time when the Senior SS and Police Leader appeared in France in May 1942, the collaboration between the GFP and the French police was absolutely loyal, correct, and legal.

End of Army Control: Absorption of the GFP into the SS Security Apparatus

Until mid-1942, the GFP remained actively engaged in investigating the French civilian population, working in conjunction with local French forces such as the *Gendarmerie*. Notably, in retaliation for resistance activity by *Maquisards*, the GFP, in collaboration with the SD, participated in mass executions in Nantes and Bordeaux on 15 December 1941. Between ninety-five and ninety-eight hostages were executed – many of whom were either Jews or members of the French Communist Party. Although roughly three-quarters of the victims had links to communist organisations, more than half were Jewish, suggesting that racial motives, particularly anti-Semitism, were interwoven with political repression in the selection of victims.

A significant structural change occurred in the first half of 1942. On 9 March, a *Führerbefehl* (Leader's Decree) formally transferred repressive authority in occupied France to the *SiPo* and the SD. This was further cemented by a second decree on 25 April 1942, which reassigned all executive authority over the GFP from the OKW to the RSHA, the central security office of the SS. These actions marked the effective end of Army control over internal security operations in France. After this reorganisation, the GFP units that remained under military jurisdiction were significantly reduced in both size and scope. Typically composed of no more than ninety men, these residual formations were relegated to traditional military police functions: apprehending deserters, investigating theft of military property, monitoring black market activity, and repairing or investigating sabotage of communication infrastructure – particularly the frequent cutting of telephone lines. Direct engagement with Resistance groups such as the *Maquis* was no longer part of their remit.

By early 1942, the Army's security and intelligence roles in France had been sharply curtailed. The *Abwehr* and GFP, formerly responsible for monitoring foreign agents and saboteurs within occupied territories, were increasingly marginalised. Their focus was redirected toward safeguarding military installations rather than overseeing broader civilian affairs. This transformation reflected a deliberate SS strategy to centralise and ideologically unify the apparatus of repression in Western Europe. As early as 1942, elements of the GFP were integrated into the SS-controlled *SiPo*/SD structure, a move which was both operational and symbolic. Younger, fitter GFP personnel were transferred to the Eastern Front, where they served alongside SS formations in rear-area security and extermination campaigns. Older or less physically capable members remained in France, where they were often incorporated into new or existing SD field offices. Between 1940 and 1941, approximately thirty-five GFP units had operated across France, Belgium, and the Netherlands. By the end of 1942, only twelve to thirteen remained active under Army command.

This absorption marked not just a bureaucratic shift, but a profound recalibration of Nazi counterinsurgency policy. Former GFP officers – now reconstituted under SS command – brought expertise in interrogation, field surveillance, and criminal investigation to the expanding political policing apparatus. Their skills enhanced the SS's capacity to combat resistance movements, enforce anti-Semitic and racial policies, and dismantle underground political organisations. In cities such as Paris, Lyon, and Bordeaux, these individuals played crucial roles in coordinating arrests, deportations, and extrajudicial killings in cooperation with the Vichy regime and its paramilitary wing, the *Milice*. The 1942 integration of the GFP into the RSHA's operational structure symbolised the growing convergence between *Wehrmacht* administrative frameworks and the SS's totalitarian vision. This fusion blurred the distinction between conventional military policing and ideological state terror. The resulting security regime not only facilitated the intensification of repression in France but also provided a model for SS-dominated governance across occupied Europe. The surviving GFP units under Army command continued to perform limited policing functions, but the central role in internal repression had definitively passed to the SS, whose militarised political police would spearhead the war against the French Resistance until the end of the occupation.

The GFP and Resistance Suppression in Occupied France

Between 1940 and 1942, the GFP played a crucial role in suppressing opposition and Resistance activity throughout occupied France. Early on, it was central to efforts aimed at disrupting organised dissent. One of their first major coordinated actions occurred in June 1941, coinciding with the launch of Operation *Barbarossa*, Nazi Germany's invasion of the Soviet Union. In anticipation of potential unrest, the GFP carried out the mass arrest of approximately 600 known communist activists across France, pre-emptively targeting individuals viewed as likely to organise or inspire resistance. Throughout the second half of 1941, the GFP intensified its operations in the Paris region, with many actions directed by *Feldpolizeidirektor* Kurt Moritz. In one significant operation in Caen, the GFP, acting in support of the local

Gestapo office, arrested roughly eighty suspected Resistance members in a targeted round-up.

These efforts were closely coordinated with German military intelligence, the *Abwehr*. Between June and October 1941, the *Abwehrstelle* in Paris oversaw a major counter-Resistance operation that successfully infiltrated and dismantled an underground network. The GFP served as the primary enforcement arm during this crackdown, conducting arrests, interrogations, and surveillance. By 1942, the growing influence of the *SiPo* and SD began to shift the balance of repressive power away from the military. Nevertheless, the GFP continued to collaborate with the SD and *Gestapo* in key operations. Their contribution was particularly notable in the tracking and apprehension of French Resistance leaders. The GFP played a supporting role in the broader German security effort that resulted in the capture of Jean Moulin – instrumental in unifying Resistance groups – who died under torture on 8 July 1943.

Likewise, the arrest of General Charles Delestraint, leader of the *Armée Secrète* (Secret Army), marked another major blow to the Resistance. Deported to Germany, Delestraint died in Dachau concentration camp just days before its liberation in April 1945. In the aftermath of these arrests, GFP units across France took part in extensive follow-up operations to apprehend exposed members of these Resistance networks. In southern France, including the Vichy-controlled zone, the GFP remained highly active. They monitored rail sabotage, arms depots, and clandestine printing presses, often working alongside the *Abwehr* and SD. Field reports from GFP patrols led to several successful raids, particularly in the Rhône-Alpes region, where Resistance activity was notably dense. The GFP also played a role in counter-operations against the *Armée Secrète*, including surveillance, arrests, and interrogations facilitated by infiltration and the recruitment of informants.

Beyond their efforts against French partisans, the GFP was instrumental in tracking agents of the British SOE. Collaborating with both the *Abwehr* and *Gestapo*, they monitored local populations, intercepted communications, and coordinated raids that led to the arrest of SOE operatives and their French contacts. Although their methods were often less visibly violent than those of the SS or *Gestapo*, the GFP's work in intelligence gathering, interrogation, and counter-sabotage was vital to the overall Nazi security architecture in occupied France. In the months preceding the Allied invasion in June 1944, the GFP, operating increasingly under the command structure of *Heeresgruppe B*, escalated their activities in Normandy and other key regions. These units were tasked with preventing sabotage to railways, bridges, and communication networks vital to the German war effort.

Though often viewed as occupying a secondary or support role relative to the SS, the GFP's activities were deeply embedded in the day-to-day functioning of German repression. Their integration with other agencies blurred institutional boundaries, and as a result, many of their specific operations have remained less well-known – obscured by the overlapping jurisdictions and rivalries among Nazi security forces. Nevertheless, the role of the GFP in occupied France – from intelligence and surveillance to arrests and interrogations – was essential to the functioning of the German counterinsurgency regime. Their work not only contributed to the tactical defeat of Resistance networks but also enabled the SS and SD to extend their political and racial agenda deeper into the fabric of occupied society.

Chapter 3

THE SS ENTERS THE PICTURE

Helmut Knochen and the SD Arrive in Paris

In mid-June 1940, *SS-Sturmbannführer* Dr. Helmut Knochen arrived in Paris, accompanied by a small detachment of the SD. Although the SD held no official mandate in occupied France at the time, Knochen was sent as a representative of the Chief of the Security Police and the SD, *SS-Obergruppenführer* and General of Police Reinhard Heydrich. Following the consolidation of the SD and the *SiPo* (comprising the *Gestapo* and the *Kriminalpolizei*) into the RSHA on 27 September 1939, Heydrich assumed direct control of this powerful new institution.

With the Nazi security apparatus fully operational, Heydrich tasked Knochen with identifying and neutralising perceived enemies of the Reich within France – chief among them communists, Freemasons, and particularly Jews. The Jewish Affairs section of the Paris *Gestapo* was initially directed by *SS-Obersturmführer* Theo Dannecker and later, from July 1942, by his deputy, *SS-Untersturmführer* Heinz Röthke.[1] *SS-Sturmbannführer* Karl Bömelburg was also assigned to France and would eventually ascend to lead the *Gestapo* in Paris, representing the RSHA.[2] Initially, however, Bömelburg served as the deputy commander, with specific responsibility for Section IV-J, which oversaw Jewish deportations.

At the time of his arrival, Knochen lacked any formal executive authority in France, effectively operating without official orders or legal jurisdiction. Despite this, he began to organise intelligence operations, including the recruitment of French informants to identify Resistance groups in Paris. These early efforts yielded limited success, primarily resulting in the denunciation of a small number of Jews by local collaborators. On 15 June 1940, Knochen approached Roger

Langeron, the Prefect of Police in Paris, to request access to files on known communists, Freemasons, and foreign nationals residing in France. He also inquired whether the police maintained a registry of Jews living in the capital.

Tensions Between the German Military and the SS in Occupied France

In spite of Knochen's demand, Langeron categorically refused to relinquish any files in his possession to the *Gestapo*. In a concerted effort to protect sensitive information, Langeron and other members of the Paris police later destroyed thousands of documents to prevent them from falling into the hands of German security services. Upon his arrival in Paris, Knochen possessed no autonomous authority; all activities conducted by the SD and *SiPo* were subject to the approval of the German military city commander, General Otto von Stülpnagel, in accordance with the military governance of occupied France. It was not until 2 January 1941 that the *Gestapo* and other RSHA-affiliated forces received limited authorisation to operate independently, and even then, their powers were restricted to conducting arrests and searches only in cases deemed urgent.

From the outset, Knochen's relationship with Stülpnagel was fraught with conflict. In response to these tensions, Knochen appealed to *Reichsführer-SS* Heinrich Himmler, prompting Himmler to dispatch a senior SS officer to Paris to lobby the German Army for broader operational autonomy for the RSHA in France. Stülpnagel, with the support of Admiral Wilhelm Canaris, head of the *Abwehr*, firmly resisted these overtures.[3] Stülpnagel was determined to maintain the Army's primacy as the principal intelligence authority in France and insisted on retaining operational control over the 2,500 personnel of the GFP, as well as the *Feldgendarmerie*. He argued that these units were functioning effectively in collaboration with the French police and that no further intervention by the RSHA was necessary.

On 24 August 1940, *SS-Brigadeführer* Dr. Max Thomas was appointed as *Befehlshaber der Sicherheitspolizei und des Sicherheitsdienstes* (Commander of the Security Police and the SD) for Belgium and France. Thomas brought with him a team of SS officers, including *SS-Obersturmführer* Theodor Dannecker, who would later play a central role in the deportation of French Jews. To counter the increasing influence of the SS in the occupied territories, von Stülpnagel secured the backing of General Alexander von Falkenhausen, the *Militärbefehlshaber für Belgien* (Military Commander for Belgium). Von

Falkenhausen, in turn, enlisted the support of *SS-Brigadeführer* Eggert Reeder, Head of Military Administration on the Belgian military staff. Although Himmler had conferred an honorary SS rank on Reeder, the latter was a staunch Prussian traditionalist who aligned himself with the conservative military establishment rather than the SS leadership.

Himmler's frustrations extended beyond Reeder. He was also disappointed by *SS-Brigadeführer* Dr. Werner Best, who, prior to becoming Reich Plenipotentiary for Denmark in November 1942, had served as Head of the Military Section on the staff of the German Military Commander in France. Best appeared sceptical of the SS's hardline approach, believing that an overly repressive strategy would be counterproductive. He frequently sided with the Army in disputes over jurisdiction and authority. Best ultimately departed France following the appointment of SS-General Karl Oberg, who arrived in Paris in 1942 to assume the newly created post of *Höhere SS- und Polizeiführer Frankreich* (Higher SS and Police Leader 'France'). Himmler had seized the opportunity created by Otto von Stülpnagel's resignation on 17 February 1942 to consolidate SS authority, appointing Oberg to the position on 3 March 1942.

The Hostage Crisis and the Escalation of Resistance and Repression in Paris

As previously noted, it was only after the launch of Operation *Barbarossa* – the German invasion of the Soviet Union on 22 June 1941 – that the Soviet Comintern directed the *Parti Communiste Français* (PCF) to initiate acts of resistance against the German occupying forces in France. In response, during the summer of 1941, the PCF began recruiting and training a small cadre of approximately twenty young activists who would form the nucleus of the *bataillons de la jeunesse*, or communist youth battalions. Motivated by patriotism and the fervour of youth, members of this group staged a bold demonstration at the Strasbourg-Saint-Denis metro station on 13 August 1941. On that day, roughly 100 young communists emerged from the station singing *La Marseillaise* and waving the French tricolor. Their overt display of national defiance prompted an immediate response from both the French police and German military forces. The protest was quickly suppressed, and two demonstrators – Henri Gautherot and Samuel Tyszelman – were apprehended, sentenced to death, and executed in the forest of Verrières on 19 August 1941.

In retaliation for these executions, the French Communist Party authorised its first direct attack against the German occupation authorities. On 21 August 1941, German naval midshipman Alfons Moser was assassinated at the Barbès-Rochechouart metro station in Paris by Pierre Georges and Gilbert Brustlein, both members of the communist youth battalions. While Georges would later be killed in action in 1944, Brustlein survived the war and lived until 2009. This assassination marked the PCF's entry into armed resistance. The German response was swift and severe. On 22 August 1941, the military command in Paris declared that all individuals currently imprisoned for offences against the German Reich or its interests would be designated as hostages. These individuals could be executed in retaliation for any further attacks on German personnel. Despite this declaration, acts of resistance continued.

On 3 September, *Feldwebel* (Sergeant) Ernst Hoffman was assassinated, followed by the killing of *Leutnant* Wilhelm Scheben in central Paris on 15 September. Infuriated by the growing number of attacks, *SS-Sturmbannführer* Helmut Knochen sought to deliver a symbolic and punitive blow to what the Nazi regime termed the 'centres of resistance'. Adhering to the Nazi narrative that conflated Jewish and communist activities under the term 'Judeo-Bolshevism', Knochen orchestrated a coordinated campaign of synagogue bombings in Paris. Between 2 and 3 October 1941, explosives were planted at six synagogues, including the Grand Synagogue de Paris, and the synagogues located on Rue Copernic, Rue Pavée, Montmartre, Rue Nazareth, and Rue des Tournelles. The attacks were executed by members of the SD in collaboration with the *Mouvement Social Révolutionnaire* (MSR), a far-right collaborationist organisation founded in September 1940. These bombings, framed as retaliatory acts against alleged centres of anti-German agitation, were part of a broader SS strategy to link resistance activity to Jewish and communist networks, thereby legitimizing intensified anti-Semitic and repressive measures under the pretext of maintaining order.

Escalation of Reprisals and the Strain on German Military Authority in France

The MSR, the far-right fascist organisation that assisted the SD in the October 1941 synagogue bombings, had been founded by Eugène Deloncle. Prior to the war, Deloncle had already come to the attention of French authorities due to his leadership of the *Comité Secret d'Action Révolutionnaire* (CSAR), a clandestine, ultra-nationalist group responsible for politically motivated assassinations of left-wing journalists and politicians during the 1930s. The French Resistance responded swiftly to the synagogue bombings and increasing German repression. On 20 October 1941, *Oberstleutnant* Karl Hotz, the German military commander (*Feldkommandantur*) of Nantes, was assassinated. The following day, *Major* Hans Gottfried Reimers, an officer of *Feldkommandantur 529* in Bordeaux and Head of the Department of Labour Allocation (*Abteilung Arbeitseinsatz*), was also killed. These attacks intensified tensions between the German occupation authorities and the French population.

In the wake of Hotz's assassination, fifty hostages were selected for execution as a reprisal measure. However, this initial group was spared following an intervention by the German military commander in France. In late October 1941, facing heightened surveillance and repression in the capital, the Resistance began shifting its operational focus from Paris to provincial regions. The situation escalated dramatically when Adolf Hitler ordered the execution of between 100 and 150 hostages in retaliation for the killings of Hotz and Reimers. Additionally, he authorised a reward of one million gold francs for information leading to the arrest of those responsible. Despite interrogating approximately 7,000 individuals, German authorities failed to identify the perpetrators. Ultimately, only one of Hotz's assassins was betrayed – denounced by a Frenchman hoping to claim the financial reward – and subsequently arrested.

General der Infanterie Otto von Stülpnagel, the *Deutscher Militärbefehlshaber in Frankreich*, or German Military Commander in France, had held this important position since 25 October 1940. Believing that harsh treatment would be counterproductive, he now attempted to delay the executions. Nonetheless, under direct orders from Hitler, he was compelled to proceed. Although fifty hostages had been slated for execution, only forty-eight were ultimately killed, as two of the individuals on the list were not in custody. Hitler then imposed a draconian reprisal policy mandating the execution of 100 hostages for every German soldier killed, forcing Stülpnagel to comply with further mass shootings. By late November and early December 1941, a renewed wave of Resistance attacks – including further assassinations of German personnel – placed increasing pressure on the German military administration. These developments undermined the prestige of the German Army in France and further strained its relationship with the SS.

Heydrich and Himmler capitalised on these tensions by portraying Stülpnagel and the military administration as either ineffective or overly lenient. On 5 December 1941, Stülpnagel submitted a proposal to the OKH recommending that an additional 100 hostages be executed in retaliation for the latest Resistance actions. He also suggested the imposition of a punitive fine of one billion francs on the Jewish population of Paris. Furthermore, he proposed the arrest and deportation of 1,000 Jews and 500 communist youths to the East. While it remains uncertain whether Stülpnagel was fully aware of the fate awaiting deportees, this suggestion occurred prior to the formalisation of the Final Solution at the Wannsee Conference in January 1942.

Nonetheless, rumours regarding mass killings in the East began circulating within the German military bureaucracy in France during the spring of 1942, although such accounts were typically dismissed as hearsay at the time. On 15 December 1941, Stülpnagel ordered the execution of ninety-five hostages – consisting primarily of Jews and communists. In the aftermath, he reportedly suffered a nervous collapse, exacerbated by the immense psychological and political pressure associated with balancing military command responsibilities and Nazi reprisal demands. Later that month, he formally submitted his resignation. In February 1942, Otto von Stülpnagel was succeeded by his cousin, *General der Infanterie* Carl-Heinrich von Stülpnagel, the former commander of *17. Armee*. Otto returned to Berlin, where he remained in semi-retirement with his wife for the remainder of the war. Despite his formal cooperation with Nazi policies, Otto von Stülpnagel's tenure as military commander in France was marked by attempts to mitigate or delay the extreme retaliatory measures advocated by the SS and Nazi leadership. Nevertheless, under mounting pressure, he ultimately capitulated and authorised the execution of numerous hostages, suggesting a complex legacy shaped by both institutional resistance and eventual complicity.

The 'Hostage Crisis' and the Path to Genocide in Occupied France

Although the initial proposal for deportations in France originated with General Otto von Stülpnagel in the autumn of 1941, this should not be interpreted as evidence that the German military authorities in occupied France were actively pursuing the objectives of the Final Solution. Stülpnagel's recommendation was more a desperate attempt to curb the spiralling cycle of assassinations and retaliatory executions that was increasingly destabilising the occupation. Nonetheless, entrenched anti-Semitic and anti-communist attitudes within the German officer corps meant that Jews and communists were routinely selected as targets for reprisal actions, reinforcing Nazi ideological goals even within the ostensibly more conservative military establishment.

It was not until the spring of 1942, when the SS was formally granted primary responsibility for suppressing resistance in France, that the full machinery of Nazi repression – and ultimately genocide – was activated on French soil. This transfer of authority marked a fundamental shift in the occupation's character. After the war, Otto von Stülpnagel was arrested by Allied authorities and extradited to France to face charges for war crimes. While imprisoned at Cherche-Midi, he took his own life on 6 February 1948. His cousin and successor, *General der Infanterie* Carl-Heinrich von Stülpnagel, had died earlier – executed by the SS on 30 August 1944 for his involvement in the 20 July plot to assassinate Hitler. Like other conspirators, he was hanged with piano wire, a method chosen personally by Hitler to inflict maximum suffering, emblematic of the Führer's sadistic retribution.

The resignation of Otto von Stülpnagel in December 1941 and his formal departure in February 1942 reflected growing dissatisfaction within the Nazi hierarchy – including Hitler, Himmler, and Heydrich – with the *Wehrmacht*'s handling of internal security in France. This dissatisfaction opened the door for the SS to assert dominance over occupation policy. While both Hitler and Field Marshal Wilhelm Keitel (representing the OKW) accepted Stülpnagel's request for relief from command, it was likely because they had come to view him as an impediment to effectively suppressing the intensifying resistance movement. Even before Carl-Heinrich von Stülpnagel could officially assume command, Hitler issued a sweeping directive in April 1942 mandating that, for every future assassination attempt, 500 communists and Jews would be deported to the East.

At the same time, under pressure from Himmler, a new SS-dominated security structure was established in France. This took the form of the office of *Höherer SS- und Polizeiführer* (HSSPF), to which *SS-Brigadeführer and Generalmajor der Polizei* Carl-Albrecht Oberg was appointed on 5 May 1942. He was formally granted executive authority over police matters on 29 May 1942, including the power to order executions. Oberg remained in this position until 28 November 1944. Although nominally subordinate to the MBF, Oberg in practice operated with complete independence from the Army. His brutal reign would later earn him the nickname 'the Butcher of Paris'.

The so-called hostage crisis of 1942 marked a decisive turning point in the internal struggle for control of occupation policy between the *Wehrmacht* and the SS. On 9 March 1942, Hitler's appointment of Oberg as HSSPF effectively sidelined the military administration and established a parallel SS authority tasked with enforcing Nazi security policy. From this point onward, Oberg was vested with exclusive control over reprisal measures against the civilian population. Significantly, the military hierarchy did not resist this reallocation of responsibility, perhaps viewing it as a relief from a morally and politically burdensome task. While Oberg occasionally cited Heydrich's orders as justification for limiting large-scale hostage executions, his appointment undeniably marked the institutionalisation of SS control in France. Though not all aspects of the occupation changed overnight, one catastrophic development did follow shortly thereafter: beginning in the spring of 1942, the systematic deportation of Jews from France to extermination camps in the East commenced in earnest. Under Oberg's tenure, the machinery of genocide – until then only latent in France – became an active and horrific reality.

Chapter 4

THE VICHY FRENCH GOVERNMENT AND SECURITY FORCES

Président du Conseil des ministers

The position equivalent to prime minister in the new Vichy Government was called the *Président du Conseil des ministers* (President of the Council of Ministers), which was the standard title for French prime ministers under the Third Republic and retained under Vichy. The first Prime Minister in the Vichy government was Philippe Pétain, who acted both as Chief of State and President of the Council. He held both posts from 11 July 1940 to 18 April 1942. Pierre-Étienne Flandin briefly served as Prime Minister from 13 December 1940 to 8 February 1941 between Pierre Laval's first dismissal and Darlan's appointment. The former French Chief of the Naval Staff, François Darlan, then assumed the post and was Prime Minister from 9 February 1941 to 18 April 1942. Then Pierre Laval ruled as Prime Minister from 18 April 1942 to 20 August 1944. He did so with expanded authority and effectively led the Vichy regime under Pétain's nominal leadership. It was Laval who traded French industrial specialists in exchange for French POWs being held by the Germans in the Reich.

The First Cabinet under Pierre Laval (13 October 1940–13 December 1940)

Pierre Laval's first cabinet lasted exactly two months, which indicates that tensions in that cabinet soon led to the end of this first Vichy government. The principal members of the cabinet were:[1]

- Pierre Laval: Vice-President of the Council (Prime Minister), Minister of the Interior, and Minister of Foreign Affairs. Laval was the central

51

figure in this cabinet and would later become the head of government in his second cabinet. In this role, he played a pivotal part in shaping the collaborationist policies with Nazi Germany.

- Marcel Déat: Minister of National Education and Youth Déat was a former Socialist who became a staunch supporter of collaboration with Nazi Germany. He later became a leader of the pro-German *Rassemblement National Populaire* (RNP, National Popular Rally).
- Édouard Daladier: Minister of National Defence. Though he was removed from the post in the autumn of 1940 after the French defeat, his influence in the cabinet remained notable.
- François Darlan: Minister of the Navy and the Colonies. Darlan was a high-ranking officer in the French Navy and was initially a key member of the Vichy government before he later held the position of Vice-President of the Council in 1941.
- Philippe Pétain: Head of State (President of the Council). Although Pétain had already been appointed head of the Vichy government earlier in 1940, Laval's role was increasingly significant, and Pétain would serve as the figurehead of the regime while Laval handled much of the day-to-day governance.
- Pierre-Étienne Flandin: Minister of the Economy. Flandin was involved in overseeing economic issues, including relations with Germany.
- Robert Schuman: Minister of Finance. Schuman was a conservative politician who would later play a central role in the creation of the European Union after the war.
- René Bousquet: Secretary General of the Police Bousquet would play a significant role in organising the collaborationist police force, which became infamous for its role in deporting Jews.

Pierre Laval's key role in this first cabinet, as both Vice-President of the Council and Minister of the Interior, gave him influence over both domestic policies and foreign relations. His tenure marked a significant shift in the Vichy government's collaboration with Nazi Germany. In addition to these individuals, Laval's cabinet was composed of a mix of both more conservative, pro-German individuals, as well as former French political figures. Laval was appointed at a time of crisis, and the early stages of the Vichy regime were marked by internal strife, uncertainty, and the ongoing occupation of France by Nazi forces. The cabinet would later evolve as Laval's influence grew, especially after Pétain's increasing reliance on Laval's leadership. Pierre Laval's first cabinet ended on 13 December 1940, after he was forced to resign as Vice-President of the Council (Prime Minister) and Minister of the Interior. This resignation was part of the political manoeuvring within the Vichy government at the time. Laval had been a controversial figure, with some factions within the Vichy regime dissatisfied with his policies and the increasing influence of the Nazi occupation in French affairs. There were several key reasons for his dismissal.

First, there was growing internal opposition to Laval because of his strong support for collaboration with Nazi Germany alarmed many within the Vichy regime, including more moderate or traditional conservative elements. In addition, some Vichy officials feared Laval was too close to the Germans and might compromise French sovereignty further than necessary. Another reason was that Laval had conflicts with Marshal Pétain. Laval had his own ambitions for power and sought to expand his influence, sometimes clashing with Pétain's authority. Although Laval had been instrumental in setting up the collaborationist framework, Pétain became increasingly wary of Laval's independent political manoeuvring, fearing he might dominate the regime or align France too tightly with the Nazis. There was also pressure from ultra-conservatives and the military within the Vichy French government. Laval's perceived opportunism and radical collaborationist stance alienated traditional right-wing and military figures in the regime.

General Maxime Weygand and Admiral François Darlan, among others, were unhappy with Laval's dominance and growing German sympathies. Following his resignation, Pétain took on more direct control, and the cabinet was reorganised. Laval's departure from the cabinet didn't mark the end of his political career. He would return to power in April 1942 when he formed his second cabinet and became the head of government again, solidifying his role in collaborating with Nazi Germany during the war. Although Laval was pro-German, at this stage in late 1940, even the German authorities did not fully trust him yet. Laval believed collaboration would eventually allow France a stronger position in post-war Europe, but the Germans were not ready to commit to that vision. His efforts were viewed as premature by some in both Berlin and Vichy.

The Second Cabinet under Pierre Laval
(April 1942–August 1944)

Pierre Laval returned to power on 18 April 1942, with increased authority, essentially functioning as Prime Minister under Pétain, though the regime was deeply authoritarian and collaborationist with Nazi Germany. The key ministers in Laval's new cabinet were as follows:

- Pierre Laval – President of the Council (Prime Minister), Laval also held the portfolio of Foreign Affairs, showing his control over both domestic and international collaboration policy.

- Abel Bonnard – Minister of National Education. Bonnard was a fanatical collaborationist and member of the fascist *Groupe Collaboration*. Later expelled from the *Académie française* after the war.
- Jean Bichelonne – Minister of Industrial Production and later Minister for the Economy. Bichelonne was a career technocrat who cooperated with the Germans on labour and industrial matters.
- Joseph Barthélemy – Minister of Justice. Barthélemy oversaw the legal framework of repression, including courts like the *Section spéciale*.
- Jacques Le Roy Ladurie – Minister of Agriculture. Ladurie managed rural policy, often cooperating with the STO logistics.
- François Lehideux – Minister of Industrial Production, was an industrialist and technocrat.
- René Bousquet – Secretary-General of the Police.[2] Bousquet coordinated closely with the *Gestapo*, especially on Jewish deportations. He was the architect of the *Vel' d'Hiv* round-up (July 1942).
- Pierre Pucheu – Minister of the Interior (earlier under Darlan), He was predecessor to later hardline ministers, responsible for creating *Courts martiales*. Nevertheless, he too was executed after the war.
- Marcel Déat – Minister of Labour and National Solidarity (from 1944). Déat was a former socialist turned fascist, co-founder of the RNP. Déat was strongly pro-German.[3]
- Jean Leguay – Deputy to René Bousquet. Leguay was a key figure in organising Jewish deportations.

Joseph Darnand's Role in the Vichy Regime

Darnand was never the formal head of government (i.e., not a Prime Minister or President of the Council). However, his rise in 1943–4 marked the militarisation and radicalisation of Vichy's repression, especially against the Resistance. Key positions held by Darnand included:

- Leader of the *Milice française* (from 30 January 1943). This was a paramilitary force created to combat the French Resistance. It operated with extreme brutality, often in cooperation with the *Gestapo*.
- Secretary of State for the Maintenance of Public Order (from 1 January 1944). This was an elevated cabinet-level post, answering directly to Laval. It gave Darnand control over the police, internal security, and the repression of the resistance.
- Secretary of State for the Interior (briefly in 1944). Darnand held this position briefly, and gave him nominal oversight of all internal affairs. This post marked the peak of his formal authority.

Joseph Darnand's influence cannot be underestimated. He brought the *Milice* under state control and made it a key pillar of Vichy repression. He personally swore allegiance to Adolf Hitler in 1943, when he joined the *Waffen-SS*, highlighting his fanatical collaboration. Darnand also oversaw mass arrests, torture, executions, and deportations of Jews and Resistance personnel. Darnand supported the creation of the 33. *Waffen-Grenadier-Division der-SS 'Charlemagne'*, made up largely of French volunteers. The division was formed in the autumn of 1944, combining units such as the *Légion des volontaires français contre le bolchevisme* (LVF, Legion of French Volunteers Against Bolshevism), members of *La Milice*, and French members of the *Sicherheitspolizei* and *Gestapo*. Darnand promoted SS recruitment in France, especially from the *Milice*, Resistance defectors, and collaborationist youth. Soon after the war ended, Darnand was captured by British forces on 25 June 1945, in Merano, northern Italy. He had fled there from Sigmaringen, Germany, after the collapse of the Vichy regime. Following his capture, he was extradited to France, where he was tried for treason for having collaborated with the Germans and crimes against the French people. He was found guilty on all counts and was executed by firing squad on 10 October 1945.

As for Laval, he fled to Spain in August 1944, but the Spanish authorities refused him asylum. He then travelled to Austria and later to Germany, where he was briefly held by the Germans. After Germany's defeat, Laval tried to fly to Spain again. On 31 July 1945 his plane was forced to land in Austria by an American fighter plane from the 79th Fighter Group of the US Ninth Air Force. He had left the Spanish city of Barcelona in a German Junkers Ju 188 aircraft, piloted by two *Luftwaffe* officers. Upon landing at Hörsching Airport near Linz on 31 July 1945, Pierre Laval and his wife were apprehended by American troops from the 65th Infantry Division and immediately taken into custody. They were then transported to Innsbruck, where they were handed over to French authorities by Brigadier General John E. Copeland, the assistant commander of the 65th Infantry Division. Laval was tried for treason and found guilty on all counts.

He was executed on 15 October 1945. Many other ministers who had fled to Germany with the retreating Vichy government were later tried in France. In the case of lower-ranking Frenchmen who collaborated with the Germans, retribution was equally swift, although not very legal. There were many instances where individual French officers and troops took it upon themselves to exact immediate retribution and vengeance on groups of captured French soldiers serving on the

German side. The most infamous case involved one of the highest-ranking officers in the French 1st Army, led by General Jean de Lattre de Tassigny. The episode involved General Philippe Leclerc.

It occurred when French troops captured the town of Bad Reichenhall on 4 May 1945. There the men of the French 1st Army encountered several fellow Frenchmen who had volunteered to serve in the *33. Waffen-Grenadier-Division der SS 'Charlemagne'* – an SS division composed of primarily of French citizens. When Leclerc inspected these French SS men, he stopped in front of one of them and asked *'Pourquoi portez-vous un uniforme allemand?'* ('Why are you wearing a German uniform?'). The private looked at General Leclerc and replied, *'Vous êtes très beau dans votre uniforme américain, mon general'* ('You look very handsome in your American uniform, general'). Leclerc's judgmental and loaded question was met with a pointed and not-so-subtle accusation of hypocrisy. The private's ironic reply turned the general's own implication back on him. Enraged by the insolence, Leclerc ordered the immediate execution of all the prisoners – without trial.

The *Courts Martiales*

The *'Courts Martiales'* (Courts Martial) were a brutal and legally dubious judicial innovation by the collaborationist Vichy French government conceived principally by Pierre Pucheu, and approved by both Pierre Laval and Joseph Darnand. These special courts were designed specifically to bypass the more lenient or reluctant civilian judiciary and accelerate the repression of the French Resistance and political opponents, including communists and Gaullists. In all instances, these judges that had remained in the French government and were now working for Vichy were relieved that the burden of imposing a death sentence against a member of the Resistance, was now out of their hands. By 1941, the Vichy regime was facing increasing internal resistance. Traditional courts and judges, many of whom still maintained Republican values or sympathies with the Resistance, were often unwilling to impose the harsh penalties – especially the death penalty – that the Vichy government wanted.

To overcome this, the regime established special courts through a law passed on 14 August 1941, with the explicit purpose of swiftly and harshly repressing resistance activity. These courts were fundamentally military in structure but were created to deal with civilians accused of acts against the state, including sabotage, the distribution of anti-Vichy or anti-German propaganda, or direct participation in armed resistance. Each court consisted of three military officers – not professional judges. These officers were personally selected by Vichy officials, notably from those judged to be completely loyal to the regime or ideologically aligned with its authoritarian and anti-communist principles. They were often hand-picked by the prefect (representative of the central government) or other high-ranking Vichy officials such as Pierre Pucheu, Vichy's Minister of the Interior in 1941, who was a key architect of this system. In some cases, officers were selected from active-duty military units, including those collaborating with the Germans.

No legal defence was allowed for the defendants. The process explicitly denied defendants the right to legal counsel. Trials were typically held in secret and lasted only a few hours, sometimes less. No appeals were permitted. Once sentenced – especially to death – execution followed swiftly, often within 24 hours. As far as what charges could be brought before these special courts and what evidence was needed for a conviction, the accused were charged based on often flimsy or coerced evidence. Accusations could include 'undermining national morale', aiding the enemy, distributing clandestine newspapers, or attacks on police or military personnel. Due process was not respected; the system prioritised efficiency and severity over justice.

The first and most infamous application of these *Courts Martiales* occurred in Châteaubriant, in October 1941, where twenty-seven hostages were executed in retaliation for the killing of a German officer. These included prominent young communists and workers. Many of those sentenced had been arrested *before* the incident and had no connection to the killing. The courts were used to send a message through exemplary punishment. The *Courts Martiales* remained in use through 1942, but they were increasingly criticised, even by some within the Vichy administration, for their arbitrariness and political nature. By mid-1942, under growing German control and influence, and amid restructuring of collaborationist police and military repression units (like the *Milice*), the *Courts Martiales* were replaced or absorbed into other mechanisms of repression, including German military tribunals and the *Section spéciale* of the Vichy courts, which still had a veneer of legality but were just as politically motivated. The Vichy *Courts Martiales* were a mechanism of terror, designed to deliver swift and irreversible punishment to those deemed enemies of the regime, bypassing the judicial safeguards that would have protected many innocent or minor offenders. These 'courts' were clearly outside of what could be termed good judicial policy. They represent one of the clearest examples of state repression during the German occupation and remain a dark stain on the legal history of France.

The *Section spéciale*

The *Section spéciale* was another infamous judicial mechanism established by the Vichy regime. Unlike the more explicitly extrajudicial *Courts martiales*, the *Section spéciale* was nominally part of the regular legal system, but it operated with a clear political purpose, which was to repress and criminalise all Resistance activity, political dissent (especially communist activity), and so-called 'subversive acts'. Its jurisdiction was retroactive – a clear breach of normal legal norms – and could prosecute offences committed before the law's enactment. It was empowered to try civilians, mainly suspected communists, Gaullists, trade unionists, or Resistance sympathisers. The types of crimes prosecuted included distribution of clandestine newspapers, participation in strikes acts of sabotage, and holding anti-German or anti-Vichy meetings.

The composition of the *Section spéciale* included a panel of five judges, three magistrates from the judiciary and two lay assessors (*assesseurs*), usually selected by the *prefect* (the regional representative of the Vichy regime). All judges had to be vetted for political reliability. Independent-minded or liberal judges were systematically excluded. The procedural characteristics were also outside of normal law rules. There was to be no trial by jury. Verdicts and sentences were rendered by the panel alone. While the defendants could have legal representation, the trials were clearly politically motivated. Lawyers who defended the accused were placed on a secret list which labelled them anti-Vichy and pro-Gaullist. Proceedings were often secret or semi-public and heavily influenced by police dossiers and reports, often with no material evidence. In contrast to the *Courts martiales*, the '*Section spéciale*' allowed limited legal defence, but outcomes were largely pre-determined, and few French lawyers were willing to stick their neck out defending the accused, knowing that they would be targeted by the regime.

The *Police Nationale*

The *Police Nationale* created by the Vichy French government was a central part of the regime's efforts to consolidate internal security and enforce authoritarian control during the German occupation of France. Below is a detailed description of its creation and organisation. Before 1941, French policing was split between various local and national forces, including the *Sûreté Nationale*, the *Garde Républicaine Mobile*, and municipal police units. However, under the Vichy regime, led by Marshal Philippe Pétain, the government sought to centralise and streamline police functions to better control the population, enforce collaboration with Nazi Germany, and suppress dissent. The *Police Nationale* was created on 23 April 1941.

The legal basis for its creation was the Law of 23 April 1941, which created the *Police Nationale*. It was initiated by Vichy's *Ministre de l'Intérieur* (Minister of the Interior), Pierre Pucheu, who was a technocrat with fascist sympathies. The purposed of the *Police Nationale* was to bring together all civilian policing under a single national authority (except in Paris, where the *Préfecture de Police* remained semi-autonomous). The centralisation made the police more efficient but also more politically aligned with the authoritarian and collaborationist goals of Vichy. It allowed for easier control of the French populace, greater ability to suppress Resistance activities, and easier handling of the deportation of Jews in coordination with the *Gestapo* and the other organs of Nazi control in France.

Organisation of the Police Nationale

The *Police Nationale* was structured to ensure both internal order and political repression, and its organisation reflected both administrative needs and ideological control:

I. Direction Générale de la Police Nationale (DGPN).

This was the central authority overseeing all police operations under the Ministry of the Interior. The key departments within the DGPN were (1) the *Sûreté Générale* (General Security), which performed normal criminal investigations, but also did intelligence gathering, and surveillance of political dissidents. There was also the (2) *Police Judiciaire* (Judicial Police), which investigated serious crimes and functioned similarly to a criminal investigation department. The third department was (3) the *Renseignements Généraux* (RG), or General Intelligence. This department was involved with domestic intelligence, including monitoring political groups, unions, and Jewish communities. Finally, the fourth department (4) was the *Police des Questions Juives* (Jewish Affairs Police). It was a special department created to enforce anti-Jewish laws, identify Jews, confiscate their property, and organise round-ups. Many of the personnel in this fourth department had volunteered for this kind of work and were fascist or fascist-leaning.

II. The Uniformed Branches.

IIa. The *Groupes Mobiles de Reserve*

Following the creation of the *Police Nationale*, Admiral Darlan created the *Groupes Mobiles de Reserve* (GMR, Mobile Reserve Groups) on 7 July 1941.[4] He did so because he realised that in spite of dismissals of suspected anti-Vichy personnel, the police forces would still contain many officers and constables who would most likely ignore orders originating from Vichy. The GMR was to be the reliable police tool of Vichy for several years, and were heavily armed, militarised police units designed to counter guerrilla resistance. The GMR was composed of police reservists, often veterans or retired army personnel. Initially at least, the overwhelming majority of its members were loyal to the Vichy regime. The various GMR units were stationed in rural areas and moved as needed. They played a key role in rural anti-Resistance operations, particularly in coordination with German security forces and, beginning in 1943, the *Milice.*

This new force was initially staffed with 6,931 officers and enlisted men. The GMR was divided into regional groups of 217 men each and each group was a self-contained formation, capable of independent action. Each unit was named for the region in which it operated. The GMR were armed with rifles, pistols and light machine guns. At least three GMR groups were mounted on horses. By 1944, there were 11,200 men in the GMR divided into fifty-nine separate units operating throughout the French countryside.[5] The GMR also organised within the *Gendarmerie Nationale,* creating nine legions from what initially were 200 Rural Police officers and 6,000 Rural Police constables. Later on in 1944, this force reached a top strength of 300 officers and 9,000 men.[6] The units were stationed as follows:

> *1ère Légion de la Garde Mobile* – stationed in the city of Lyon
> *2e Légion de la Garde Mobile* – stationed in the city of Marseille
> *3e Légion de la Garde Mobile* – stationed in the city of Montpellier
> *4e Légion de la Garde Mobile* – stationed in the city of Riom
> *5e Légion de la Garde Mobile* – stationed in the city of Limoges
> *6e Légion de la Garde Mobile* – stationed in the city of Toulouse

The following units were located outside of Metropolitan France:

> *7e Légion de la Garde Mobile* – stationed in Algeria
> *8e Légion de la Garde Mobile* – stationed in Tunisia
> *9e Légion de la Garde Mobile* – stationed in Rabat

Obviously, when North Africa came under the complete control of the Allies in the spring of 1943, whatever police and army forces which the Vichy government had in this area were either disbanded, imprisoned, or (more likely) joined the Free French forces of General Charles de Gaulle. Thus, by the summer of 1943 the 7th 8th and 9th Legions no longer existed.

IIb. The *Garde Mobile*
The *Garde Mobile* (Mobile Guard) was a paramilitary police force used for crowd control, counter-insurgency, and the suppression of Resistance actions. It was absorbed into the *Gendarmerie* on 31 March 1941 by decree of the Vichy government. The *Garde Mobile* was supervised by regional prefects, who in turn, reported to the central Ministry. The Departmental and Municipal Police were subordinate to the *Police Nationale*, especially in the unoccupied zone. The commissariats were the local station posts that were managed by *commissaires* (inspectors/commissioners).

IIc. The *Gendarmerie Nationale*
The *Gendarmerie Nationale* (National Rural Police) was organised as 'legions' of battalion strength each, all named after the region in which they operated. This changed on 9 January 1943, when their regional names were replaced with a numerical system. One *Gendarmerie* battalion was actually armed with light tanks and was designated as the *75e Bataillon de Chars Légers de la Gendarmerie*. The unit was stationed at Montrouge. The following list includes all of the *Gendarmerie* legions (each roughly battalion in size), which existed in France as of February 1943. These were stationed as follows:

1e Legion des Flandres-Lille
2e Legion de Picardie Amiens
3e Legion de Normandie – Rouen
5e Legion de l'Orleanais- Orleans
6e Legion de Châlons-sur-Marne (now called Châlons-en-Champagne)
8e Legion de Bourgogne-Dijon
9e Legion Poitou-Poitiers (later transferred to Chateauroux)
10e Legion de Bretagne-Rennes
11e Legion d'Anjou-Nantes
12e Legion du Limousin-Limoges
14e Legion du Lyonnais-Lyon
16e Legion du Languedoc-Montpellier
17e Legion de Gascogne-Toulouse
18e Legion d'Acquitaine-Bordeaux
45e Bataillon de Chars Legers-Montr
Le Garde Personnelle du Marechal.
Garde Republicaine de Paris-Paris.

The *Garde Republicaine de Paris* was actually four legions (battalions) with 2,933 men. Of that number, 776 were mounted on horseback and comprised one of the four battalions of the *Garde Republicaine de*

Paris. On 18 February 1943 these men were placed at the disposal of the Chief of the Paris Prefect, Amédée Bussière, and absorbed into the Municipal Police force. As for the *Le Garde Personnelle du Marechal*, it was a force only concerned with the safety of Marshal Philippe Petain. This escort battalion was created on 19 August 1942. When the head of state was not travelling, the battalion formed the presidential guard at the town of Vichy. Initially it contained 420 men, but by 21 February 1943 the battalion strength had increased to 559 officers, NCOs and enlisted men.

IId The *Polices Spéciales*
The *Polices Spéciales* (Special Police) were specialised branches of the Vichy national police force (*Police Nationale*). It was created or expanded by the Ministry of the Interior during the Occupation. These were not regular police or *gendarmerie* units – they were civilian investigative and surveillance forces tasked with politically sensitive or repressive duties, often in direct cooperation with German security forces like the *Gestapo* and SD. Shortly after Adolf Hitler invaded the Soviet Union on 22 June 1941, communists' groups in France began sabotage and guerrilla attacks against the Germans. Interior Minister Pierre Pucheu realised that in order to fight the highly organised communists, the Vichy government needed a specially trained and dedicated anti-communist police force. Vichy did not trust their own regular police who often times would warn suspects of an impending arrest, ignore obvious fake documentation at checkpoints, and would even be members of the Resistance.

As time wore on, these acts against Vichy increased in frequency. The effectiveness of the regular Vichy police can be gauged on a sliding scale over the years 1940–4. The later the year, the less effective was the regular Vichy police force. It was essential therefore, even as early as the summer of 1941, that a select faction of trusted police officers be grouped and formed into a special unit which Pucheu titled the *Police Spéciales* (Special Police). There were two main sub-commands of the *Police Spéciales*. The first was called the *Service de Police Anti-Communiste* and the other was the *Brigades Spéciales*. The *Service de Police Anti-Communiste* often worked under cover and had paid informants. They had two main sections, one for unoccupied France where Vichy's rule was complete, and one for the occupied zone, where the German Army was master. The section in occupied France had twenty men under *Intendant de Police* Jurquet de la Salle, while the section in unoccupied France had an equal number of men and was led by *Intendant de Police* Charles Detmar.[7]

On 28 September 1942 the *Service de Police Anti-Communiste* was disbanded and its personnel drafted into a new French Vichy police department called the *Service des menées anti-nationales*, which would turn out to be the Vichy-French version of the *Gestapo*. When liberation came, a number of the members of the *Polices Spéciales* were able to reintegrate into the new Gaullist police force. Some however, whose hands had been tainted too much, were tried and sentenced. Some escaped in the late summer and early fall fled primarily to Germany, specifically to the Sigmaringen enclave in southwestern Germany (in Baden-Württemberg).[8] There the Germans established the Vichy government in exile. The Germans chose Sigmaringen because it was securely behind German lines and could serve as a propaganda tool to claim that Marshal Pétain and his ministers were still 'leading' France.

The Police Nationale as a Tool of Nazi Repression

The *Police Nationale* employed various security organisations which sought the interest and security of the Vichy-French government. The *Police Nationale* during the Vichy regime's term in office (1940–1) cooperated extensively with the *Gestapo*, *SiPo* and SD. It played a key role in the Vel' d'Hiv round-up (July 1942), arresting over 13,000 Jews in Paris. It also was complicit in the suppression of Resistance networks and pro-Gaullist sympathisers. The *Police Nationale* also targeted communists, Freemasons, and foreign refugees by performing surveillance on them. They were sometimes tasked with arresting individuals that were selected to be hostages to be shot. In this case, communists, Jews and lastly, Freemasons would be chosen.

Reorganisation of the French Police

The French *Gendarmerie* had always enjoyed the fact that it was led by professional military officers and never took orders from appointed civilian officials. A decree of 24 June 1942 redefined the role of the French *Gendarmerie* service and was geared to bring it closer to Vichy and to help fight the growing Resistance. The Ministry of Defence longer controlled it, and the *Gendarmerie* was now to be controlled by any ministry which required its assistance. Of course, the Ministry of the Interior would be its principal head, but any Vichy civilian official, most usually the local Prefect, could now command the men of the *Gendarmerie*. The only stipulation was that the order had to be given in writing. The men of the *Gendarmerie* resented this very much. In addition, the order that *Gendarmes* operating in the occupied zone were to only carry a pistol as their sole weapon was still left in place.[9]

Over all, the attempt to bring the *Gendarmerie* in line with the pro-German policies of Vichy failed. Orders were executed late, or not at all, or improperly. Men ignored orders altogether, and later still, joined the Resistance. In order to have better control of the regional police forces, the Vichy government assigned regional Prefects who were to take charge of the various police forces and departments and seek out those within their ranks and within the various communities who were either sabotaging impeding Vichy's rule. The Prefects were assisted in this by the Service de police were proving more and more ineffective, the Vichy regime continued its creation of special police forces that were ideologically in tune with its pro-German tendencies and policies, like the *Groupes Mobiles de Reserve*, the *Police Spéciales*, and later still the *Service des menées antinationales* (Service for Anti-National Activities) that replaced the *Service de Police Anti-Communiste*.

The *Service des menées antinationales* a French government surveillance and intelligence service tasked with monitoring and combating subversive, anti-national, or politically radical activities, especially during times of political tension. This type of agency was concerned with threats to national unity or internal security, such as espionage, communist agitation, or other perceived ideological threat. During the Vichy regime (1940–4), the *Service des menées antinationales* played a significant and troubling role. It became one of the tools of state repression, aimed at suppressing not just 'anti-national' activities in the traditional sense, but also resistance movements, communists, Jews, Freemasons, Gaullists, and others deemed enemies of the Vichy state or Nazi Germany. The service worked closely with the German authorities (*Gestapo* and SS) to identify and dismantle Resistance networks and arrest dissidents. It helped compile lists, conduct surveillance, and organise arrests. The service was heavily involved in rooting out communists (especially after the German invasion of the USSR in 1941) and played a part in Jewish persecution, though the bulk of that was handled by other Vichy institutions like the *Commissariat général aux questions juives* (General Commissariat for Jewish Affairs). It was a key arm of the Vichy regime responsible for implementing and overseeing anti-Jewish laws and policies during the Nazi occupation of France. Established in March 1941 by the Vichy government under German pressure – but it was also an expression of Vichy's own homegrown anti-Semitism. Its primary duties included:

1. Drafting and enforcing anti-Semitic legislation (e.g., the *Statut des Juifs*).
2. Organising the 'Aryanization' of Jewish property – seizing Jewish-owned businesses, homes, and assets and transferring them to non-Jews.

3. Compiling registries of Jews in France.
4. Coordinating with German authorities in the identification, arrest, and deportation of Jews to concentration and extermination camps.

The first head of the *Service de Police Anti-Communiste/Service des menées antinationales* was Xavier Vallat (a Catholic nationalist), later replaced by Louis Darquier de Pellepoix, a virulent antisemite and Nazi collaborator. Though it was a French institution, the *Commissariat Général aux Questions Juives* worked closely with the German SS and *Gestapo*, especially in organising the mass arrests of Jews (like the Vel' d'Hiv round-up in 1942). In addition to creating special police forces and assigning reliable prefects to the various regional police headquarters, the Vichy French government passed numerous decrees which made it mandatory for all French police headquarters in the occupied zone to coordinate their efforts with the local German military government garrison commanders (*Feldkommandanturen* and *Kreiskommandantur*).

Table 3. Comparison of Vichy French Police and Security Forces, 1941–1944

Force	Date Established	Absorbed/ Changed	Role	Affiliation
Garde Mobile	1921	Absorbed into the *Gendarmerie* on 31 March 1941	Public order, crowd control	Military (Ministry of War/ Defence)
Gendarmerie Mobile	March 1941	Result of *Garde Mobile* absorption	Rapid-reaction force, paramilitary policing	Military
Groupes Mobiles de Réserve	7 July 1941	Dissolved in 1944	Internal security, anti-*Maquis* repression	Civilian (Ministry of Interior)
Milice	30 January 1943	Dissolved in 1944	Political repression, anti-Resistance	Political, paramilitary under Vichy Govt.
Polices Spéciales	March 1941	Dissolved in August 1944	Surveillance, suppression of Jews, communists, Freemasons, assisting the *Gestapo*	*Police Nationale* (Ministry of the Interior)

The headquarters of these military governors were the equivalent of regimental and battalion staffs and had a small cadre of army personnel and some rear area security forces. However, whether this order was followed or not depended on the allegiance (or lack thereof) of the local Vichy police commander. As 1942 turned into 1943, the political atmosphere within the Vichy police began to change. By 1944 most people knew that Germany was likely going to lose the war. This, more than anything else, caused many members of the French police to question their loyalty to Vichy. On the date of the Allied landings in France on 6 June 1944, the strength of the police forces in metropolitan France stood as follows:

Table 4. Vichy French Police Forces, 6 June 1944

Formation	Southern Zone	Northern Zone	Grand Total
Police de Corps Urbains	14,081	15,102	29,183
Groupes Mobiles de Réserve	7,860	3,757	11,617
Garde Republicaine de Paris	n/a	2,758	2,758
Garde Mobile	5,840	n/a	5,840
Gendarmerie Mobile	19,088	17,518	36,606
Total:	46,869	39,135	86,004

The above figures do not include 5,493 firefighters and 2,666 Reserve Firemen and 7,033 *Gardes de Communications* (Communications Police), plus the thousands of *Francs Gardes* of the *Milice*. The *Francs-Gardes* were distinct in that they were uniformed, armed, and had a para-military organisation, often participating directly in anti-Resistance operations and, later, in combat alongside German units (including the *Waffen-SS*). The *Milice* overall had around 25,000 members by 1944, but not all were *Francs-Gardes*. The *Francs-Gardes* likely numbered between 7,000 and 10,000 men at their peak in strength.

The Fall of Vichy

The end of an actual, semi-independent Vichy France came to an end in November 1942. In that month, the German Army in occupied France sent in elements of the *1. Armee* and the *7. Armee*. The *1. Armee* was the main force moving into southern and southwestern France from the north. At the time, *1. Armee* was led by *Generaloberst* Johannes Blaskowitz.

The headquarters of *1. Armee* was located in the Bordeaux area. The *7. Armee*, led by *Generaloberst* Friedrich Dollmann, was mostly stationed in Brittany and Normandy. The *7. Armee* basically sent whatever mobile units they had for the operation.

These were detached to aid in the occupation. In particular, the *335. Infanterie-Division*, a static unit assigned to coastal guard duty, was useful in the occupation. This division had been stationed near the Vichy-occupied zone border since mid-1941. It helped to occupy Marseilles. The *7. Panzer-Division* – nicknamed the *Gespensterdivision* ('Ghost Division') reached Toulon on 11 November, entering on 27 November. The *II. SS-Panzerkorps*, which made its appearance in France in August 1942, employed its three divisions in the occupation of southern France. At the time, *II. SS-Panzerkorps* was composed of *1. SS-Infanterie-Division (mot.) 'Leibstandarte SS Adolf Hitler'*, *2. SS-Infanterie-Division (mot.) 'Das Reich'*, and the *3. SS-Infanterie-Division (mot.) 'Totenkopf'*.[10]

Elements of the *Wehrmacht*'s security divisions, *Feldgendarmerie*, and *Gestapo*/SD accompanied the army units in order to establish control over the countryside and conduct surveillance. The German police forces were particularly interested in capturing the entire files section of the Vichy-French police. The civilian and personnel files would later prove vital to the Nazis, as they began to search what had been unoccupied France, for foreigners, Jews, communists and freemasons. When the Germans occupied the previously unoccupied Vichy zone during Operation *Anton*, they were able to successfully access and make use of Vichy French police and administrative files. These records became instrumental in the escalation of Nazi repression in southern France.

Between July 1940 and November 1942, the Vichy regime had compiled detailed surveillance records, including the identity files on Jews and foreigners (especially after the *Statut des Juifs* of 1940–1). The records also included all police surveillance done to political dissidents, particularly communists and Gaullists. It also included files from every local prefecture, records held by the numerous police inspectors, and the intelligence services (e.g. the *Renseignements Généraux*). The Vichy government also had the Masonic lodge registries. Once the *Wehrmacht*, *Gestapo*, and SS moved into the Free Zone, they worked closely with the existing Vichy-French police, particularly with the virulently anti-Semitic French *Milice* (after 1943) and Vichy's Ministry of the Interior, to exploit all of these files and lists. The end-result was mass arrests and deportations of Jews, foreign and domestic. They also rounded up former Spanish Republican members who had been living in southern France since the fall of the Spanish Republic in March 1939.

These men and women were now arrested and sent to concentration camps in Germany. With these pre-existing Vichy registration files, the Germans were able to identify and locate Jews in southern France using (from both 1940 and 1941). These records enabled the Nazis to perform targeted round-ups, especially from 1943–4, like *Unternehmen Frühlingsbrise*, (Operation Spring Breeze), which was the German codename for a large-scale round-up of Jews in France during spring–summer 1942, including the infamous Vel' d'Hiv' round-up in July 1942. The Drancy transit camp, which had previously held mostly Jews from northern France, began to receive detainees from the south as well. Arrests of foreigners and refugees only increased as time went on. Not only were Spanish Republicans apprehended, but also Polish Jews, German political exiles, and other refugee groups who were tracked down and arrested – all because of the Vichy registration files – often from internment camps like *Gurs, Rivesaltes*, and *Les Milles*.

Many people were handed over to the Germans under the German-French police cooperation agreements, including the 1942 Oberg-Bousquet protocol. The files also aided the Nazis in suppressing the civilian population and in combating the Resistance. Local police intelligence files also allowed the Germans to crack down on Resistance groups, communist cells, and networks like the communist-run FTP. This intensified after the creation of the *Milice* in 1943, as this paramilitary force, loyal to Vichy, but deeply integrated with German security operations, began to take part in raids, anti-partisan operations and in patrolling the city and rural regions of France.

The operation to occupy Vichy French territory had actually been prepared by General Adolf Heusinger as early as December 1940. It was then that the codename 'Attila' was first used in a document dated '10.12.40' (10 December 1940).[11] *Unternehmen Attila*, planned in December 1940 under Führer Directive No. 19, was the German strategic contingency for a full occupation of the Vichy 'unoccupied zone' should France align with the Allies or the Western Mediterranean become threatened. The *Luftwaffe* (Air Force) and *Heer* (Army) were to coordinate in seizing the French airfields and coastal installations. The *Wehrmacht* and *Luftwaffe* were to secure military assets – especially airfields and naval ports – and prevent the French fleet from defecting or joining the Allies. *Unternehmen Lila* (Operation Lila), was a parallel operation that was to take place during 'Attila'.

The purpose of *Unternehmen Lila* was to seize the French fleet at Toulon intact. '*Unternehmen Attila*' was planned, but never executed in its original form. Instead, the similar *Unternehmen Anton* was executed from 11–27 November 1942, following the Allied landings in North Africa – codenamed Operation Torch. When '*Anton*' was executed, German forces allocated for the operation included German divisions from *1. Armee* and *7. Armee*. These division were to advance from Atlantic and central France. In addition, the Italian 4th Army was to occupy the southern coastal areas bordering the Italian-French frontier of August 1940. During the operation, the Vichy Army offered only token resistance but quickly complied with the German order to disarm.

Although *Anton* went without a hitch, *Lila* failed. The French scuttled their fleet on 27 November 1942, just as German tanks from *7. Panzer-Division* entered the port of Toulon. The loss of the Vichy fleet at Toulon was a painful one. The Germans were hoping to grab the three battleships, seven cruisers, and twenty-eight destroyers which were moored at Toulon. In addition, there were twenty submarines that the *Kriegsmarine* was dying to get their hands on. Had the Germans obtained these subs, they could have created three or four wolfpacks that could threaten Allied shipping in the Mediterranean. As it happened, the Vichy-French naval command, employing a ruse, was able to delay the Germans long enough for the ships to be scuttled, thus preventing the entire fleet from falling into the hands of the Nazis. The German occupation of Vichy France in November 1942 unlocked direct access to a wealth of police and administrative files, which had already been compiled under the Vichy regime. These were quickly exploited by Nazi authorities, significantly enhancing the repression and deportation efforts in southern France.

Chapter 5

INDEPENDENT PRO-GERMAN MILITIAS

La Milice

The origins of the *Milice* date back to the *Service d'ordre Legionnaire* (SOL) which was created by Joseph Darnand in 1941 and operated in unoccupied France.[1] The SOL had the 'blessing' of Vichy Interior Minister, Joseph Darnand, and his Interior Secretary, Pierre Pucheu. Initially the formation was a patriotic organisation but in reality, it was geared to promote Petain's version of a Fascist New Order in France. In fact, a month after Germany invaded the unoccupied southern zone (November 1942), Adolf Hitler met with Pierre Laval. This meeting occurred on 19 December 1942. Hitler basically told Laval that Germany was not satisfied with the reliability of the French police and that the Vichy government should create a brand-new police force, whose loyalty would not be questioned.[2] Laval did not waste any time, speaking with Darnand in early January 1943 and proposing to use the SOL to create the *Milice*.

On 31 January 1943 a decree changed its title to *La Milice*. The headquarters of the organisation was in Vichy. Initially, the *Milice* was to have a table of organisation strength of 29,000 members, although its membership remained around 25,000 militiamen throughout its existence, meaning that those number of volunteers went through the ranks as full or part-time *Milicien*.[3] While many members were part-time *Milicien*, there was a permanent armed barracks police force within the *Milice* called the *Franc-Garde*. The *Franc-Garde* therefore, was the armed wing of the *Milice*. It was established in June 1943. It was organised into tiers of generic formation names rather than numbered battalions:

- *main* (one chief + four men)
- *dizaine* (10–15 men, a combat group)
- *trentaine* (30-man section, one per provincial capital)
- *centaine* (100 to 120-man company, in regional capitals; 'mobile' or 'normal')
- cohorte (300 to 360-man battalion)
- centre (900 to 1,080-man regiment, made of multiple *cohortes*)

In early 1944, there was a *cohort* stationed in the town of Vichy, and a *centaine* each in the cities of Lyon, Marseille and Toulouse. In addition, there was a *trentaine* section in each of the forty-five southern departments of Metropolitan France. While the strength of the *Milice* never exceeded more than 15,000 men at any one time, the strength of the *Franc-Garde* peaked at just under 4,000 men by June 1944. Some sources differ as to the number of active *Franc-Garde* members. These estimates range from 1,700 to as many as 6,000.[4] Although the *Milice* had been ordered created by the Germans, they did not trust the French enough to initially arm it in January 1943. This now came back to haunt the Germans as militiamen began to be assassinated by the French underground. In fact, during the summer of 1943, the *Maquis* had received specific orders from British intelligence regarding the *Milice*: 'They are unarmed, hit them now! They have nothing to shoot back with'. The *Milice* lost seventy men before the Germans realised they had better arm them or they would lose more volunteers. In April 1943 permission was granted for selected Vichy French political and military movements to parade openly, and in September 1943 the SS allowed the *Milice* to establish training camps in order to train members in policing matters.

In this way, an initial batch of 600 *Miliciens* began training under SD officers.[5] Joseph Darnand's post as second in command of the *Milice* was titled as either 'Executive Commander of the *Milice*' or 'National Chief of the *Milice*'.[6] In addition to the *Franc Garde*, the *Milice* had two other departments – the *Avant Garde Milicienne* (*Milice* Youth Section), and '*Les Miliciennes*' (*Milice* Women's Section).

While the youth sections were later tapped for volunteers in the *33. Waffen-Grenadier-Division der-SS 'Charlemagne'*, and the female members were used in a support role, the bulk of the fighting performed by the *Franc-Garde*. Within the *Franc-Garde*, you had the *Franc Garde Permanente* and the *Franc Garde Non permanente*. The *Franc Garde Permanente* was the 'permanent' (quartered in barracks) troops and the *Franc Garde Non permanente* was the part-time volunteer force.

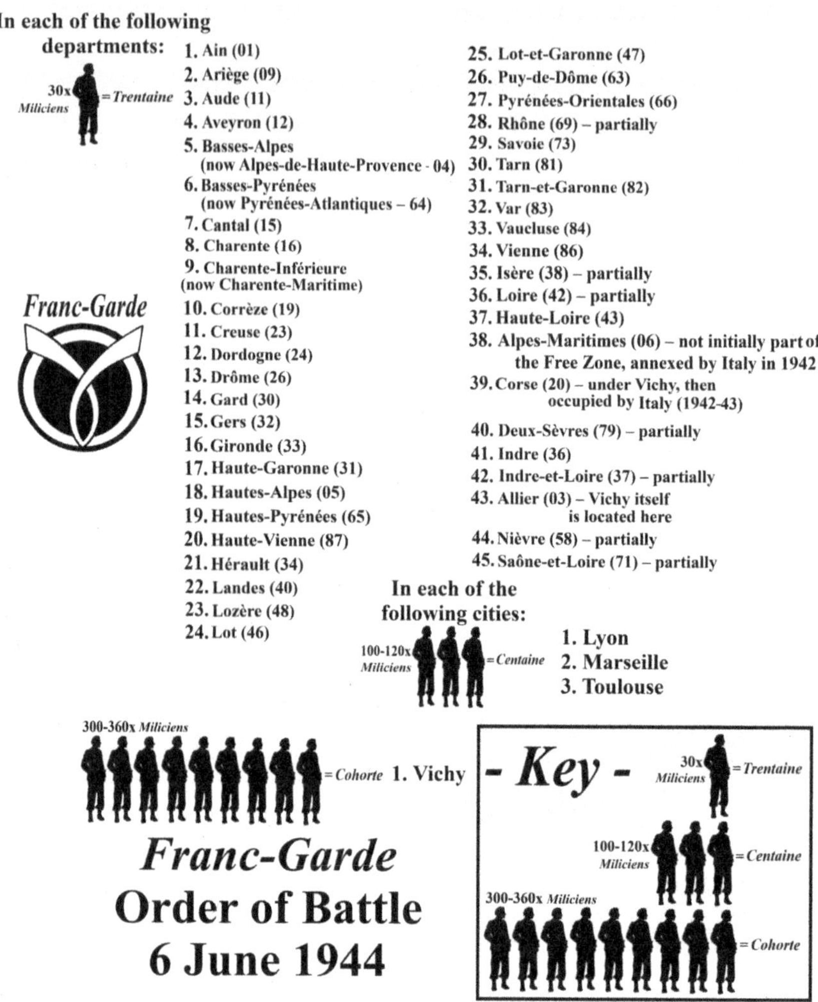

Figure 4. The *Franc-Garde* Order of Battle for 6 June 1944.

The insignia of the *Milice* was the letter 'Gamma' in the Greek alphabet. It had been chosen since this Greek letter in the zodiac was represented by the Ram, a symbol of power. In addition, the Ram symbol in the zodiac also stood for spring in the seasonal year. Thus, in one fell swoop, the *Milice* use of the Gamma letter was meant to represent power associated with rebirth and strength.[7]

When the Allies landed in Normandy on 6 June 1944, the *Milice* was put on alert. Seven days later, on 13 June a general call-up of all active and part-time volunteers was announced. A total of 6,695 *Miliciens* heeded the call-up. Of this number, 4,740 were part-time volunteers while 1,955 were the full-time *Franc-Garde*. It appears then, that only a small number of the estimated 25,000–29,000 *Miliciens* who served at one time or another heeded the call-up. An average of three men out of four decided it was time to either seek anonymity or to join the *Maquisards* in the hope that their collaboration would go undetected. Before 6 June 1944, about 100,000 French citizens collaborated in one way or another with the Germans. On 7 June 1944 these people suddenly declared they were for General De Gaulle and tried to blend in. After the Allied invasion of France, the Germans found it wise to transfer the Vichy government to Alsace-Lorraine, near the pre-war Franco-German border. But by late summer that region was also threatened by the Allied advance.

At the end of August 1944 about 6,000 surviving *Miliciens* and 41,000 of their dependents (who feared retribution by association) withdrew from Belfort, France.[8] Their arrival in Alsace-Lorraine had been dramatic. The local French population (that part which had not been deported in 1940), had initially greeted the *Milice* as friends and liberators, but upon realising that these men were not Free French troops, their praise and waving had turned to shouts of insults or looks of disapproval. Many in the *Milice* had mistreated their countrymen horribly. For their crimes, many *Miliciens* which were caught by the FFI and civilian population in general, were destined to suffer terrible and gruesome torture before being killed. One *Maquisard* kept a diary of the actions of his partisan unit. He wrote how he witnessed the horrors perpetrated on a captured *Milicien* in July 1944. His account says it all:

> Aged twenty-nine, married three months ago, made to saw wood in the hot sun wearing a pullover and jacket, made to drink warm salted water, ears cut off, covered with blows from fists and bayonets, stoned, made to dig his grave, made to lie in it, finished off with a sharp blow in the stomach from a spade, two days to die.[9]

Most women who collaborated with the Germans got off a lot easier. They were stripped of their clothes in public and their heads were shaved. In many cases a Swastika was either painted or carved into their foreheads. In the most extreme cases, women were also killed. After having withdrawn from many regions of France, *Milice* militiamen and other collaborators converged in the area of Belfort. It was there that the Vichy government in exile was now located. Most of the *Milice* had been operating in what had previous to November 1942, been the unoccupied zone in southern France. Some *Milice* were operating in the northern region of France, but the overwhelming number were in the south. When the call-up had come on 13 June 1944, 415 *Franc-Garde* came from the north, while 1,540 *Franc-Garde* were moving from southern France. They now followed Marshal Petain, who was a virtual prisoner of the Germans by now, as well as other Vichy leaders. They all withdrew from Belfort for Sigmaringen, Germany where the Vichy government in exile was to be relocated.[10]

They travelled through Mulhouse, Struthof, and Ulm. Of the 6,000 *Milicien*, about 2,500 were deemed physically fit and were sent to join the forming French *33. Waffen-Grenadier-Division der-SS 'Charlemagne'*, while 400 more remained at Sigmaringen and became the 'palace guard' for Marshal Pétain.[11] Joseph Darnand kept 250 men as his personal bodyguard. He left with this small force for northern Italy on 12 March 1945. Darnand attempted to escape into Switzerland but was captured by Italian partisans at Tirano. He was tried by a French court and executed on 10 October 1945. Many other *Miliciens* were executed at the end of the war. Those who were spared lived because by then the anger and thirst for revenge by the Free French had been basically satisfied. Those lucky enough not to be killed were given the choice of being jailed or to serve in Indochina as part of the *Légion étrangère française* (French Foreign Legion). In cases where a *Milice* member was judged to have collaborated more closely with the Germans, he was either killed or, in some rare instances, allowed to join the *Légion étrangère*. All those who were given a choice, chose service in the Legion, either in Indochina or in France's African possessions. Many died there serving in the French Foreign Legion. A good number were killed at the battle of Diem Bien Phu in 1954.

La Police Allemand (Carlingue)

The *Police Allemand* was established in 1941. The *Carlingue*, as they were more commonly known, was led by Pierre Bonny, a former French police officer. Later, Henri Lafont and Pierre Loutrel, both professional criminals, took over its operations.[12] The group was based at 93 rue Lauriston, in Paris. The term *'Police Allemand'* actually came from the manner in which these French operatives of the *Gestapo* would announce themselves. When approaching a suspicious person who needed to be questioned, or whether they were knocking on the door of a suspect's apartment, they would always announce themselves as

'*Police Allemand!*' ('German Police!'). The *Carlingue* operated under the direction of the SD. The *Gestapo* was an integral part of the German SS and police forces which helped to control France and which fought the partisans.

The *Gestapo* was an instrument of repression and terror, which became even more effective by the recruitment of local French men (and some women) into its organisation. The *Gestapo* recruited these French citizens regionally and employed them in the areas where they lived. This was done because it was thought the volunteers would know their own regions but more importantly, they would know the local people. The theory was that local agents would be more effective in rooting out Jews, communists, Allied sympathisers and just about anyone who opposed the Nazis or the Vichy government. Many French authors have tried to paint these *Gestapo* volunteers as simply being recruited from the dregs of human society, such as common criminals, sadists, opportunists, smugglers, and the like.

While many who served in the *Gestapo* were indeed ruffians and criminals, many others were believers in the Nazi-Fascist cause and were everyday, run of the mill Frenchmen. It is a whitewash to simply say that every French citizen employed by the *Gestapo* came from the criminal caste. It may be painful for the French nation to accept, but the truth is that many who served, served because they believed in what they were doing. Most were fascists, or fascist-leaning. The *Carlingue*'s primary role was to assist the *Gestapo* in identifying and arresting members of the French Resistance. Members of the *Carlingue* often operated in plain clothes, blending into French society to infiltrate resistance networks. They were involved in intelligence gathering, conducting raids, and interrogating detainees. Their activities were marked by brutality and a lack of due process. They utilised torture and other coercive methods to extract information from suspects.

The *Gestapo* had regional offices where the French volunteers were recruited and stationed. The recruiting offices were located in the following cities: Anger, Chălon sur Marne, Poitiers, Saint-Quentin, Rouen, Nancy, Orleans, Rennes, Bordeaux and Dijon. In each of these regional offices a *Kommando* was established that contained a number of French volunteers assisting the local German *Gestapo* unit.[13] For organisational purposes, these *Kommandos* were under the local *Kommandeur der Sicherheitspolizei* (KdS). These KdS commands were located throughout occupied France, with one located in Vichy (in unoccupied France) to represent the RSHA. The KdS commands were as follows:

1. KdS Paris
    *   Location: Paris
    *   Area of Responsibility: The most prominent KdS, overseeing the capital and surrounding regions, dealing with political repression, the persecution of Jews, and coordination with the Gestapo.

2. KdS Lyon
    *   Location: Lyon
    *   Area of Responsibility: Lyon was a key city in the French Resistance movement. The KdS here managed intelligence gathering and suppression of local Resistance activities. It was involved in many of the arrests and deportations of Resistance members and Jews.

3. KdS Marseille
    *   Location: Marseille
    *   Area of Responsibility: Marseille was a vital port city, and the KdS office here focused on maintaining control over the southern French coast, controlling Resistance movements and dealing with deportations.

4. KdS Bordeaux
    *   Location: Bordeaux
    *   Area of Responsibility: Bordeaux, located in southwestern France, was a significant location for the Gestapo, handling repression, arrests, and deportations.

5. KdS Lille
    *   Location: Lille
    *   Area of Responsibility: This region, in the north of France, was important for monitoring both industrial output and local Resistance groups. It had strong coordination with the German military and the local collaborationist forces.

6. KdS Toulouse
    *   Location: Toulouse
    *   Area of Responsibility: Toulouse, in southwestern France, served as an important hub for the KdS, overseeing political repression, particularly in the rural areas of the region.

7. KdS Rennes
    - Location: Rennes (Brittany)
    - Area of Responsibility: Rennes, located in the western part of France, was home to a key KdS office overseeing parts of Brittany. This area was known for significant Resistance activity and efforts to infiltrate local groups.

8. KdS Nancy
    - Location: Nancy
    - Area of Responsibility: Nancy was in the northeastern part of France, close to the German border. The KdS here monitored movements, especially in regions like Lorraine, which had significant industrial importance.

9. KdS Strasbourg
    - Location: Strasbourg
    - Area of Responsibility: Situated on the Franco-German border, Strasbourg was an area of particular interest for the SD and KdS. It was responsible for coordinating the repression in the region of Alsace and Lorraine, especially after they were annexed by Germany.

10. KdS Vichy
    - Location: Vichy (Vichy France, unoccupied zone)
    - Area of Responsibility: The KdS in Vichy was responsible for maintaining control over the southern part of France, which was technically under the Vichy government's control. The KdS collaborated closely with the Vichy regime, conducting surveillance and controlling internal opposition.

11. KdS Clermont-Ferrand
    - Location: Clermont-Ferrand
    - Area of Responsibility: The KdS here managed the central regions of France, where Resistance groups were active. The area was also crucial in military and logistical operations for the Germans.

12. KdS Nantes
    - Location: Nantes (Western France)
    - Area of Responsibility: This KdS office was involved in monitoring the western regions of France, especially in the Brittany and Pays de la Loire regions.

The total number of personnel stationed in a KdS command could vary widely depending on the size and significance of the city or region. Based on the structure of personnel outlined above, the total number of personnel in a typical KdS office would be approximately:

- Small KdS offices (in smaller towns or less strategically important areas): 50–100 personnel, including administrative staff, officers, and some police. These numbers were for German personnel only, and did not count French members of the *Gestapo* or *SiPo*.
- Larger KdS offices (in major cities or key resistance hotspots like Paris, Lyon, and Marseille): 150–300 personnel, including officers, investigators, enforcement, and auxiliary forces. As above, these numbers were for German personnel only, and did not count French members of the *Gestapo* or *SiPo*.

These figures reflect the average staffing levels, but larger or more significant KdS offices could have had more personnel, especially if the area was highly active with Resistance or Resistance suppression operations. Initially there were eleven (then twelve) KdS commands in France but by August 1944 there were a total of twenty such KdS headquarters all over occupied France. In addition to the KdS commands listed previously (Paris, Lyon, Marseille, Bordeaux, Lille, Toulouse, Rennes, Nancy, Strasbourg, Vichy, Clermont-Ferrand, Nantes), the other KdS commands that were established or expanded by August 1944 were:

Additional KdS Commands:

13. KdS Caen
    - Location: Caen, Normandy
    - Area of Responsibility: The KdS office in Caen was important for controlling the Normandy region, particularly as the area became a critical point for Resistance activities. This office was involved in the suppression of Resistance movements in the wake of the Allied invasion in 1944.

14. KdS Rouen
    - Location: Rouen, Normandy
    - Area of Responsibility: Rouen, also in Normandy, had a significant KdS presence. The region was vital for Nazi logistical operations, and the KdS here was responsible for managing intelligence gathering and Resistance suppression.

15. KdS Angers
    - Location: Angers
    - Area of Responsibility: This city in the Loire region was significant for monitoring Resistance groups and carrying out arrests related to anti-German activities.

16. KdS Dijon
    - Location: Dijon
    - Area of Responsibility: Dijon, located in Burgundy, was an important KdS site for controlling the central-eastern part of France, coordinating with military units and addressing growing Resistance threats.

17. KdS Tours
    - Location: Tours
    - Area of Responsibility: Tours was a key city for military operations and internal security, overseeing a large area of central France, including parts of the Loire Valley.

18. KdS Besançon
    - Location: Besançon, Franche-Comté
    - Area of Responsibility: Besançon was a strategic city in eastern France, close to the Swiss border, and its KdS had an active role in monitoring the movement of Resistance groups, intelligence activities, and border control.

19. KdS Toulon
    - Location: Toulon, Provence-Alpes-Côte d'Azur
    - Area of Responsibility: Toulon was a significant naval base, and the KdS here was responsible for overseeing the security of the Mediterranean region and dealing with Resistance movements, especially following the Allied invasion in 1944.

20. KdS Montpellier
    - Location: Montpellier, Languedoc-Roussillon
    - Area of Responsibility: Montpellier, located in southern France, was important for the management of Resistance groups and intelligence-gathering in this region, which saw increased partisan activity.

Altogether, the *Sicherheitspolizei* (the *Gestapo* and *Kriminalpolizei*) could count on 2,500 Germans in the whole of France. These were assisted by some 30,000 Frenchmen (some in uniform, some in civilian clothes). Therefore, the ratio of Frenchmen to Germans in these *Kommandos* was around 12:1. That is, twelve French *Gestapo* volunteers to one German *SiPo*, SD, or *Gestapo* member. There were several unique French-manned formations serving the local *SiPo*/SD/*Gestapo* units. One of these French *Kommando* units was a 'self-defence police force' which was created in 1943 and called the *Selbstschutzpolizei*. The following section mentions some of the principal collaborationist formations which operated under the SS command.

The *Selbstschutzpolizei*

The *Selbstschutzpolizei* was born from an idea by the *Höhere-SS und Polizeiführer Frankreich* (Higher SS & Police Leader France), *SS-Gruppenführer* Karl Oberg, in the spring of 1943. As stated earlier, official permits for pro-German Frenchmen to bear arms were severely restricted. Oberg had the idea to group those Frenchmen who wanted to defend themselves into a *Selbstschutz* (self-defence) formation. Of course, this new unit would not be under the control of the Vichy government, but would be run directly by the German *SiPo* and SD command. At the same time the German police needed more and more French volunteers to assist them in the fight against the growing Resistance. In the spring of 1943 Oberg ordered *SS-Standartenführer* Dr. Hermann Bickler to organise what would become the French *Selbstschutzpolizei* (Self Defence Police).[14] Bickler was an Alsatian lawyer who was born in Germany in 1904. He later became a French citizen after 1918, when the province of Alsace was returned to France.[15]

Since 1926, he had been an activist within Alsatian separatist groups who wanted Alsace to be returned to Germany. At the beginning of the war, Bickler was mobilised as a sergeant in the French Army. He was found guilty of pro-German propaganda and was arrested and sent to jail in Nancy. Later he was incarcerated in Carcassonne. After the Franco-German armistice, he was liberated and returned to Alsace, which was now part of Germany once again. He joined the NSDAP and rose quickly in the ranks to become 'Kreisleiter' (District Leader) in the city of Strasburg. The position of *Kreisleiter* came with many responsibilities. For example, the *Kreisleiter* was responsible for supervising all Nazi Party activity within the district. They managed political propaganda, membership, and party discipline.

They reported up the chain to the *Gauleitung* (regional office). *Kreisleiter* were often involved in coordination with the *Gestapo* and SS on security matters and ideological enforcement, especially after the war began. They were also responsible for aspects of implementing anti-Jewish policies, including persecution or deportation, in coordination with Nazi security agencies. In 1943 Bickler became an *SS-Standartenführer* and was posted to Paris in May as the new Chief of *Abteilung VI* (Intelligence) of the *SiPo* and SD. He was assisted by *SS-Hauptsturmführer* Weizel and *SS-Obersturmführer* Hans Keller.[16] Bickler seized three French castles whose former proprietors were Jewish in the region of Taverny, northwest of Paris.

The three castles were: (1) Château Vaucelles, (2) Château Haut-Tertre, and (3) Château Jäger. This three-castle complex became the *'Taverny SD Schule'*. On 3 July 1943, in Château Vaucelles, Bickler organised a meeting between eighty German intelligence officers and collaborationist Frenchmen. The French were *SiPo*/SD agents and the Chiefs of security from numerous Fascist parties; such as the French Popular Party (PPF) and its 'Y-Bureau', French Party, and the *National Popular Regroupement* (RNP), plus some smaller right wing ultra-groups like the 'Youth of New Europe'. They agreed that each volunteer would have to go through an interview with Bickler or one of his assistants in their Parisian office, located at 55 Lannes Boulevard. After that, the French volunteer's file would be analysed by Bickler himself, who would give the final approval or denial to the man's application. The ones who were accepted were called and sent on to the Taverny School where they were to take part in an intensive two-week course. After that, the volunteer returned home with an automatic pistol, a gun permit, and a special *Ausweiss* (pass) giving him the right to be assisted by and to help the German police in any situation.

By this time the commander of the school was designated. He was a Frenchman named Jacques Duge de Bernonville. He was assisted by a former LVF Lieutenant named Sorel de Neufchâteau. In 1944 both men were removed from their posts by the Germans. Jacques Duge de Bernonville went on to serve in the *Milice*, where he took control of those forces in the city of Lyons. On 12 February 1944 the *Selbstschutzpolizei* (SSP) was completely reorganised by Bickler as noted in an order numbered '186/44' from the *Höhere-SS und Polizeiführer* Karl Oberg to *Befehlshaber der Sicherheitspolizei und SD* (Supreme Commander of the Security Police and SD) *SS-Standartenführer* Helmut Knochen and *Befehlshaber der Ordnungspolizei* (Supreme Commander of the Order Police), *SS-Brigadeführer und Generalmajor der Schutzpolizei* Paul Scheer.[17]

Initially, *Generalmajor der Polizei* Bolko von Schweinichen had led the *Orpo* in Paris beginning in May 1942, but he had been replaced by *Oberst der Schutzpolizei* Walter Schimana in March 1943. Schimana left in May 1943 and *Generalmajor der Polizei* Paul Scheer then assumed command. Scheer had been commander of the *Orpo* in Kiev, in the Ukraine in 1941.[18] The new commander of the Taverny School as of 1 January 1944 was *SS-Sturmbannführer* Georg Best. Best had been charged with overseeing the French police in the occupied part of France which was under the German military government.[19] When the southern part of France was occupied in November 1942, his duties were expanded to include those French police forces in this region as well. The training and administrative personnel of the Taverny School were as follows:

Hauptmann der Schutzpolizei der Reserve Rambacher.
SS-Obersturmführer und Oberleutnant der Schutzpolizei Riedinger, Chief of Operations.
Polizeiinspektor Stranz, Police Secretary.
Meister der Gendarmerie der Reserve Rosse.
Meister der Gendarmerie Gneist
Meister der Gendarmerie Senkbeil
Zugwachmeister der Schutzpolizei Caspar.
Zugwachmeister der Schutzpolizei Hoffman.
SS-Hauptscharführer Reichert, *SiPo/SD*.
SS-Unterscharführer Buchmeier, *SiPo/SD*.
Ms. Anna Grunwald, German translator.
A French administrative employee (name unknown).

In May 1944, as Chief of Operations, *SS-Obersturmführer* Riedinger was assisted by *SS-Obersturmführer* Brayer and *SS-Hauptscharführer* Freuntzel, a.k.a. 'Max Jakob', including many trainers, former LVF volunteers and other Russian Front veterans, like Captain Madec, Warrant Officer Lacroix, Sergeant Florea, and Sergeant Buisset. We can note that all German personnel were career (professional) police officers & officials. The *Selbstschutzpolizei* was dependent on the *Orpo* for training, weaponry, and administrative affairs, but had to refer to the *SiPo/*SD for any political matters. Training and the use of the *Selbstschutzpolizei* in missions were expanded while the regular training course began to be monthly, with a three-week duration period. The students received pay for those three weeks and learned the techniques of sabotage, radio operation, and right-wing political philosophy and ideology. When they returned home, they had to keep secret their activities and training.

The French volunteers were liable to be called into active duty only by a personal order of the *Höhere-SS und Polizeiführer Frankreich* Karl Oberg, for special missions or to protect any objectives like railways, factories, political offices, important persons, etc. Around 5,000 young

Frenchmen were eventually trained in Taverny, including many foreigners like White Russians, Spaniards, Italians, Serbians, Flemish and Walloon volunteers from Belgium, and Arabs from North Africa and elsewhere. The best students were asked to stay as full-time policemen. About 150 remained permanently stationed at the Taverny School, with fifty full-time members grouped into each large town, or city close to the respective castle. Those permanent forces included some French-speaking foreigners, the more notable being a French-Canadian, and a Kabyle, Amar Irguiz, who was actually a former member of the *Waffen-SS*. Amar Irguiz was from the Kabyle Tribe – who were the first descendants of the first real North Africans. The Kabyle Tribe were Berbers (Amazigh), particularly from the Kabylie region of northern Algeria. The Kabyle Tribe hid in the mountains during the Arab invasion, so Islamisation had been slow and superficial.

Many of them were Christians. The Germans considered the Kabyles to be of 'Aryan' origin, and many were actually blond and blue eyed. After the war, Amar Irguiz was to be jailed and sent to Indochina, with the BILOM, a French penal battalion. The acronym BILOM stands for *Bataillon d'Infanterie Légère d'Outre-Mer*, which translates in English to 'Overseas Light Infantry Battalion'. This was a French military unit formed after the war, primarily composed of former German prisoners of war and French collaborators, including members of the *Milice* and the LVF. The battalion was established on 27 May 1948, following a directive from French Minister of Justice André Marie. The unit was conceived as a means to provide a form of 'expiation' for individuals who had been involved in collaborationist activities during the war. They were offered the opportunity to serve in the French colonial army in exchange for a temporary pardon, allowing them to reintegrate into French society. Amar Irguiz survived the First Indochina War, taking part in many battles. Deemed rehabilitated, he re-entered society and later became a prominent businessman.

Selbstschutzpolizei members wore a special blue uniform. The battle dress was a former blue uniform used by French mountain troops – the blue garrison cap with the *Kriegsmarine* (German Navy) soft cover, with a small metallic German police insignia. On the left arm they wore a yellow cuff band with black lettering spelling the word '*Selbstschutz*'. Sometimes they would go into action with German *SiPo*/SD uniforms, but they mostly worked in civilian clothes primarily for undercover tasks. With the blue uniform, the full-time members received an 8mm calibre French Model 1892 revolver. They also carried a French Model 1892 carbine. It is possible that individuals may have also carried other types of arms. Both were obsolete First World War weapons. While the British were arming the FFI with the latest submachine guns, the Germans were equipping their French collaborationist forces with mostly outdated equipment.

In the months of April and May 1944, three mobile groups (*Rollkommandos*) were formed with full-time *Selbstschutzpolizei* members and sent to the cities of Dijon, Toulouse, and Rennes. From the Taverny School, these cities were located northeast, southwest, and west (respectively). The *Toulouse Kommando* left Taverny Headquarters with nine men on 15 April 1944. The Dijon *Kommando* left by 30 April with eight men under the command of SD Sergeant Haus. The *Rennes Kommando* arrived in that city on 8 May and had with them thirteen men under the command of *SS-Hauptscharführer* Freuntzel, (a.k.a. 'Max Jakob'). There they were stationed in the city and were allocated to garrison 76 Boulevard de la Duchesse Anne. They had their meals at the local SD station, located at Jules-Ferry Avenue.

After July 1944 the *Selbstschutzpolizei* was dissolved. Some full-time members eventually enlisted in the *8. Kompanie, II. Bataillon, Brandenburg Regiment 3, Brandenburg-Division*.[20] This included Jacques Dugé de Bernonville, the former French commander of the Taverny School.[21] The majority of the Frenchmen at the Taverny School followed the withdrawal of the German Army from France in the late summer of 1944 and eventually joined the French *33. Waffen-Grenadier-Division der-SS Charlemagne* that was in the process of forming at *Truppenübungsplatz Wildflecken*, located in the Rhön Mountains of Bavaria. Some of the bolder members chose to remain behind Allied lines to try and provide intelligence. At the end of the war, few members of the *Selbstschutzpolizei* were caught and tried, even though the FFI had infiltrated two of its members into the organisation in 1944 and these two men had actually seized the negatives of most of the *Selbstschutzpolizei* identity cards.[22]

The Bezen Perrot Group

The Bezen Perrot group was named after Abbot Jean-Marie Perrot, a prominent Breton priest and cultural figure who promoted Breton identity and independence for Brittany. Abbot Jean-Marie Perrot was assassinated in 1943, by the French Resistance, who saw independence for Brittany as divisive and against the interest of France. The group was driven by Breton nationalism, not simply pro-German sympathies. Its members believed that supporting the Nazi regime would help achieve independence for Brittany from France. The Bezen Perrot group was the military faction of the BNP.

The origins of the Bezen Perrot military unit comes from the creation of the 'Lu Brezhon' ('Brittany Army') in October 1943.[23] That declaration is what likely prompted the French Resistance to target the Abbot for assassination. The 'army' initially had twelve members and later was raised to some eighty or ninety men. Initially, there was talk of establishing a *'Bretonische Waffenverband der SS'* (Breton Group of the Armed SS), but there were such small numbers of volunteers that the Germans never considered this but once. This is rather odd, given that the British Free Corps, raised by the SS, never exceeded three-dozen men (British, Irish, Canadian and South Africans). The SS even took the time and trouble to create a *Waffen-SS* cuff band for this English-speaking unit. It was the only *Waffen-SS* cuff band that was written in English. The words 'British Free Corps' were written in silver thread on a black cloth background.

So why would the SS take the time and trouble to nurture three dozen traitors from the United Kingdom and its Commonwealth, and ignore almost three times the number of Breton separatists? The answer is that for propaganda purposes, it was more worthwhile to see an Englishman wearing the uniform of the *Waffen-SS* than a Breton separatist. In the end, the eighty to ninety or so volunteers were armed and clothed by the local SD command. Another source however, states that only around seventy men were serving in the Bezen Perrot Group.[24] Of these, 65 were between the ages of 18 and 25. During the initial stages of the German occupation (1941–2), the Bezen Perrot group operated under the auspices of the local German *Feldgendarmerie* unit of *Feldkommandantur 148*. This military government staff was led by *Oberstleutnant* Baron von Gebsattel.[25] In April 1943 the group was taken over by the local KdS command under *SS-Obersturmbannführer* Hartmut Pulmer. Pulmer, who had been born on 9 November 1908, was 35 years old in 1943.[26]

He assigned his adjutant to run the day-to-day affairs of the Bezen Perrot unit. He was *SS-Sturmbannführer* Fritz Barnekow, who had been promoted to his present rank on 1 May 1942. Barnekow was older than his commander, having been born on 18 December 1899.[27] He was thus 44 years old in 1943. The Bezen Perrot group was split into two sections of about forty to fifty men each. The first section was under the command of Leon Jasson, while the 2nd Section was led by Alan Heussaf.[28] Each of these two sections contained four groups. These 'groups' numbered perhaps about fifteen to twenty men each and were allocated to the Security Police and SD or the local *Gestapo* unit, based on need.

The use of French locals greatly increased the effectiveness of the German SS/SD units and that is one of the main reasons why collaborators were so hated and despised by the *Maquis*. Another irritating factor for the French was that service in many of these pro-German collaborator forces paid extremely well. Each member of the Bezen Perrot Group, for example, received an amazing 3,900 francs per month. The Germans therefore, made it very profitable for a Frenchman to betray his countrymen. Eventually, it was not just the small separatist groups or French Fascist types that joined the *Gestapo*. Now men who wanted money at any price, adventurers, and even common criminals would join the local SS and SD command in order to obtain the great benefits which service in these units offered.

Pay was high, food was plentiful, and many times houses, offices, and personal property of persons apprehended were looted. In July 1944 the 1st Section of the Breton of the *SiPo*/SD command in Brest. Both sections were withdrawn and eventually reached Alsace-Lorraine but not before many of its members had deserted, since they felt that their interest lay in Brittany and not in Alsace-Lorraine or Germany. What was left of the force was initially transferred to the *Abwehr* under the *Brandenburg* commandos, and later, under *SS-Obersturmbannführer* Otto Skorzeny's commando force. Skorzeny assigned them to *SS-Jagdverbände Südwest*. The initial unit these men joined was *Streifkorps-Südfrankreich*. In the summer of 1944, the unit was at Ales, Cevennes, France.

In September 1944 it was still located there. It included the 8th 'Legionary' Company, which consisted of 180 Spanish and French volunteers, among them, some Bretons. The unit was eventually transferred to northwestern Italy and fought Italian partisans on the French-Italian border until January 1945. It then carried out deep reconnaissance behind the lines of the 7th US Army in the Black Forest region. It was finally withdrawn to Austria, where it was to join up with the other *SS-Jagdverbände* in Linz. However, that plan failed to materialise. *SS-Jagdverbände Südwest* ended the war in the region of Bressanone (Brixen), in the province of South Tyrol. After the liberation of France, many members of the Bezen Perrot fled, were arrested, or were tried and convicted for collaboration.

Le Mouvement National Antiterroriste de Lyon
This organisation was the creation of a member of the *Parti Populaire Français* (PPF, French Popular Party, a fascist and collaborationist political organisation led by Jacques Doriot) from Lyon named Francisque André. The first we hear of this 'anti-terrorist' formation is

in November 1943, when posters were plastered all over Lyon stating that because of the ineffectiveness of the local police at stopping the growing assassinations and other murders in the city, the 'people' were taking matters into their own hands and would start killing known *Maquisard* leaders every time another Lyonnaise citizen would be killed. Andrě was a Fascist of the Jacques Doriot persuasion. Like Doriot, he had been a long-time communist who had eventually joined the fascist PPF in 1937, three years after Doriot left the Communist Party (1934). Andrě was a cripple who had suffered debilitating injuries as a child in a car accident.

According to various sources, the size of this group was never larger than 80–150 men. What all sources state is that *SD-Hauptsturmführer* Rudolf Moritz of the Lyon KdS eventually helped to fund and support this group. This SD officer should not be confused with August Moritz, of the Security Police in Marseilles.[29] After the Allied landings in Normandy this unit did not remain in Lyon for very long. By August 21st 1944 the unit had been withdrawn through Nancy and was on its way to Germany. The unit, still under the control of Andrě and Moritz, met up with Doriot at Mengen. Andrě was captured in northern Italy in captured in northern Italy in July 1945 and returned to Grenoble where he was tried for the murders of about 120 *Maquisards* from the Grenoble-Lyon areas. He was found guilty and shot in March 1946.

La Hauskapelle Bordeaux

This unit was created from a group of former plutŏt Anarchists. They were mainly young men and were each paid by the local Bordeaux KdS the fantastic amount of 4,000 Francs per month. The first leader of this group was a local named Ferdinand Vincent, but it was a German SD commander named Friedrich Wilhelm Dohse, who spoke fluent French, who actually directed the actions of the unit. The twenty-nine-year-old Dohse (born 22 July 1913) had arrived in Bordeaux on 26 January 1942. By 1942, Helmut Knochen's powers extended to the whole of occupied France and Belgium. Friedrich Dohse was promoted to *SS-Standartenführer* and became the *Befehlshaber der Sicherheitspolizei und des Sicherheitsdienst* of this transnational zone.[30]

Dohse operated from *Gestapo* headquarters located at 224 Avenue de la Libération (formerly Cours du Maréchal Pétain) in Le Bouscat, a suburb of Bordeaux. Between 1942 and 1944, he oversaw a network of over 200 agents, many of whom were French collaborators. Among them was Pierre Poinsot (born in 1907) who was commissioner for Jewish affairs. He established what came to be known as the 'Poinsot Brigade', which was composed of about twenty men, including fifteen inspectors and his two brothers, Henri and Jean Poinsot. The 'Poinsot Brigade' established its headquarters in the Hôtel du Parc Lardy in May 1944 when Poinsot was appointed to the sub-directorate of general intelligence, in what remained of the Vichy government. Claude Bonnier, who had been arrested, was taken to the *Gestapo* headquarters in Bouscat to await Dhose's arrival and interrogation. He was locked in a cell, handcuffed behind his back.

The greatest success of the *Hauskapelle* was the destruction of a local *Maquisard* band and the capture and use of British weapons taken from a parachute drop that was meant to support the local FFI. The parachuted weapons were eventually used by the group as well as other *Gestapo/SiPo*/SD forces. On 24 August 1944 the unit left Bordeaux in a large convoy of SD trucks and vehicles which carried the SD commands and their collaborators from Bordeaux, Bayonne, and Mont-de-Marsan.[31] In August 1944, as Allied forces advanced, Dohse was transferred to Danzig and then to Denmark, where he was captured by British forces. He was subsequently handed over to French authorities and imprisoned at the Fort du Hâ in Bordeaux. In 1953, Dohse was tried alongside other *Gestapo* officials for war crimes, including the arrest, deportation, and execution of Resistance members.[32] He was sentenced to forced labour but was released shortly after the trial due to time already served. Dohse died in 1995 in Kiel, Germany, without expressing any remorse for his actions during the war.

Le Corps Franc Français

This force was created using remnants of volunteers from the Bordeaux section of the *Mouvement Social Révolutionnaire* (MSR, Social Revolutionary Movement), a staunchly anti-Semitic, anti-Freemason, anti-communist and anti-Anglo-Saxon political party whose bulk of its members returned to Marcel Deat's RNP. The unit was created in 1943 by André Besson, whose nom de guerre was Besson Rapp. The local *Abwehr* unit, which was headed by *Hauptmann* Gartner, supported the Corps Franc Français. The unit was later loosely tied to the SD, since the SD absorbed all GFP units in 1942 and the entire *Abwehr* in August 1944. In fact, the unit assisted GFP *Gruppe 644* quite effectively against the local communist partisan units of the in exile in Germany. The force was never larger than 90–100 men. When the withdrawal to Germany was ordered, André Besson was recuperating from shrapnel wounds. In Alsace, the group was integrated into the *33. Waffen-Grenadier-Division der-SS 'Charlemagne'*.

La Phalange Raciste

This was founded on 9 July 1940, in Bordeaux and the Gironde region. This unit was given the bigoted title of 'The Racist Phalanx'. The leader of this group was a Frenchman named Pierre Paparan.[33] The bulk of its members were French university students who had been emboldened by the seemingly invincible force of arms of the Third Reich. Later in the group's history, the son of Pierre Paparan, Jacques Paparan, assumed control of the group. From the very beginning, SD officer Friedrich Wilhelm Dohse of the Bordeaux KdS used its members for various espionage and spying missions. In March 1943 the local guerrilla group, which was overwhelmingly manned by ex- adherents of the Spanish Republic, ambushed a squad of *La Phalange Raciste*, killing most.[34] Pierre Paparan himself was caught by the Free French in early 1945 and tried for working for the Bordeaux KdS. He was tried and executed on 25 February 1945.[35]

Pro-Axis French Arab units: *La Brigade nord-africaine*

In April 1944 a new anti-communist formation, *La Brigade nord-africaine*, was created using a core of Muslim volunteers from North Africa who had been living in France. The idea to create this force had been the brainchild of the SS Security Services' Paris HQ and assistance was sought from the Algerian leader, Mohamed el-Maadi, in January 1944.[36] As such, it was affiliated in any way with the Vichy French government. Maadi was the editor of the Arab language magazine *Er Rashid* ('The Messenger'). As such he was in a position to greatly influence his fellow Algerians and others in Muslim communities in France. In this way he was able to recruit 400 Arab men for the new formation, of which only 300 were chosen since the other 100 or so had such terrible criminal records that even the SD was unwilling to hire them. This all changed later, as the need for more manpower grew and soon even common criminals were being accepted into the *Brigade nord-africaine*. The effect this had was that the unit eventually received a reputation as looters and rapists within the French community. Even the hated *Milice* did not want to be associated with them, although initially it was simply out of racism. In fact, the SD had been trying to get these Muslim volunteers into the *Milice* since 1943, but to no avail. The commanders of the various companies within the *Brigade nord-africaine* were all Frenchman who wore the SD uniform, while their Muslim volunteers wore a similar uniform to the *Milice*.

Henri Lafont

The overall commander of the brigade was a Frenchman by the name of Henri Chamberlain, who used the *nom de guerre* of Henri Lafont and had a long history before the war of criminal behaviour. He had the rank of an *SS-Hauptsturmführer* and split the unit into five companies. His father died when Lafont was 11 and on the day his father was buried, his mother abandoned him. He grew up on his own and was forced to fend for himself. In 1940, while in a French jail, he met two *Abwehr* agents who befriended him and suggested he work for the Germans. Lafont initially got a position with the French police through his connection with the *Abwehr*. However, he surrounded himself with former criminals and even some corrupt policemen, like his second in command, Pierre Bonny, and went into business for himself, extorting people and stores. The last straw for his police boss came in July 1940, when he forcibly freed twenty-seven criminals from French jails and made them a part of his growing criminal gang. He was only spared from being jailed or killed because he managed to locate and arrest the Belgian spymaster Otto Lambrecht and hand him over to the *Gestapo*, who thereupon protected LaFont. The *Abwehr* then approached Lafont and asked him to help insert two agents into French-controlled Algeria, in North Africa.

However, Lafont botched the mission. The agents were arrested and the Vichy French government sentenced him to death, although they could not reach him in occupied France, and the Germans refused to extradite him. From late 1940 through to the beginning of 1942, the *Gestapo* employed Lafont and his 100 or so associates to counteract the French Resistance. Lafont and his men excelled at hideous ways to torture his fellow countrymen.[37] As a result, he and his band of criminals gained a terrible reputation with the French Resistance as being the worst of the worst of all of the *Carlingue*. For a detailed description of the *Carlingue*, please refer to the section in this chapter titled 'La Police Allemand'.[38] In 1942 Lafont's trouble with the French police ended when he became a member of the German *Devisenschutzkommando* (Foreign Exchange Protection Command), which was supposed to be in charge of overseeing the banks and fighting the Black Market. In this position, he enriched himself while also ingratiating himself with top Nazi brass, including the head of the Paris SD, *SS-Standartenführer* Helmut Knochen.

Creation of the Brigade nord-africaine

In the beginning of 1944 Lafont contacted Mohamed el-Maadi, who was a former French colonial captain, and proposed the creation of an organisation called *La Légion nord-africaine*. Mohamed el-Maadi was rabidly anti-communist and was an active member of the secret French Army organisation, *La Cagoule*. Members of this group had taken part in assassinations of important left-wing politicians and newspaper editors during the period of the Third Republic and into the Vichy French period. The more than 300 Arabs chosen for this battalion were grouped into platoons and were dressed in the uniform of the *Milice française*. The men of the battalion initially operated in the region of the Dordogne, although it is known that the *Première Compagnie* (1st Company) and *Troisième Compagnie* (3rd Company) also operated in Montbéliard.[39] Three platoons of the *Brigade nord-africaine* fought the *Maquis* in the region of Corrèze and Tulle. One company fought in the region of Dordogne, Mussidan and Sainte-Marie-de-Chignac, while another fought in the area of Brantôme and in Franche-Comté, in eastern France.

In July 1944 the *Brigade nord-africaine* was reformed and soon disbanded because of desertions by Arabs within the unit. The reason for the desertions was that it was clear the war was turning against the Germans. Some of its former members travelled to Germany with Capitaine el-Maadi, while others joined the *Freies Indien Legion* (Free India Legion). The India Legion was the *Infanterie-Regiment 950 (indisch)* of the German Army, which was now making its way towards the relative safety of southern Germany. The Arab companies were now basically reduced to the size of platoons of perhaps twenty-five to thirty Arab volunteers each. Each platoon was named as a section. Therefore, the 1st Platoon was referred to as the 1st Section, the 2nd Platoon was the 2nd Section, etc. These sections were commanded by the same SD company commanders as follows:

1 Section, SS-Untersturmführer Charles Cazauba
2 Section, SS-Untersturmführer Paul Claviě
3 Section, SS-Untersturmführer Paul Millebuaux
4 Section, SS-Untersturmführer Alex Villaplana
5 Section, SS-Untersturmführer Lucien Prěvost

Desertions continued throughout the withdrawal and by the time the remnants of *Brigade nord-africaine* reached Grenoble, on their way north to the German border, barely thirty Arabs remained within the unit. All except one of the French SS second lieutenants who had served in the battalion ended up joining the 33. *Waffen-Grenadier-Division der-SS 'Charlemagne'*.

Chapter 6

THE FRENCH RESISTANCE

French Resistance: Early Beginnings
By late 1940, various Resistance groups had formed within occupied France. These groups were diverse in political ideology – ranging from communists to conservatives – and operated independently, which made coordination difficult. Charles de Gaulle, leading the Free French from London, recognised the importance of unifying these groups to create a stronger and more effective resistance. In 1942, de Gaulle sent Jean Moulin, a high-ranking civil servant loyal to the Republic, into occupied France with a critical mission to unify the Resistance movements, create a central council to represent them and establish a link between the internal resistance and the Free French government-in-exile. Moulin used his diplomatic skills to bring together leaders of the main resistance groups, despite deep ideological differences. On 27 May 1943, the *Conseil National de la Résistance* (CNR, National Council of the Resistance) held its first clandestine meeting in Paris. It included representatives from major Resistance movements, various political parties (socialists, communists, radicals, etc.), and trade unions. The CNR aimed to coordinate Resistance activities, support the Allied war effort, and plan for post-liberation governance. In 1944, it published what was called the 'Programme of the CNR', outlining ambitious social and economic reforms for post-war France, including social security, nationalisation of key industries, and a free press – many of which went on to shape modern French society. The CNR also worked hand-in-hand with British and Free French forces.

The SOE Free French Section
The Free French Section of the SOE was formed around 1940–1. Its purpose was to recruit, train, and insert French-speaking agents into occupied France to conduct sabotage, espionage, subversion, and

support local Resistance networks (*Maquis*). This section was part of the broader SOE structure initiated by Winston Churchill with the aim to 'set Europe ablaze'. During the war, the special 'Section F', as it was referred to, eventually trained over 400 agents and inserted them into France. Their missions varied, and included sabotage of German industry and infrastructure, including the rail system, and assassinations of important collaborators and German officers. They also coordinated arms and supply drops by the British and later, the Americans, to support the French forces of the interior. They were also tasked with gathering intelligence. This became a priority about six months before the Normandy landings. Some notable agents who were members of the SOE Free French Section included Violette Reine Elizabeth Szabo, who conducted sabotage missions. She was deemed ready to conduct operations in early 1944. Unfortunately, she was captured on 10 June 1944 during her second operation in France. Because of poor intelligence on the part of the local *Maquis* in the Limoges community, SOE was unaware that *2. SS Panzer-Division 'Das Reich'* was in the area. By 1944 many of what had been considered elite SS panzer divisions, like the *'Das Reich'*, had gone through a physical transformation.

This was primarily due to heavy losses, which required more and more replacements. The Germans began recruiting ethnic-Germans from all across Europe as early as 1941. In the spring of 1944, the *2. SS-Panzer-Division 'Das Reich'* had been withdrawn from the Russian front and sent to France to recuperate and reconstitute. At this time, it received 9,000 ethnic-German recruits, some of which arrived in the division area as late as May 1944. A good number of these men were *volksdeutsche* from Alsace and from eastern territories in Poland that had been annexed by Nazi Germany. Thus, a good portion of these recruits were former French or Polish citizens whose allegiance was questionable.[1] The reorganisation of this SS division with these new recruits occurred in the Montauban-Toulouse area.

Although after the D-Day landings on 6 June 1944, the Germans had forbidden the French population from using motor vehicles, Szabo and her companions, two members of the local Resistance, were driving in a Citroen when they encountered a *Waffen-SS* checkpoint.

A day earlier, on 9 June, *SS-Sturmbannführer* Helmut Kämpfe of the *'Das Reich'* SS division had been captured by the local *Maquis*. In retaliation for his capture a day later, on 10 June 1944, men from this SS division perpetrated the Oradour-sur-Glane massacre. In total 643 men, women and children were killed at Oradour-sur-Glane. Incensed, the local Resistance commander, Colonel Georges Guingouin, who was an ardent communist, ordered that Kämpfe and several other captured German soldiers be executed. The execution took place in front of numerous French citizens, who watched as *SS-Sturmbannführer* Kämpfe and the other hapless German soldiers who happened to have the bad luck of being captured, had their arms and legs tied and were thrown inside a truck. Guingouin's men then poured petrol all over the lorry and set fire to it, with the result that the men inside burned to death.

It was under this highly-charged emotional situation that Szabo and her two companions encountered the *'Das Reich'* road block on 10 June. Having sprained her ankle, she knew she could not get away, so she decided to stay and delay the Germans long enough for one of her companions to escape. Using a Sten gun and several magazines, she managed to kill an *SS-Unterscharführer* (corporal) and wounded three others before she ran out of ammunition and was captured. She was arrested and eventually sent to Ravensbrück concentration camp, where she was condemned to death and executed on 5 February 1945.

Another notable figure in 'Section F' was Noor Inayat Khan, who was a wireless operator stationed in Paris. She was one of the most remarkable and heroic agents of the SOE during the Second World War. Khan was a Muslim who was of Indian-American descent, but was a British citizen when the war broke out. Her story stands out not only for her bravery and tragic end, but also because of her background and personal convictions. Khan arrived in France on 16 June 1943 and was sent to Paris to support the 'Prosper' network (also known as the 'Physician' network) as a wireless operator. Her codename was 'Madeleine'. She became the only functioning wireless operator in Paris after most of the network was rolled up by the *Gestapo* – an incredibly dangerous position as her transmissions could be triangulated by German direction-finders.

The same day that Khan landed in France, Francis Suttill (code-named 'Prosper'), the network leader, was arrested by the *Gestapo* in Paris. Eight days later, on 24 June, Andrée Borrel (code-named 'Denise'), who was Suttill's second-in-command, was also arrested. Over the following days and weeks, dozens of SOE agents and French Resistance members linked to the 'Prosper' network were captured due to compromised safe houses, infiltration, and possibly betrayal (the exact cause is still debated). The arrests decimated the 'Prosper' network, which had been one of the largest and most active SOE circuits in France. Many agents, including Noor Inayat Khan, were left isolated in occupied territory with no direct support. The *Gestapo* used captured radios to send *'funkspiel'* (radio games) – false messages – to London, deceiving the SOE and leading to further agent losses. After the 'Prosper' network was dismantled in June 1943, Khan chose to remain in Paris rather than be exfiltrated, despite orders.

She therefore became the only active SOE wireless operator in Paris, moving constantly and transmitting messages to London under extremely dangerous conditions. On 13 October 1943 Noor Khan was arrested by the *Gestapo*. Her arrest was the result of betrayal, possibly by a French collaborator. She was held at the headquarters in Paris for the SD (located at 84 Avenue Foch). She was interrogated repeatedly by Ernst Vogt, a *Gestapo* officer, but she refused to give any information even after torture. She even refused to give her real name. She even attempted to escape twice from her prison, once by loosening the bars on her window and climbing out, demonstrating both ingenuity and determination. According to the most plausible theory, Khan was betrayed to the *Gestapo*, reportedly by René Garry, the brother of a Resistance member who was a contact for Khan. Garry may have acted out of financial motive or personal jealousy.

Another theory suggests a man named Henri Déricourt, who was a double agent for the *Gestapo*, may have contributed indirectly to her capture, though this remains unconfirmed. The *Gestapo* arrested her at a safe house on Rue de la Faisanderie in Paris. The *Gestapo* had been monitoring her movements and possibly intercepted one of her radio transmissions. Noor tried to fight and escape but was overpowered. Throughout her nearly year-long incarceration, she endured torture and was kept in shackles. Subsequently, she was transferred to the Dachau concentration camp near Munich, where she was executed in 1944 alongside three other SOE agents. Several others, including Suttill and Borrel, were later executed at Dachau, but most were taken to Natzweiler or Flossenbürg Concentration Camp. It should be noted that Francis Suttill was also an important member of the French SOE section. In Paris he headed the largest, if not one of the largest SOE networks in France, before being betrayed and captured. The collapse of Prosper was one of the most devastating setbacks for SOE operations in France.

The *Franc-Tireurs* and the FTP: Two Currents of French Resistance

The term *franc-tireur*, originally used during the Franco-Prussian War to describe irregular sharpshooters or guerrilla fighters, was revived during the Second World War by multiple French Resistance factions opposing the Nazi occupation and the collaborationist Vichy regime. Most notably, it became associated with two distinct resistance movements: the *Franc-Tireur* group and the *Francs-Tireurs et Partisans*

(FTP). Though they shared a name rooted in irregular warfare, these movements emerged from different ideological traditions and operated with varying strategies and objectives.

The Franc-Tireur Movement

Founded in the Free Zone (*Zone libre*) in Lyon in late 1940 under the original name *France Liberté*, the *Franc-Tireur* movement was a non-communist Resistance organisation. It was established by a group of intellectuals, journalists, and activists deeply opposed to both Nazi occupation and the Vichy government's collaboration. One of its key founders was Jean-Pierre Lévy, who would later play a significant leadership role in the broader Resistance.

Initially focused on intellectual and political resistance, the movement emphasised the dissemination of underground newspapers – most notably *Franc-Tireur* – and the organisation of opposition networks throughout southern France. In 1943, as part of Jean Moulin's efforts to unify the disparate Resistance movements, *Franc-Tireur* merged with *Combat* and *Libération-Sud* to form the *Mouvements Unis de la Résistance* (MUR), which laid the groundwork for the *Forces Françaises de l'Intérieur* (FFI).

The Francs-Tireurs et Partisans (FTP)

The *Francs-Tireurs et Partisans* (FTP), by contrast, emerged in April 1942 as the armed wing of the French Communist Party (PCF). Although communist cells had existed earlier, significant armed activity only began after Germany's invasion of the Soviet Union in June 1941 (Operation *Barbarossa*), which reoriented communist policy toward active resistance. The FTP evolved into a highly organised paramilitary force marked by ideological militancy, decentralised structure, and broad inclusivity – including French nationals, former soldiers, political radicals, and large numbers of foreign anti-fascists such as Jewish émigrés, Spanish Republicans, and members of the *Main-d'œuvre immigrée* (MOI). Operating primarily in small autonomous cells, the FTP employed classic guerrilla tactics: sabotage of transportation and communication infrastructure, assassinations of German officers and collaborators, raids on armouries, and urban ambushes. The FTP-MOI, its foreign-born contingent, was particularly noted for daring acts of resistance, including high-profile assassinations and sabotage in cities such as Paris and Lyon. Quite often in the major cities the female branch of the communist party would take advantage of the Germans' use of bordellos in order to obtain information from the enemy. For example, it was feared that French Resistance groups could use female agents on German *Wehrmacht* members.[2]

Resistance and Liberation

While the *Franc-Tireur* emphasised political unity, coordination, and propaganda, the FTP specialised in direct armed confrontation. After 1943, both movements were increasingly integrated into the centralised Resistance framework promoted by Jean Moulin, though tensions often persisted – especially between the FTP and more conservative or Gaullist factions – over issues of political authority and military coordination. In the summer of 1944, in the wake of the Allied landings in Normandy, FTP units played a pivotal role in the liberation of France. Their operations disrupted German troop movements, sabotaged infrastructure, and instigated uprisings in both rural and urban centres, including decisive actions in regions such as Limousin, the Massif Central, and Île-de-France. In urban centres like Paris, Toulouse, and Lyon, FTP militants launched coordinated insurrections that often coincided with or preceded Allied advances.

Table 5. Comparison Chart: *Franc-Tireur* vs. *Franc-Tireurs et Partisans*.

Aspect	*Franc-Tireur* Movement	*Francs-Tireurs et Partisans* (FTP)
Founding Date	Late 1940	June 1941
Base Location	Lyon	Paris
Political Affiliation	Moderate/Republican, MUR	French Communist Party (PCF)
Focus	Propaganda, underground press, civil resistance	Armed struggle, sabotage, assassinations
Key Activities	Publishing the *Franc-Tireur* newspaper, political organisation	Attacks on German troops, railway sabotage, urban guerrilla warfare
Key Figures	Jean-Pierre Lévy, Jean Moulin	Charles Tillon, Missak Manouchian
Integration	Merged int MUR in 1943	Merged into FFI in 1944
Legacy	Promoted unity of non-communist resistance groups	Known for bold operations and foreign volunteer fighters

Major French Resistance Operations, 1940–1941

Between 1940 and 1941, the French Resistance initiated several significant operations against German forces and their collaborators. These included sabotage of infrastructure, assassinations, and acts of defiance. An important operation which was undertaken in June 1941 by the SOE Free French section, took place in the region of Pessac, near Bordeaux. Pessac is a commune in the Gironde department in Nouvelle-Aquitaine in southwestern France.

**Table 6. Timeline for the *Franc-Tireur* Movement
and the *Francs-Tireurs et Partisans*.**

1940	*Franc-Tireur* movement founded in Lyon after German occupation.
1941	FTP formed by the PCF after Germany invades the USSR (June 1941).
1942	FTP becomes increasingly active in urban guerrilla warfare.
1943	*Franc-Tireur* merges with *Combat* and *Libération-Sud* to form the MUR.
1944	Both groups contribute to the liberation of French cities and regions. FTP and other groups are unified into the *Forces Françaises de l'Intérieur* (FFI).
1944–5	Both groups contribute to the liberation of French cities and regions.

The target of one of the earliest important operations by 'Section F' was the transformer station located at Pessac, near Bordeaux. By 1941, Bordeaux was already a key logistical and naval hub for the Germans, especially as the Atlantic U-boat war intensified. The submarine base and military use of port facilities made it a critical site for Nazi Germany's war strategy, which is why it also became a target for Resistance and SOE activity. The codeword for the attack was 'Josephine B'. On the night of 7–8 June 1941, the operation was carried out successfully by Sergeant Jean Forman, Sub-Lieutenant Raymond Cabard, and Sub-Lieutenant André Varnier – all of whom had parachuted into France for this sole mission. They first neutralised a small contingent of German guards then entered the transformer station, planted magnetic incendiary devices on six of the eight transformers, and later escaped on bicycles. The destruction of this large transformer was important because it was a key electrical infrastructure in the entire region.

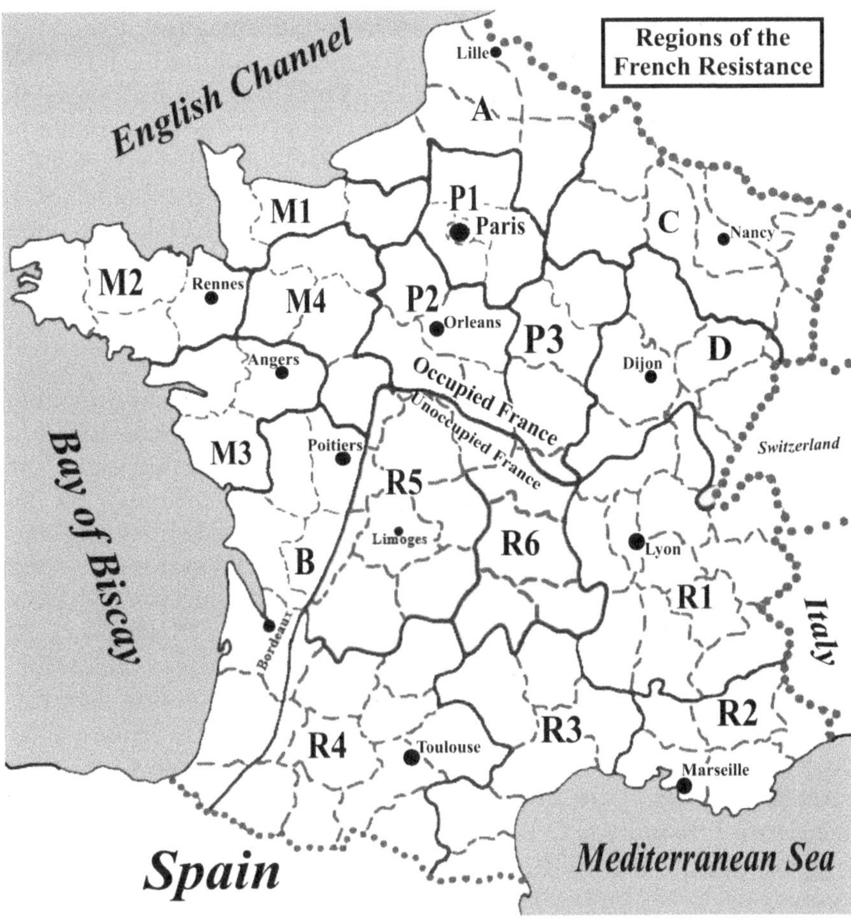

Figure 5. The French Resistance, although varied, was eventually brought under a blanket organisation which tried to coordinate attacks against the German occupation forces. (Author's line drawing)

The loss of the transformer station impacted German operations, and significantly delayed work on the U-boat (submarine) base, where the *Kriegsmarine* 12th U-boat Flotilla was to be stationed. In addition, the Germans had requisitioned factories and shipyards in and around Bordeaux for ship repair and refitting, manufacture of military goods, including rubber and chemicals. These too were impacted by the sabotage. When it became operational, this port became the most important naval base in southwest France. From Bordeaux, attacks were made by the 12th U-boat Flotilla in the Atlantic against Allied shipping. The destruction of the transformer station was serious enough to delay the final completion of this *Kriegsmarine* submarine base well into 1942. A month earlier, the SOE Free French section had struck in Le Palais-sur-Vienne, a commune in the Haute-Vienne department of the Nouvelle-Aquitaine region in west-central France. The target of the attack was the rubber production facility located there. French SOE operatives overpowered the two night-watchmen, tied them up, then proceeded to lay explosives that blew up the facility's boilers. This sole act halted rubber production for five whole months.

The French Resistance Zones

During the occupation, the French Resistance divided metropolitan France into zones or regions for better organisation and coordination of underground activities. In 1941 the regions were created under the leadership of the CNR. These divisions were used primarily by the *Mouvements Unis de la Résistance* (MUR), the *Armée Secrète* (AS), and later the *Forces Françaises de l'Intérieur* (FFI). The regional system reflected both geographic necessity and military-operational concerns. The Paris Region was divided into Paris (central), and sectors P1 (Paris 1), P2 (Paris 2), and P3 (Paris 3). This subdivision helped manage clandestine operations in different parts of the capital and surrounding suburbs. Northwestern France was divided into four regions: M1 (Brittany), M2 (Normandy), M3 (Anjou-Maine), and M4 (Poitou). These areas were strategically significant due to Atlantic ports, naval installations, and later, their proximity to D-Day landing zones. Unoccupied France, was initially under Vichy control until the German invasion of the entire country on 11 November 1942 (Operation *Anton*).

The former Vichy territory was divided by the Resistance into six regions: R1 (Toulouse), R2 (Marseille), R3 (Montpellier), R4 (Clermont-Ferrand), R5 (Lyon), and R6 (Limoges). There were four additional regions designated A–D. These were created as special operational or transitional areas, often for command, coordination, or areas that didn't neatly fall into other designations. Their exact use varied over time, but generally were divided as follows. The region of the Northern Alps was categorized as 'A', Eastern France (Alsace-Lorraine) was labelled 'B', the region of the Southern Alps was 'C', while Region 'D' was often designated for the Mediterranean coastal area or Corsica, although Corsica had its own resistance peculiarities due to its early liberation in 1943. This regional system allowed for a more efficient command and control for the FFI and MUR. It also facilitated coordination of actions like sabotage, intelligence, and logistics. Communication between the Resistance and the Allied forces was also improved, particularly in preparation for Operation Overlord – the Normandy landings on 6 June 1944, and Operation Dragoon, the Allied invasion of southern France on 15 August 1944.

Major French Resistance Operations, 1942–1943

Between 1942 and 1943, the French Resistance significantly increased its activities, evolving from mainly intelligence-gathering and propaganda organisation, into more direct sabotage, assassinations, and armed operations. The Resistance also involved itself in trying to help people who the Nazis were seeking, like downed Allied pilots and Resistance leaders on the run. In particular, Jews were hidden by members of the Resistance. A principal target was the rail system in France. The blowing of tracks significantly slowed the flow of troops to and from France. In addition, derailing German military trains also helped to win the war.

While blowing up rail lines and sabotaging trains was a broad resistance tactic used to delay German logistics – including military and supply movements – there is evidence that some of these acts directly affected deportation trains carrying Jews to Nazi death camps, especially to Auschwitz. For example, in August 1943, a train carrying Jewish deportees from Limoges (in Vichy-controlled southern France) to Drancy, the transit camp near Paris, was delayed multiple times due to rail sabotage. The Resistance had destroyed sections of the tracks, which forced German and Vichy authorities to reroute or hold trains for days. In this instance, several deportees managed to escape, either during chaotic transfers or after the train was temporarily halted near small towns where local *Maquis* groups and sympathisers were active. The delay also bought time for Resistance networks to attempt rescues or hide people from further arrests.

The Resistance was well aware that the *Société Nationale des Chemins de fer Français* (SNCF, French National Railway Company) was heavily used by the Nazis to transport Jews to Drancy, and from there to extermination camps like Auschwitz, Sobibor, and others. Resistance groups, particularly the FTP and members of the *Jeunesses Communistes* (Young Communists), increasingly focused on blowing up train tracks, derailing trains, attacking rail yards to destroy facilities or rolling stock, and cutting communication lines used by the railway system. While these actions often aimed to slow military transport, they also affected deportation logistics – delaying transports and, in some cases, causing enough confusion for individuals to escape or be rescued. It's also worth noting that many French railway workers covertly aided Jews and Resistance fighters by leaking transport schedules, deliberately slowing down trains, sabotaging equipment, and helping people jump from deportation trains. Some were part of broader resistance networks like *Résistance-Fer* ('Railway Resistance'), which became more active in 1943.

The French Resistance was also responsible for spectacular acts against the Germans and their Vichy-French allies. One such operation was the mass escape from the Vichy Camp of Le Vernet in late 1942. Le Vernet, in southern France, was a detention camp holding political dissidents, Jews, and foreigners. In late 1942, resistance networks helped coordinate the escape of a significant number of detainees before the Germans could deport them to concentration camps. The operation was supported by underground escape networks like the *Réseau du Musée de l'Homme* and *Réseau Garel*, often working with church organisations and local sympathisers. The brazen prison break had a great impact on the morale of the French populace opposed to the Vichy government. The attack on the detention camp was part of a broader movement to protect Jews and political refugees, showcasing how humanitarian aid and resistance overlapped.

Resistance groups like *Combat*, *Franc-Tireur*, and *Libération-Sud* regularly produced and distributed illegal newspapers named after their organisation. In 1942–3, distribution networks for these illegal newspapers expanded massively, reaching tens of thousands of readers. The French communists also had their underground newspaper, called *L'Humanité* ('Humanity'). *Libération-Sud* was founded by Emmanuel d'Astier de la Vigerie. The paper had ties to socialists and other left-leaning resisters. The basic content of each issue did *exposés* on German actions, Vichy complicity, calls for solidarity, and denunciations of anti-Semitic laws. To distribute these illegal newspapers the Resistance used networks of teachers, postmen, students, and railway workers. Papers were sometimes pasted secretly on walls at night or left in cafés, mailboxes, or factory locker rooms. The newspaper, *Défense de la France* was created by Catholic students from the Sorbonne in 1941. These Catholic students and their supporters had distributed up to 450,000 copies of the newspaper by 1944. The students used portable printing presses hidden in Paris apartments. Then there was *La Voix du Nord* ('The Voice of the North'), which originated in occupied northern France and was connected to Gaullist supporters, especially in the city of Lille.

One of the important operations undertaken by the Resistance in 1943 was the destruction of the Bussy-Varache Viaduct near Limoges. French Resistance operations in the region of Limousin began as early as late 1940, with members cutting telephone lines, establishing

Resistance cells, and organising guerrilla activities. Brive-la-Gaillarde and Limoges were the regions where the *Maquis du Limousin* were headquartered. There were multiple major sectors within the *Maquis du Limousin*. These included the sectors of Haute-Corrèze (at Neuvic-Ussel), Moyenne-Corrèze (at Tulle), and Basse-Corrèze (at Brive-la-Gaillarde), as well as the partisans and *Maquis Francs-tireurs* located between Dordogne and Corrèze. Then there were the *Creusois Maquis Armée secrète* at Guéret and Saint-Gilles-les-Forêts, and the *Maquis Francs-tireurs et partisans* in Limousin. What is strange is that a report from June 1944 by SOE agent Philippe Liewer found that the local *Maquis* in the Limoges region were apparently poorly led and less prepared for combat than London had counted on.

Beginning in early 1943, *Maquis* sabotage operations in this region increased dramatically. Then beginning in the second half of 1944, operations shifted to performing large-scale attacks against German occupation troops. The plan to destroy the Bussy-Varache Viaduct was conceived and led by Georges Guingouin, a French communist and the leader of the *Maquis du Limousin*. Other notable figures of the French Resistance in this region included André Malraux, Gontran Royer and Edmond Michelet. Guingouin understood the value of the viaduct to the German war effort. If it could be significantly damaged, German forces would be forced to divert rail transport for a hundred kilometres or more, significantly delaying troop movements and other rail transport. Simply destroying the rail was not going to do this, as repairing a rail line was moderately easy and could be achieved relatively fast.

On the night of 13 March 1943 Guingouin and a squad of men from the *1ère Brigade de Marche Limousine* (1st Limousin Marching Brigade) approached the viaduct. There they laid sufficient explosives to destroy a pier between two arches of the viaduct on the line from the Palais to Eygurande-Merlines. The railway lay suspended in the void for several tens of metres, preventing any train traffic. The explosion was heard miles away, notifying the local German garrison that the *Maquis* had struck again. The destruction of the viaduct was so complete that it was rendered unusable by the German for the rest of the war. This attack on the viaduct significantly disrupted German logistics in the region. Its destruction forced the Germans to undertake lengthy cargo transfers between the two areas, which were now isolated from one another. Thus, by this one act of sabotage, the occupying forces were severely hindered until the liberation of France by the Allies. The destruction of the Bussy-Varache Viaduct was one of the most spectacular and most successful operations carried out by the French Resistance during the war.

On the night of 10–11 September 1943, a pivotal operation was orchestrated by Henri Romans-Petit, a prominent Resistance leader. It resulted in the capture of the *Chantiers de la Jeunesse* supply depot in Artemare, Ain. This mission marked the first significant military action undertaken by the *Maquis* de l'Ain, a clandestine resistance group. The *Chantiers de la Jeunesse* (Youth Work Camps) were established by the Vichy regime to indoctrinate young men into its ideology. These camps were strategically located across France, including Artemare, and served as logistical hubs for the regime's operations. The depot in Artemare housed essential supplies, including uniforms, equipment, and provisions, which were vital to the Vichy administration's control over the region. Henri Romans-Petit, a former military officer with extensive experience, had been actively involved in organising resistance activities in the Ain department.

By September 1943, he had established a network of *Maquisards* and had begun to coordinate more assertive actions against German and Vichy targets. The operation in Artemare was part of a broader strategy to disrupt enemy logistics and demonstrate the growing strength of the French Resistance. Under the cover of darkness, a group of approximately sixty *Maquisards*, led by Romans-Petit, approached the Artemare depot. The element of surprise was crucial to the mission's success. The Resistance fighters, dressed in civilian clothing to avoid detection, infiltrated the area and swiftly overpowered the guards. They then seized control of the depot, capturing a significant quantity of supplies intended for the Vichy regime's use. The operation was executed with precision and minimal resistance, highlighting the effectiveness of the *Maquisards'* training and coordination. The captured supplies were subsequently distributed among the local Resistance groups, bolstering their capacity to conduct further operations against the occupying forces.

The successful capture of the Artemare depot had several immediate and long-term effects. It demonstrated the growing capability and organisation of the French Resistance, serving as a morale booster for both fighters and the civilian population. The operation also disrupted the logistical operations of the Vichy regime, depriving them of essential resources.

In the broader context of the Second World War, this action contributed to the weakening of Axis control in France and provided a foundation for subsequent Resistance efforts. The success of the Artemare operation was followed by other significant actions, including the capture of the Vichy army's administrative depot in Bourg-en-Bresse later that same month. Henri Romans-Petit's leadership and strategic acumen were instrumental in these operations. His ability to coordinate complex missions and inspire his fellow Resistance fighters earned him recognition and respect within the movement. Later, he would play a key role in organising the *Maquis de Haute-Savoie* and coordinating with Allied forces for further resistance activities. The capture of the *Chantiers de la Jeunesse* supply depot in Artemare stands as a testament to the courage, ingenuity, and determination of the French Resistance during a critical period of the Second World War.

In late September 1943, the Resistance achieved a significant victory in Bourg-en-Bresse, located in the Ain department of southeastern France. Under the leadership of Henri Romans-Petit, alias 'Romans', the *Maquis de l'Ain* executed a daring operation to seize the Vichy army's administrative depot in the city. Like the previous attacks, this action was part of a broader strategy to destabilise Vichy authority and demonstrate the growing strength of the Resistance. The operation was meticulously planned and executed. Henri Romans-Petit, who had previously organised training camps for Resistance fighters in the region, coordinated the action. On the night of the operation, Resistance fighters infiltrated the depot, which was largely unguarded due to the recent withdrawal of German forces. They swiftly loaded approximately ten tons of supplies, including uniforms and equipment, into trucks. The entire operation was completed in under 20 minutes, showcasing the efficiency and precision of the *Maquis*. This capture was a pivotal moment for the *Maquis de l'Ain*. It not only provided essential supplies but also served as a powerful symbol of the Resistance's capabilities. The uniforms obtained from the depot were later used in the 11 November 1943 parade in Oyonnax, where *Maquisards* marched openly, demonstrating their military organisation and defiance against the Vichy regime.

The year 1943 ended with an incident that occurred in the town of Oyonnax. When Marshal Philippe Pétain's administration outlawed any celebrations of the 1918 armistice, *Maquis* leaders in the region chose to defy the prohibition and stage a procession through the town of Oyonnax. The Resistance leaders managed to obtain the support of the town police commissioner and the gendarmerie captain. The telephone lines were also cut, to prevent any collaborator from warning the Germans. Resistance men, all in uniform and fully armed, paraded through most of the town. The uniforms had actually been taken from the Resistance raid on the *Chantiers de la Jeunesse* supply depot in Artemare, Ain. This parade was an iconic event in the history of the French Resistance, as well as the Ain and Haut-Jura *Maquis*.

It was a memorable march which took place on 11 November 1943. Wreath-laying ceremonies commemorating the French victory in 1918 were also held in thirteen other towns. The entire country soon found out about the act of defiance put on by the Ain and Haut-Jura *Maquis*. It was not only a slap in the face to the Germans but an embarrassment to the Vichy government of Pierre Laval. The Vichy government immediately sent 500 GMR men. Soon after another 1,000 GMR troops entered the region. However, the commanders were reluctant to go head-to-head with the *Maquis*. An agreement was struck where the Resistance men would temporarily leave the area, so the GMR could claim a victory.

The Germans, however, were not taken in by this obvious ruse. Instead, they proceeded to send their own reinforcements into the region. The punishment meted out by the German command included the arrest of 120–130 residents, and the execution of the town's doctor, Émile Mercier, who was denounced as the leader of the Secret Army's Ain region. There were also numerous deportations to the Reich. The town's mayor and one of his deputies were later shot by the *Gestapo*. The local *Maquis* also suffered losses, as the Germans brought in additional forces into the region. The parade however, had repercussions as far away as London, where the act of defiance finally convinced Prime Minister Winston Churchill of the need to supply the French Resistance with more weapons. The *Maquis de l'Ain's* activities culminated in the liberation of Bourg-en-Bresse in September 1944, marking a decisive end to the Resistance's operations in the area. The actions taken in 1943, including the capture of the administrative depot, were instrumental in laying the groundwork for this success a year later.

Resistance to Compulsory Labor and the Rise of the *Maquis*

As the German occupation authorities intensified efforts to conscript French citizens for compulsory labour in Germany under the STO, increasing numbers of young French men began to evade the draft. This phenomenon became particularly widespread from the autumn of 1943 onward. Upon being summoned, many would choose to go into hiding to avoid forced labour service. The majority of these so-called 'work resisters' sought refuge in rural areas. Those with family in the countryside often took shelter on farms owned by relatives. A smaller, yet still significant, number fled to more remote and rugged terrains such as forests, the French Alps, and other isolated regions. These individuals became known as *Maquisards*, giving rise to loosely organised resistance groups collectively referred to as the *Maquis*, which would eventually operate across various parts of France.

Going underground, however, was fraught with hardship. Despite occasional assistance from sympathetic local networks, conditions for *réfractaires* living in the *Maquis* were extremely difficult. Scarcity of food and exposure to the elements – particularly hunger and cold – were persistent challenges. Initially, these groups were not engaged in active resistance. They were poorly organised and lacked weapons, which made any form of armed opposition to the Vichy regime or the German occupiers impractical. This began to change as the broader Resistance movement recognised the potential of these young men as recruits.

As stated previously, in January 1943, Jean Moulin successfully unified the three principal Resistance movements in the southern zone under the umbrella of the MUR. Prior to this, these military organisations had already begun to consolidate under the *Armée Secrète* (Secret Army), a Gaullist paramilitary structure. As increasing numbers of *réfractaires* joined the *Maquis*, the Resistance began to mobilise this influx of manpower. In southern France, the MUR established the *Service National Maquis* (SNM), an auxiliary structure designed to integrate and support these fighters. In the north, many young men fleeing the STO gravitated toward the Communist Party and its military wing, the *Francs-Tireurs et Partisans* (FTP).

Beyond their political divergences, the MUR and FTP also differed in strategic orientation. The MUR, through its *Armée Secrète*, prioritised preparation for a future Allied invasion and focused on building capacity to support such an operation. In contrast, the FTP emphasised immediate, direct action against German forces. Resistance organisations played a crucial role in supporting the *Maquis*, initially by providing false identity papers and securing food supplies. Over time, they began to train promising recruits in guerrilla tactics. However, the ability of the *Maquis* to engage in sustained armed resistance remained limited due to a chronic shortage of weapons.

The Importance of Arms Deliveries to the Resistance

This constraint was substantially alleviated when the American Office of Strategic Services (OSS) and the British SOE revised their strategies and began to supply the *Maquis* with large-scale weapons deliveries. While limited arms drops had taken place between 1941 and 1942, it was not until 1943 that the frequency and scale of these operations increased significantly. This escalation corresponded with broader Allied preparations for the liberation of Western Europe. By the beginning of 1944, air drops of weapons intensified as part operations aimed at bolstering the Resistance in anticipation of the Allied landings.

Alongside these deliveries of arms, came Operation Jedburgh – a covert Allied mission launched in early 1944 to support the French Resistance in preparation for and following the D-Day landings. Small teams, typically composed of three men – an American, a British or Free French officer, and a radio operator – were parachuted into occupied France. Their primary tasks were to coordinate guerrilla operations, organise local resistance groups (particularly the *Maquis*), gather intelligence, and disrupt German communications and logistics. Working closely with the Resistance, the Jedburgh teams played a critical role in mobilising sabotage efforts, assisting Allied forces, and undermining German control during the liberation of France.

The SOE and OSS worked in close coordination with local resistance units and umbrella organisations such as the FFI. Resistance groups were tasked with disrupting German lines of communication, supply chains, and transport infrastructure before and after the D-Day landings on 6 June 1944. Following the landings, the volume of arms deliveries reached its peak. These efforts enabled the Resistance to transition from a largely defensive posture to active, coordinated military engagement. Large shipments of weapons, explosives, and supplies played a decisive role in enhancing the operational capabilities of the *Maquis*. Thus, while clandestine resistance had existed prior to 1943, the shift to large-scale Allied support through aerial weapons drops marked a turning point in the *Maquis'* transformation into an effective paramilitary force contributing directly to the liberation of France.

Major French Resistance Operations, 1944

Between January and March 1944 two major events occurred that were significant to the partisan and anti-partisan war. The first was a battle that took place between the *Maquis des Glières* and German security forces. This battle lasted almost an entire month, from 31 January until 26 March 1944. In this battle forces from the Gaullist *Armée Secrète* and communist *Francs-Tireurs et Partisans* took part. A daring jailbreak took place on 18 February 1944, when RAF Mosquito bombers, coordinating with the local French resistance, and SOE operatives, bombed the *Prison d'Amiens*, in northern France, breaching the prison walls. As a consequence, many prisoners being held there were able to escape. In total, 258 prisoners were able to escape, while 102 prisoners were killed, either by the bombing or the German guards. Unfortunately, about half of the prisoners were recaptured. This carefully coordinated plan was code-named Operation Jericho.

Between April and May 1944 many Resistance forces became more active, in part in anticipation of the long-awaited Allied landings. One such force was the *Corps Franc de la Montagne Noire* (Free Corps of the Black Mountain) was an elite, semi-autonomous French Resistance unit created in early 1944, known for its discipline, strong military organisation, and a politically neutral stance. It operated under the broader umbrella of the FFI, but retained a degree of independence. This force was an FFI-aligned paramilitary group created by Georges Guingouin and commander Roger Mompezat (a.k.a. 'Garrigue'). Its composition was a mixture of French resistance men, escaped Allied soldiers, and even former Spanish Republican troops.

The *Corps Franc de la Montagne Noire* was noted for its multinational makeup and professional-style structure. The unit was considered a leading combat formation because of the military training of most of its members. Because of Allied air drops, it was well-armed. The unit's area of operations was the *Montagne Noire* (Black Mountain) region of the southern Massif Central, in southern France, spanning the Tarn, Aude, and Hérault *départements*. Their stronghold was near Castres and Mazamet, with operations covering the surrounding countryside and mountain passes. Beginning on 20 April this capable combat force began setting up ambushes against German convoys. They also sabotaged roads, railway lines and bridges. German supply lines were also compromised, especially at choke points such as mountain passes.

From 20 May until 10 June the *Mont Mouchet Maquis* rose up, engaging German forces in a premature, self-initiated insurrection. Unfortunately for the Resistance fighters, a force had just been organised in the spring that happened to be stationed their area. This was *Sicherungs-Brigade 74*, more commonly referred to by its unofficial title, *Brigade Jesser*. The brigade was led by a veteran commander of the Russian front, *Generalmajor* Curt von Jesser.[3] More importantly, its units had been toughened by combat on the Eastern Front. *Brigade Jesser* was composed of the following sub-units:

Sicherungs-Brigade 74:
Sicherungs-Regiment 1000 (two battalions)
Sicherungs-Regiment 1010 (two battalions)
Aufklärungs-Abteilung 1000[4]
Panzerjäger-Kompanie 262

In addition, the brigade received a *Panzerspähwagenzug* (armoured reconnaissance platoon sent from Paris).

Added in July:

> One battalion of the Wolga-Tartar Legion / *2. Freiwilligen Stamm Regiment*
> One battalion of the Azerbaijani Legion / *2. Freiwilligen Stamm Regiment*
> *Heeres-Flak-Abteilung 958 (mot.)*

Added in August:

> *Reserve-Artillerie-Abteilung 28* (two batteries from *189. Reserve-Division*)
> *III. Bataillon der SS-Polizei-Regiment 19*

The Germans could count on over 3,000 men with Ju 88 bombers for air support. In addition, 300 *Milice* also took part in the battle. Their combined operations utilised ground combat and punitive actions against local population and the *Maquis*, ultimately overwhelming the Resistance stronghold. As a result, the approximately 2,700 *Maquis* took heavy losses, losing over 1,000 men killed and taken prisoner. Many of those taken prisoner never made it to German prisons.

In late May and early June, the FFI received orders that were to assist with the upcoming invasion of France, code-named 'Operation Overlord'. Numerous plans were laid out, directed by OSS agents in cooperation with the FFI. *Plan Bleu* listed all of the power lines that needed to be destroyed. *Plan Rouge* detailed the German ammunition dumps that had been identified and were to be attacked and destroyed. *Plan Noir* was the same, but targeted fuel depots for sabotage. The fuel depots and ammunition dumps, if at all possible, were to be destroyed using explosives. A frontal assault was considered a last resort, due to the expectedly high casualties that a frontal assault would cause. *Plan Vert* targeted the railways for sabotage. *Plan Tortue* targeted road disruptions, especially roads where German reinforcements were expected to use when reinforcing German forces in Normandy. Collectively, these plans resulted in 486 rail and road disruptions before D-Day. *Plan Violet* was to do the same for all telecommunications. This particular plan was to be activated between 5–6 June 1944. Finally, *Plan Jaune* was to employ the FFI units to strike at command centres.

On 18 June 1944, coordinated attacks were carried out by units of the FFI, in conjunction with the Special Air Service (SAS). Ambushes against German patrols throughout the Saint-Marcel region of Brittany were laid out. These actions were followed by Operation Grock, a sustained campaign of guerrilla warfare that continued into August 1944. Initiated on 13 June, the operation was designed to reinforce and support the Saint-Marcel *Maquis*, who had incurred significant losses

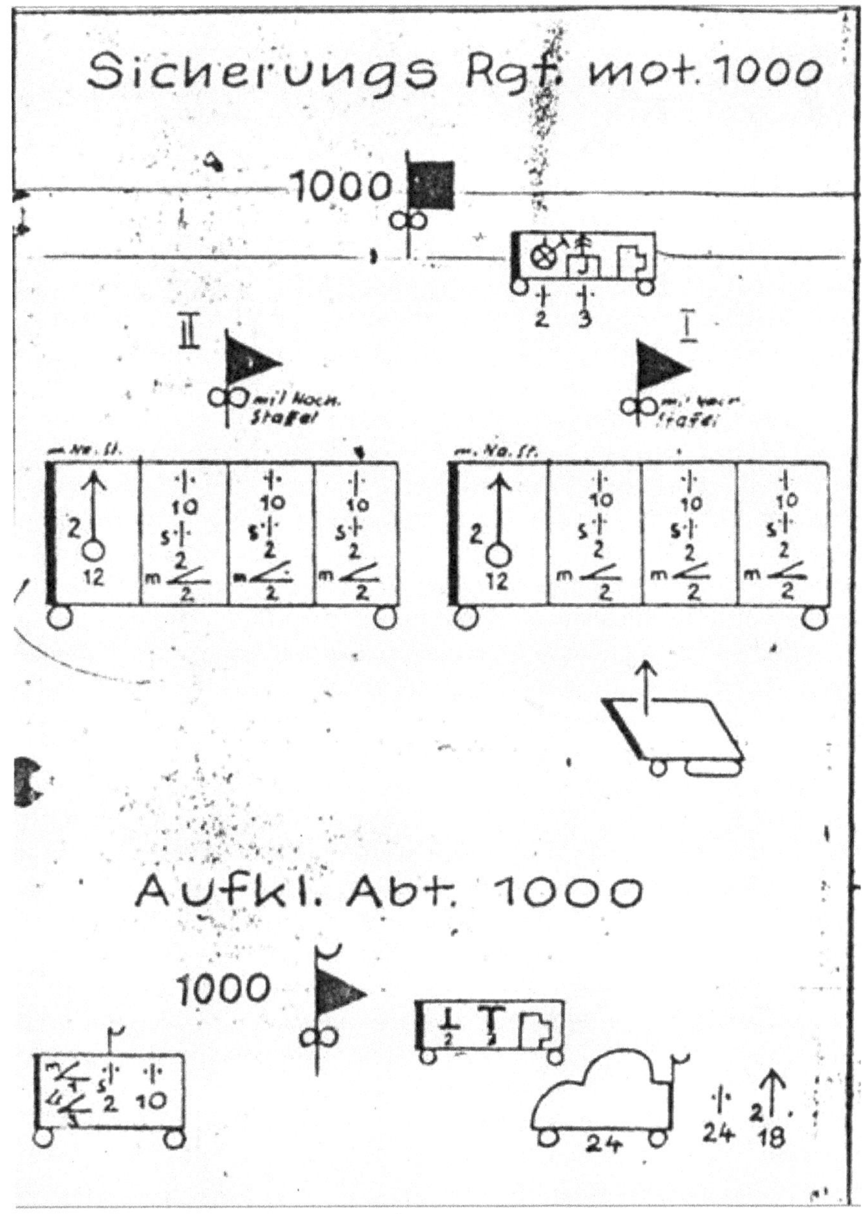

Figure 6. Table of organisation for *Sicherungs Regiment 1000,* and *Aufklärungs-Abteilung 1000.*

during earlier missions such as Operations Dingson and Samwest. Operation Grock was commanded by Captain Deplante, with Captain Leblond initially overseeing logistical support. The operation employed 58 French paratroopers of the 4th Battalion, Special Air Service (SAS) in the vicinity of Pontivy, thereby minimising the risk associated with fixed installations vulnerable to German anti-partisan operations.

Its objectives included the reorganisation of surviving resistance elements, the training of new recruits, and the distribution of arms and munitions. Operation Grock maintained the momentum of sabotage and asymmetric engagements – particularly targeting rail and road infrastructure – and served to complement broader Allied strategic goals in the region, especially in the lead-up to the breakthrough at Avranches. In July the *Corps Franc de la Montagne Noire* took part in a battle against German forces and French *Milice* troops. According to all accounts, the engagement was fierce, with neither side taking many prisoners. The battle took place at La Galaube. There the *Corps Franc de la Montagne Noire* attempted to block the withdrawal of a German panzer division. Elements of *11. Panzer-Division*, supported by infantry and armoured vehicles waded into battle. The *Milice* were also trying to withdraw alongside the German panzer division and therefore assisted in the assault, continuing its operations well into August 1944. The Resistance also fought withdrawing German forces and what Vichy French troops still remained loyal to Pétain.

In July the FFI *Maquis* in the Vercors region of southeastern France declared a 'Free Republic'. This large resistance force significantly endangered the supply and retreat route of the *19. Armee* which at the time was operating in southern France. In response, the Germans launched *Unternehmen Bettina*, which ran roughly from 21 July to 5 August. This came to be known as the Battle of Vercors. The *Maquis du Vercors* comprising almost 4,000 men, defended against approximately 10,000 German troops who launched a serious assault which included air support and even airborne glider troops (for a detailed description of *Unternehmen Bettina*, see Chapter 10).

In July the battle of Mont Gargan took place FTP forces led by Georges Guingouin who clashed with *Wehrmacht* troops in the Massif Central. In this battle, approximately 2,500 *Maquisards* participated, with casualties recorded as thrity-eight killed, fifty-four wounded, and five missing. The *1e Brigade de Marche Limousine*, plus mobile *Maquis* units, and even the *Gardes Mobiles* from Guéret took part in the battle. German forces included *Sicherungs-Brigade 74* (i.e. the *Jesser Brigade*) and *Sicherungs-Regiment 95*. In addition, the 1st and 3rd Company of the 2nd Cohort of the *Milice* assisted the German offensive. The *Milice* were under the regional leadership of Jean de Vaugelas. The battle lasted from 18–24 July 1944.

This engagement marked one of the few full-scale clashes in which the FTP confronted regular *Wehrmacht* units in open terrain. Although German forces secured a tactical victory by taking Mont Gargan, the maquisards evaded encirclement and continued their guerrilla efforts in the region. Between June-August 1944, in the region of Limousin, the *Maquis* there launched a series of attacks, ambushes, and destruction of roads and rail lines, which temporarily slowed down the movement of the *2. SS-Panzer-Division 'Das Reich'* as it was trying to move north. In these operations both the Gaullist *Armée Secrète* and the communist *Francs-Tireurs et Partisans* took part. This was followed by the liberation of Brive on 15 August. The big prize – the liberation of Paris – occurred between 19 and 25 August. In the battle for Paris the French police sided with the Resistance almost to a man.

The Massacre at Tulle
Prelude
In 1943, the city of Tulle, capital of the Corrèze department, had a population of around 20,000. Tulle became very important as an industrial centre in the region. In that year, the *Maquis* launched their first major operations against German units in the region, and these operations intensified enormously until the spring of 1944. Between 27 April and 25 May, the Tulle *gendarmerie* recorded seventy-eight 'terrorist' attacks, including fourteen on railway tracks, eight on the road, seventeen against the police, one on a factory, nineteen telephone lines cut, and seven attacks against the French militia. The rest involved raids to obtain food and weapons. The *Manufacture d'Armes de Tulle* – Weapons Factory of Tulle – abbreviated to MAT.[5] The MAT was a major arms factory situated on the outskirts of the city. It was also the target of various FTP actions, both to obtain weapons and, above all, to cause lasting damage to production.

In April 1944, a twelve-man commando unit from the SD, led by *SS-Hauptsturmführer* Friedrich Korten, arrived in the city of Tulle in the Corrèze department of central France.[6] Their mission was prompted by the intensification of local Resistance activities, particularly those carried out by the *Maquis*, who had established a strong presence in Tulle and its surrounding areas. In response to the growing instability, German command had identified the region as a priority for counterinsurgency operations. Korten was accompanied by three sections (ninety men) of the Bonny-Lafont gang, a collaborationist paramilitary group known for working in close coordination with the

Gestapo. Despite their presence, German forces lacked the manpower and resources necessary to mount a comprehensive campaign against the resistance at that time.[7]

The Military Situation in Tulle in Early June 1944

By the 1940s, Tulle had become a significant industrial hub within Corrèze. The city was home to a range of industries, including a prominent textile sector specialising in lace and several metallurgical enterprises. Most notably, Tulle had the important MAT factory. In anticipation of conflict with Nazi Germany, the factory's workforce expanded dramatically – from around 1,280 employees in 1939 to 4,760 by April 1940, nearly a quarter of whom were women. The facility produced various military armaments, including machine guns, aircraft cannons, and anti-tank weapons. Following the French defeat and the onset of occupation, employment levels at MAT declined sharply. The strategic industrial potential of Tulle, particularly its capacity for weapons manufacturing, was quickly recognised by the German authorities following the occupation of southern France.

The German administration installed a liaison staff in the city and took direct control of the MAT. The factory was subsequently integrated into the *Deutsche Waffen- und Munitionsfabriken* (German arms and ammunition factories), abbreviated to DWM. Soon, a German director was appointed to head the MAT. Production was redirected to serve the German war effort, focusing on semi-automatic firearms and aircraft engines. The Germans employed weapons from France and Czechoslovakia to equip several of its infantry divisions.[8] By 1944, the workforce had increased again, reaching approximately 3,000 employees. From the earliest days of occupation, Resistance groups began to form throughout the Corrèze department and the greater Tulle area. These groups grew significantly in size and activity following the introduction of the STO, which conscripted French citizens for forced labour in Germany. Numerous *Maquis* camps emerged in the rural outskirts of the city. The Resistance in the region was primarily divided between two factions: the Gaullist *Armée secrète* and the communist FTP. The latter, more radical and militarised, attracted a larger number of armed volunteers and exerted greater influence in Corrèze – so much so that German soldiers often referred to the department as 'Little Russia'.

By the winter of 1943, the FTP had amassed approximately 2,000 fighters in the region, a number that nearly doubled by the time of the Allied landings in June 1944.[9] Beginning in 1943, the *Maquis* initiated a series of increasingly bold attacks against German and collaborationist forces, which intensified significantly by the spring of 1944. Between late April and late May, a wave of operations targeted infrastructure, including railways, roads, factories, and communications networks. The local gendarmerie recorded dozens of attacks, including sabotage, ambushes, and raids for supplies and weaponry.[10] The MAT arms factory itself was a frequent target, both for the purpose of acquiring weapons and to hinder German production capabilities. This escalation of hostilities placed German forces in a heightened state of alert. By the spring of 1944, Tulle resembled a city under siege. Checkpoints were erected throughout the city, and German patrols – often supported by French militia units – monitored all activity. A strict curfew was enforced from 5 p.m. onwards. The population lived in a state of growing tension, and many anticipated a significant operation by the *Maquis*. That expectation was realised shortly after the Allied invasion of Normandy commenced.

The Resistance Attack on Tulle, 7–8 June 1944

At the time of the *Maquis* offensive, the Axis garrison in Tulle comprised approximately 1,375 men: the *III. Bataillon, Sicherungs-Regiment 95* (around 700 troops), 350 members of the GMR, and roughly 325 *miliciens*. Opposing them were approximately 900 Resistance fighters drawn from both the *Armée secrète* and the FTP, part of a larger regional force of about 1,400 combatants. On 7 June 1944, FTP units launched a coordinated assault on German positions in Tulle. While the timing of the attack coincided with the Normandy invasion, it had not been undertaken spontaneously. Planning had begun in mid-April, with Tulle chosen for strategic reasons: the city's population was broadly sympathetic to the Resistance; it was the smallest departmental capital in the region; the German garrison was relatively weak; and the city's lack of major transport links meant that a rapid German response would be unlikely.

The assault commenced in the early morning with FTP units advancing from three directions. In the south, they targeted the MAT factory and the Souilhac district near the train station. In the west, they attacked a school building – *École normale supérieure de jeunes filles* – where German forces had entrenched themselves. A third force engaged the city centre. Initial gains were made, but the FTP soon encountered stiff resistance and began to suffer significant casualties. In response, the local FTP commander ordered a temporary cessation of hostilities to regroup and reassess.[11] By midday, fighting had largely subsided across much of the city. One consequence of the pause was the surrender of GMR forces and the French militia, who abandoned their positions and left the city. The Resistance now controlled the centre of Tulle. However, German forces managed to re-establish control in the rail district, where they conducted sweeps for suspected Resistance members. In a brutal reprisal, eighteen railway workers hiding in a coal bunker – despite having refused to cooperate with the FTP – were summarily executed.[12]

By the evening of 7 June, the FTP had succeeded in isolating German units in the northern and southern quarters of the city. Most German forces eventually withdrew to the fortified school building, which was subsequently designated the FTP's primary objective the next day. On 8 June, heavy combat resumed. The decisive moment came in the late afternoon when a fire broke out within the school, spreading rapidly. During an attempted breakout, approximately forty German soldiers were killed by the Resistance; the remainder surrendered. Tulle was now under full FTP control. In total, the Germans lost around 120 men during the battle.[13]

For the FTP, and more broadly for the French Communist Party, this victory carried significant symbolic and strategic value.[14] It likely reinforced the belief that a Communist-led seizure of local power was achievable in the wake of the Allied landings. Nevertheless, the success was short-lived. While FTP strategists had considered the possibility of a German counter-attack, they calculated that no nearby German garrisons were positioned to intervene rapidly. Limoges, the closest major garrison, was itself engaged in combat with other Resistance units. The nearest significant German force – the 2. *SS-Panzer-Division 'Das Reich'* – was based over 200km away in the Toulouse-Montauban area and was not deemed an immediate threat. Unknown to the FTP, however, orders had already been issued on 6 June for the *Das Reich* Division to move northward in preparation for deployment in Normandy. As the division began its march, German high command instructed its units to suppress Resistance movements in southern France with immediate and uncompromising force. Tulle was named as a target for reprisal.

German Reoccupation and Repression

Only hours after the FTP had declared victory, a reconnaissance battalion from the SS *'Das Reich'* Division, under the command of *SS-Sturmbannführer* Heinrich Wulf, arrived in Tulle. At the time, the entire reconnaissance battalion contained approximately 950 troops, and was supported by armoured reconnaissance vehicles and half-tracks. These encountered light resistance from the *Maquis* and swiftly retook the city within 15 minutes. They accomplished this by using overwhelming firepower. The city centre sustained extensive destruction. Terrified civilians barricaded themselves in their homes, anticipating harsh reprisals. Faced with a mechanised and vastly superior force, the FTP troops withdrew from the city and went into hiding. Tulle once again fell under German control. Additional units and senior officers – including *SS-Hauptsturmführer* Aurel Kowatsch and *SS-Sturmbannführer* Albert Stückler, the personal representative of divisional commander SS-General Heinz Lammerding – arrived during the night. Shortly after midnight, Stückler ordered the assembly of a company to arrest all able-bodied men at dawn and concentrate them at the MAT factory.

On the morning of 9 June 1944, the first stage of the Tulle massacre began. After the war, the divisional commander of the *'Das Reich'* SS division, Heinz Lammerding, claimed ignorance of what occurred in Tulle because he only arrived after the massacre. This appears to then throw the responsibility for the killings to lower-ranking SS officers in the division. For example, Lammerding's testimony appeared to blame the SS officers in charge at the time, like *SS-Hauptsturmführer* Aurel Kowatsch and *SS-Sturmbannführer* Albert Stückler, whose involvement appears to be certain. Due to conflicting testimonies, however, it remains impossible to conclusively verify Lammerding's presence or absence at the time of the massacre. It is unlikely that *SS-Hauptsturmführer* Kowatsch would have acted alone and without the consent and approval of his superior, *SS-Sturmbannführer* Stückler.

According to several sources, the mutilation of German soldiers' corpses by FTP fighters the day before the executions (8 June) is alleged to have been a motivating factor. However, this claim remains contentious in the historiography. German scholar Dr. Bruno Kartheuser considers such allegations unsubstantiated, grounding his position in testimonies and evidence from both German and French sources. Of particular importance to Dr. Kartheuser is the statement made by the senior medical officer of the division, *SS-Hauptsturmführer* Dr. Heinrich Schmidt, who reported finding no signs of mutilation. Other testimonies alleging mutilation, in Dr. Kartheuser's assessment, proved inconclusive. He writes that these allegations often originated from individuals who did not witness the mutilations first-hand, but heard about the story second-hand. Dr. Kartheuser wrote a massive four-volume study of the Tulle massacre from archival sources and testimonies.[15]

Historian Peter Lieb, however, believes the mutilation claims to be credible. He relied on both German and French sources. The existence of mutilated bodies, in Lieb's opinion, is vital for understanding the severity of the German reprisals perpetrated at Tulle.[16] Another area of uncertainty concerns who decided on hanging 120 hostages (of which only 99 were actually hanged).[17] The number '120' did not coincide with Lammerding's directive of 5 June 1944, which specified a reprisal ratio. One belief is that initial high figure of intended hangings may have been abridged through the actions of Prefect Pierre Trouillé, who advocated for not killing the captured wounded German soldiers taken by the Resistance in Tulle. Additionally, Dr. Schmidt introduced a new angle to the story, by asserting that his medical findings – specifically, the absence of mutilation – may have influenced the decision to reduce the number of executions to 120 (of whom only 99 were ultimately hanged). On 11 June 149 people were selected to be transported via Poitiers and Compiègne to the Dachau concentration camp.[18]

So initially and by midday, the number of 120 hostages to be executed seems to have been decided upon, prompting the initiation of a selection process from among thousands of detainees. This 'sorting out' process began long before the hostages were brought to the arms factory. Railroad workers were released almost immediately, given the importance of keeping the rail system running. Next, people deemed essential to the city's administrative and economic infrastructure were exempted and were released. To assist in these selections, Mayor Gabriel Bouty was summoned to the factory by the SS. Antoine Soulier, a civilian hostage during these events, later remarked that it appeared as if Bouty was collaborating.[19] This was because the SS forced him to selecting people essential to daily life in Tulle. According to his post-war testimony, Bouty claimed that he was unaware at the time, that those not selected by him would be executed. The final decision regarding who would be hanged, however, was made by the SS. After the massacre the Germans reinforced Tulle. Several more infantry companies from *Sicherungs-Regiment 95* were stationed in the city. In addition, the Germans placed two artillery batteries on the heights overlooking the city. Until the city was liberated by the FFI on 20 August 1944, those artillery pieces loomed over the city, threatening the civilian population of Tulle with destruction.

Nazi Retribution: The Maillé Massacre, 25 August 1944

Before the Oradour-sur-Glane massacre, a company of the SS '*Der Führer*' Regiment was most likely responsible for the murder of a total of sixty-seven people in Argenton-sur-Creuse area. Fifty-six people, including women and children, fell victim to a '*razzia*' (a plundering and destructive incursion by the SS) on 9 June 1944 in the town itself, and eleven hostages were shot the following day near Limoges. Another, less well-known massacre in France occurred in Maillé.[20] On the same day Paris was liberated (25 August 1944), German forces surrounded the small village of Maillé. Over the course of several hours, German troops systematically murdered civilians – men, women, and children – using firearms, grenades, and flamethrowers. Homes were burned, and much of the village was destroyed. The violence was indiscriminate and brutal, suggesting collective punishment against the local population, suspected of aiding the French Resistance. In total, some 124 civilians, including women, children, and elderly people, were executed. The massacre appears to have been a reprisal for attacks carried out by French Resistance fighters in the region. In the days leading up to the massacre, Resistance operations had reportedly resulted in German casualties. Unlike the Oradour-sur-Glane massacre (10 June 1944), which was widely publicised, the Maillé massacre remained relatively obscure for decades.

For many years, the massacre received very limited international attention, and no major war crimes trials specifically addressed it. In 2004, on the 60th anniversary, the village was visited by then-President Jacques Chirac, who called for remembrance and historical recognition. A German court investigated the massacre in the early 2000s, and in 2008, a former German soldier, Gustav Schlueter, was identified by French authorities as possibly involved, but he died in 1965 before he could be charged. The French war crimes office in Colmar continued to investigate, and new archival research in recent decades has helped clarify the involvement of *Waffen-SS* units. Unlike Oradour-sur-Glane, which was preserved as a ruin, Maillé was rebuilt after the war, contributing perhaps to its initial historical obscurity.

Recent scholarship has finally brought to light that the *17. SS-Panzergrenadier-Division 'Götz von Berlichingen'* had a unit stationed about 25km south of Maillé in Châtellerault, in the department of Vienne (Nouvelle-Aquitaine – formerly Poitou-Charentes); in the Poitiers *Arrondissement* (and the Canton de Vouneuilsous-Biard). The *Waffen-SS* unit stationed in Châtellerault was *SS-Feldersatz-Bataillon 17* – the replacement battalion for the *'Götz von Berlichingen'* SS division. Witnesses to the massacre at Maillé stated that German units that took part in the massacre had come from Châtellerault. Some witnesses testified that the men which came from Châtellerault were very young soldiers who wore camouflage uniforms. Such uniforms were only worn by units of the *Waffen-SS* or other specific units, like the *'Herman Göring'* panzer and panzergrenadier divisions and the *'Gross Deutschland'* panzer and panzergrenadier divisions.

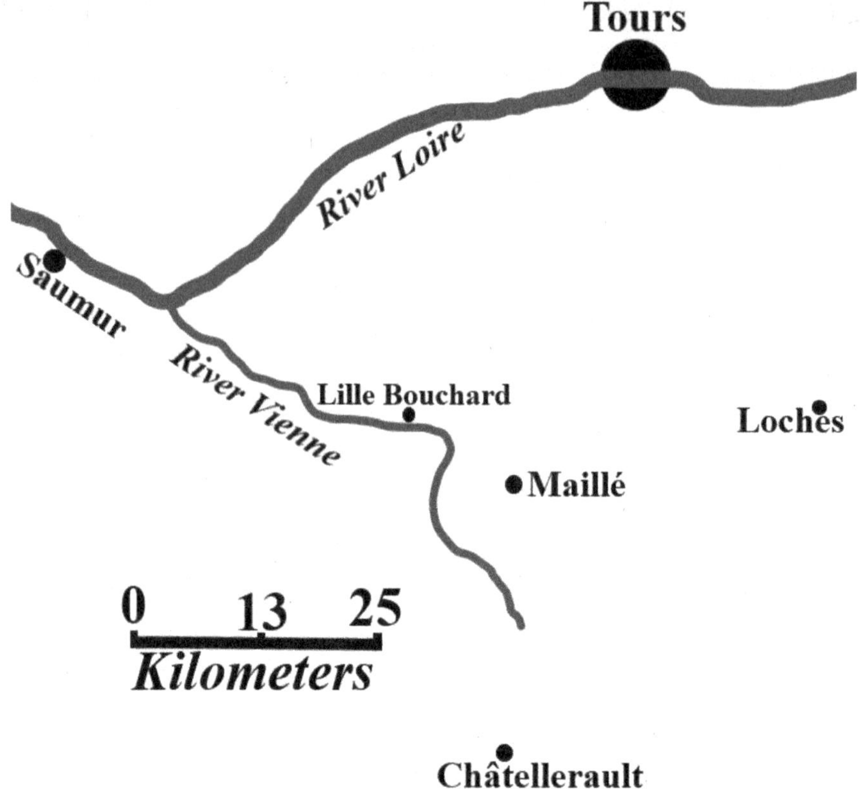

Figure 7. Location of the village of Maillé.

Given that none of these elite *Heer* or *Luftwaffe* divisions were located in the region in August 1944, we can assume with almost 100 per cent certainty, that the men which the witnesses described were from the *Waffen-SS*. Given that the only *Waffen-SS* unit located near Maillé were the three companies of *SS-Feldersatz-Bataillon 17*, we can also surmise that men from this *Waffen-SS* field replacement battalion participated in the massacre. Five days before the massacre occurred, on 20 August, the '*Götz von Berlichingen*' SS division had taken heavy losses in the attempt to extricate itself out of the Falaise pocket, at Argentan. Remnants of the division then crossed the Dives River at Chambois-Orville. Unable to reach its parent division, *SS-Feldersatz-Bataillon 17* was instead used to fight the local partisans.[21]

The *Armée Secrète*: Structure, Role, and Legacy within the French Resistance

The *Armée Secrète* (AS), or 'Secret Army', was a central military component of the French Resistance during the Second World War. It originated in 1942 through the consolidation of disparate paramilitary groups operating primarily in the southern, initially unoccupied *Zone libre* of France. These groups, which had previously functioned with limited coordination, were unified in response to the increasing need for a structured, nationwide Resistance movement capable of supporting an anticipated Allied invasion and undermining the German military presence.

From its inception, the AS was closely aligned with General Charles de Gaulle and the *Forces Françaises Libres* (Free French Forces) in London. In November 1942, de Gaulle appointed General Charles Delestraint – a retired but respected officer of the French Army – as its first commander. Delestraint was tasked with transforming the AS into a coherent underground military force, able to conduct sabotage, gather intelligence, and prepare for widespread guerrilla warfare. His leadership significantly contributed to the AS's early organisational framework, particularly in forming regional command networks and coordinating clandestine operations. The German occupation of the southern zone following the Allied landings in North Africa (Operation Torch) in late 1942 further radicalised the Resistance and accelerated the militarisation of its efforts. Delestraint travelled clandestinely across France, forging ties between resistance cells and maintaining contacts with de Gaulle's representatives in London.

However, Delestraint's arrest by the *Gestapo* in Paris on 9 June 1943, represented a severe blow to the AS. He was subsequently imprisoned, tortured, and eventually deported to Dachau concentration camp, where he was executed by the SS on 19 April 1945, mere weeks before the camp's liberation. In the wake of Delestraint's arrest, Jacques Bingen – a senior emissary of de Gaulle and delegate to the Resistance – assumed temporary oversight, ensuring the continued operational integrity of the AS. Bingen worked alongside Jean Moulin's successors in the *Conseil National de la Résistance* (CNR) to sustain coordination between the AS and other Resistance networks, especially in preparation for integration into a broader, unified national Resistance army.

By early 1944, the AS merged with other prominent armed movements, including the FTP – the Communist resistance wing – and the *Organisation de Résistance de l'Armée* (ORA), a Gaullist group composed largely of former French military officers loyal to the 1940 armistice army. This fusion resulted in the creation of the FFI, a unified command structure that greatly enhanced the strategic capacity of the Resistance during the liberation campaign. General Pierre Kœnig, appointed by de Gaulle, assumed overall command of the FFI in France in mid-1944.

Despite its eventual absorption into the FFI, the *Armée Secrète* retained its own operational identity in various regions, notably under leaders like Henri Romans-Petit, who directed AS and *Maquis* units in the Ain and Haut-Jura. AS formations were instrumental in preparing and executing coordinated acts of sabotage ahead of the Allied invasion in June 1944, including the disruption of German rail logistics, the destruction of telecommunications infrastructure, and the armed defence of liberated zones. They also provided shelter and exfiltration routes for downed Allied airmen, escaped prisoners of war, and Jewish refugees, often with the logistical support of the British SOE and the American OSS. The legacy of the *Armée Secrète* lies not only in its contribution to the armed struggle against the Nazi occupation but also in its role in fostering unity among France's ideologically fragmented Resistance factions. It helped transition the Resistance from a series of localised, semi-independent networks into a centralised national force, ultimately contributing to both the military liberation of France and the post-war legitimacy of de Gaulle's provisional government.

The *Mouvements Unis de la Résistance* (MUR): Coordination, Intelligence and Sabotage in the French Resistance

The *Mouvements Unis de la Résistance* (MUR, United Resistance Movements) was established in January 1943 through the unification of three of the most prominent resistance organisations operating in southern France: *Combat, Franc-Tireur,* and *Libération-Sud.* This unification was orchestrated under the direction of Jean Moulin, the representative of General Charles de Gaulle and a pivotal architect of Resistance coordination. Though not a singular 'operation' in the traditional military sense, the creation of the MUR constituted a foundational act of political and structural consolidation, enabling the Resistance to transition from a collection of autonomous cells into a more unified and strategic force. The formation of the MUR served several key purposes. It provided a centralised command structure, improved communication across regions, and enhanced the ability to plan and execute coordinated operations against both German occupation forces and Vichy collaborators. While much of the MUR's initial activity focused on recruitment, the expansion of underground press networks, and intelligence gathering, it increasingly took on an operational military role. Its members facilitated the transmission of vital information to Allied intelligence services in London, including detailed reports on German troop movements, infrastructure vulnerabilities, command locations, and supply depots.

This intelligence proved essential not only for the planning of sabotage missions and guerrilla actions on French soil but also for Allied strategic bombing campaigns and special operations. A particularly important dimension of the MUR's operational scope was its collaboration with *Résistance-Fer*, the network composed largely of railway workers. These agents exploited their positions within the French railway system to carry out sabotage, impede German logistics, and delay or obstruct deportation trains transporting Jews, political prisoners, and STO conscripts. Acts of resistance included the destruction of rail lines and bridges, the cutting of communication cables, and deliberate delays or rerouting of trains. In some instances, railway personnel facilitated the escape of detainees or redirected entire convoys into abandoned sidings or remote areas, often at great personal risk.

Résistance-Fer operatives also provided crucial real-time data on German military convoys, ammunition shipments, fuel stockpiles, and strategic timetables. This intelligence was transmitted to the *Bureau Central de Renseignements et d'Action* (BCRA) – the Free French intelligence and sabotage agency operating under de Gaulle's command. The BCRA, in turn, coordinated with British SOE and American OSS networks, as well as internal Resistance groups like the MUR, to orchestrate effective sabotage operations and strategic assaults. By early 1944, in preparation for the anticipated Allied landings, the MUR had become an essential node in a larger web of resistance networks. Coordinated sabotage campaigns, particularly in central and southern France, were conducted with the explicit objective of paralysing German reinforcements *en route* to the Normandy and Provence fronts. These efforts intensified in the weeks surrounding D-Day (6 June 1944), when *Résistance-Fer* agents – often acting in direct collaboration with MUR intelligence planners – systematically targeted key transport arteries in regions such as the Loire Valley, Brittany, and the Massif Central. The disruptions caused by these acts of sabotage significantly impeded the *Wehrmacht*'s ability to deploy reinforcements to contested zones.

In February 1944, the MUR, along with other major resistance organisations such as the FTP and the ORA, was integrated into the FFI, a centralised command structure for all domestic resistance forces operating under Free French authority. Though the Communist FTP retained a degree of operational autonomy, this unification marked a critical step in the transition from isolated resistance efforts to a national military campaign against the occupier. Among the notable figures in *Résistance-Fer* was Jean-Guy Bernard, who was ultimately captured and executed in 1944. Another important liaison with the MUR was Maurice Bénard, a railway worker deeply involved in sabotage coordination and intelligence transfer. Nevertheless, the majority of *Résistance-Fer* participants remained anonymous – ordinary civilians who undertook extraordinary acts of defiance under the constant threat of death or deportation. The legacy of the MUR lies not only in its contributions to the armed liberation of France but also in its demonstration of how disparate ideological groups – republican, socialist, and even conservative – could be brought together under a shared national mission. It exemplified the transition from fragmented opposition to coordinated resistance and, ultimately, national insurrection.

Chapter 7

THE GERMAN POLICE IN FRANCE

The German Police in Alsace-Lorraine

The first use of German *Ordnungspolizei* (*Orpo*, Order Police personnel occurred during the so-called '*Sitzkrieg*' (sit down war), where French and British forces faced off against third-rate German army and reserve units behind the Maginot Line in the autumn of 1939. Part of the forces allocated to garrisoning the Franco-German border region against possible Allied invasion included reserve police units. Most of the police who were assigned to the German *1. Armee* during this period were officered by a cadre of full-time police officers while the bulk of the men in these battalions were made up of part-time reservists. *SS-Gruppenführer und Generalleutnant der Polizei* Georg Jedicke was responsible for *Orpo* forces in the German Army 12th Military District. *Generalmajor der Polizei* Gerhard Winkler was in command of police forces in the 5th Military District.[1]

Both of these areas bounded the French border. The mission that had been assigned to the *Orpo* in the autumn and winter of 1939–40 in these two military districts was to cover the rear area of *1. Armee* and *7. Armee*. The *1. Armee* was under the command of *Generalfeldmarschall* Erwin von Witzleben, while *7. Armee* was led by *Generaloberst* Friedrich Dollmann.[2] These two armies formed *Heeresgruppe C* (Army Group 'C') under *Generalfeldmarschall* Wilhelm Ritter von Leeb.[3] Together, this army group contained twenty-four divisions which were not to launch their attack against the French Army units in Alsace-Lorraine until 15 June 1940.[4]

The *1. Armee*, operating from the 12th Military District, had the largest number of divisions (sixteen), while *7. Armee* which was located further south, in the 5th Military District, contained eight divisions.

However, of these eight divisions, four were static-type fortress divisions, which were only capable of limited defence and not attack.[5] Both armies were to form a pincer drive each and were to capture the provinces of Alsace and Lorraine by linking up at the Plateau de Langres.[6] The *1. Armee* was to form the right pincer of the attack, while the *7. Armee* was to launch the left. The attack planned for 15 June 1940 was directed at tying down additional French forces in the hope that they would not be diverted north and northwest, where the bulk of the German armoured and mechanised divisions were making their way south towards Paris. Germany had plans to annex the provinces of Alsace and Lorraine, which it had won after the war of 1870, but had to return to France at the end of the First World War.

In the autumn of 1939 *SS-Gruppenführer und Generalleutnant der Polizei* Georg Jedicke made an inspection tour of police forces behind the lines of *1. Armee*. He inspected the *Reserve-Polizei-Bataillon 66* and *Polizei-Bataillon 122* and found them to be at full strength. The *Reserve-Polizei-Bataillon 66* had been raised in the city of Darmstadt, while the men of *Polizei-Bataillon 122* hailed from Mannheim.[7] Both battalions had the triangular organisation of three motorised rifle companies plus platoon-sized support units like signals, anti-tank, light howitzer, and motor transport elements. *Polizei-Bataillon 66* contained 541 officers, NCOs and enlisted men. At this time, the commander of *Polizei-Bataillon 66* was *Major der Schutzpolizei* Richard Sonnenberg, while *Major der Schutzpolizei* Walther Soosten led *Polizei-Bataillon 122*.[8]

When the French campaign came to an end in late June 1940 and the German *1. Armee* entered Lorraine, *Reserve-Polizei-Bataillon 66* and *Polizei-Bataillon 122* followed in their wake. Both battalions were used to garrison the region and were initially employed in regular police duties. This soon changed however, as the region was annexed by Germany. The annexation was followed by a large displacement of the French population. Many French families were forced to leave the region, the first of which being local Jewish families whose property was now confiscated and was later redistributed to 'deserving' ethnic German families in the region. At the end of July and beginning of August 1940 *Reserve-Polizei-Bataillon 63*, under the command *Major der Schutzpolizei* Willing,[9] arrived from Poland to relieve *Reserve-Polizei-Bataillon 66*.[10] According to one source, *Reserve-Polizei-Bataillon 63* had been disbanded in January 1940 and the remaining personnel were supposedly transferred to *Reserve-Polizei-Bataillon 64*.[11] However, a more authoritative source states that *Reserve-Polizei-Bataillon 63* was not disbanded until the winter of 1942–3.[12] To add further confusion, another scholarly reference says that on 12 October 1939,

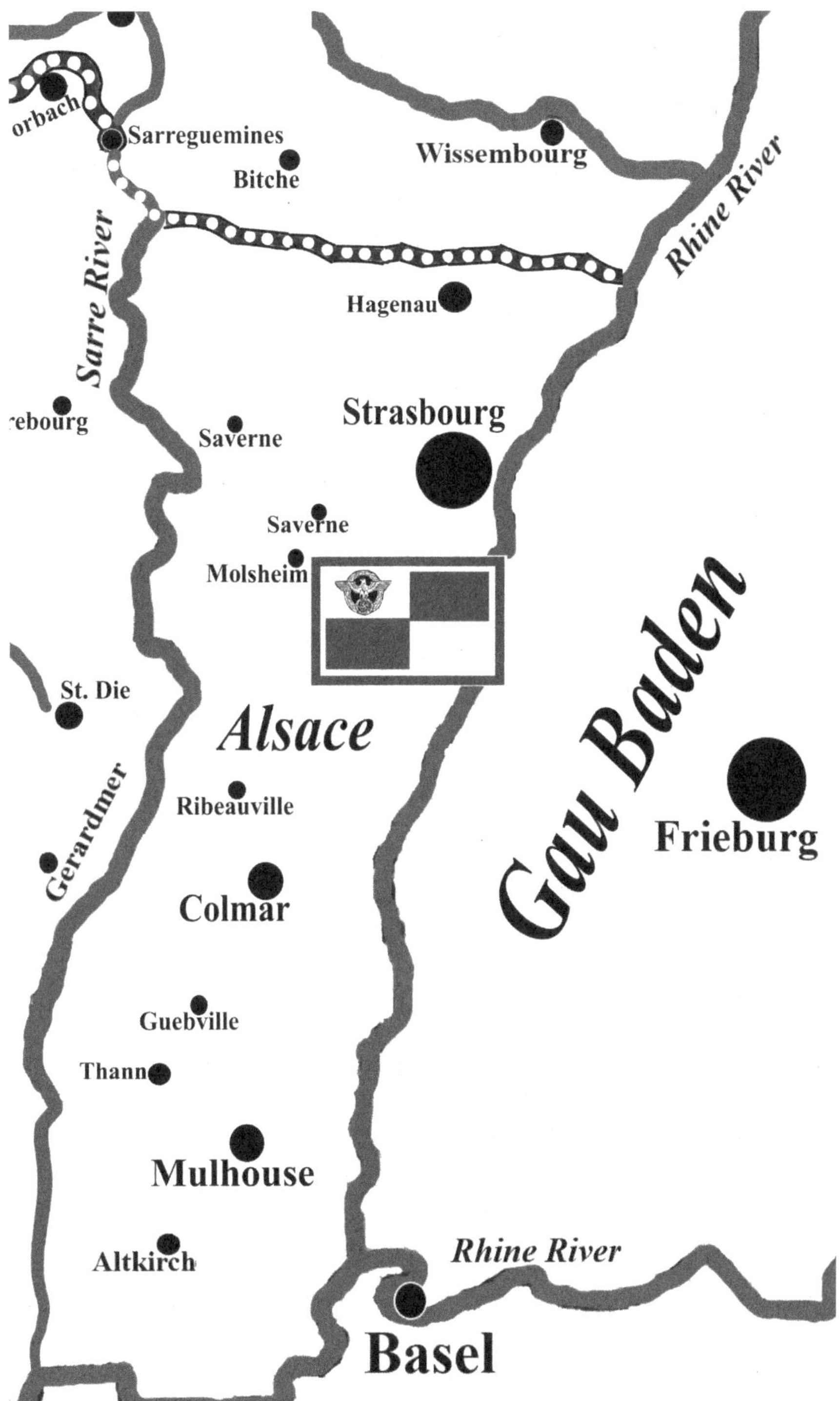

Figure 8. The region of Alsace.

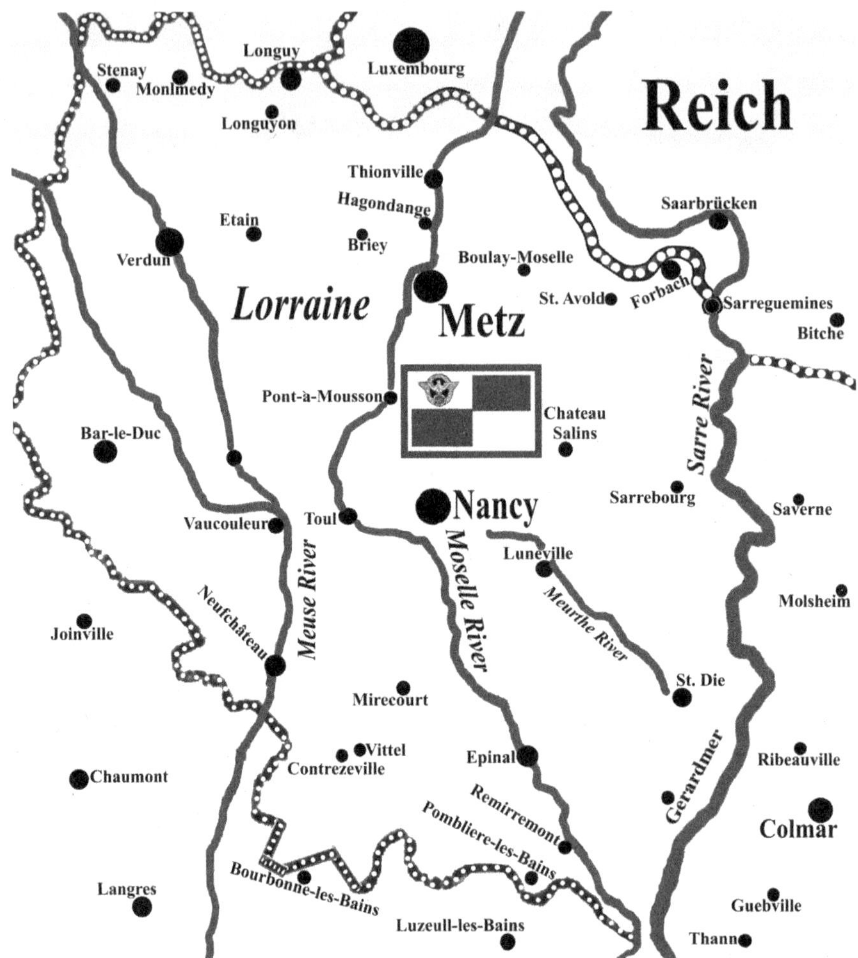

Figure 9. The region of Lorraine.

Reserve-Polizei-Bataillon 63 was re-designated as *Reserve-Polizei-Bataillon 64*, and *Polizei-Bataillon 65* became *Polizei-Bataillon 66.*[13]

While *SS-Gruppenführer und Generalleutnant der Polizei* Georg Jedicke made his inspection tour of the *Reserve-Polizei-Bataillon 66* and *Polizei-Bataillon 122, SS-Brigadeführer und Generalmajor der Polizei* Gerhard Winkler similarly inspected the police battalions under his command in *Wehrkreis V* (5th Military District). This turned out to be *Polizei-Bataillon 54*, which had been raised in Stuttgart. The *Polizei-Bataillon 54* had been formed in 1939, and had entered Alsace in late June 1940. It was stationed in Strasbourg and its environs. Another police unit, the *Polizei-Bataillon 74*, which had been created in the 7th Military

A *Sicherheitsdienst* station post, somewhere in France. The SD established posts throughout occupied France as a way of controlling the security of the region and to have a base from which to plan and launch operations. Usually, the SD commanders, like the Heer officers, would choose prominent locations, such as a four-star hotel, or a mansion or castle. In this particular place, the Army and the SD have appropriated a French château. (*Archives nationales*)

German troops arresting suspected Resistance fighters, somewhere in France. (*Bundesarchiv*)

Helmut Knocken, in the uniform of an *SS-Brigadeführer*. (*Bundesarchiv*)

Hanging convicted Resistance men. The harder the repression of the French civilian population by German security forces, the greater the number of acts of resistance.

Marseilles 1943. The German police formed a part of the Nazi security apparatus in occupied France. (*JForum.fr*)

German signpost from occupied Paris. The second listing from the top shows in which direction and exactly where the *Geheime Feldpolizei* (Secret Field Police) station post is located. The GFP was also a part of the Nazi security apparatus in France. After the war, a number of GFP officials were tried for crimes against the French people. The Hotel Matignon, where this GFP post was located, was and still is a famous locale. Today, it is the official residence of the Prime Minister of France. It is located in the 7th *arrondissement* of Paris, at 57 Rue de Varenne. (*Bundesarchiv*)

Two French members of the *Légion des volontaires français contre le bolchevisme*. After the Germans invaded the Soviet Union, an entire regiment of anti-communist French volunteers was created – *(verstärktes) Französisches-Infanterie-Regiment 638*. The regiment contained three battalions of infantry and was reinforced. At its height in strength, it contained 2,300 men. Many of the Frenchmen who served in this regiment later joined the *33. Waffen-Grenadier-Division der-SS 'Charlemagne'* – an SS division composed mostly of French volunteers. At its height, the division contained 7,840 officers, NCOs and men. (*Bundesarchiv*)

Jacques Doriot (sitting, with spectacles). Doriot was the leader of the Fascist *Parti populaire français*. When the Germans raised a regiment of French volunteers to fight in Russia, Doriot volunteered and was granted an officer's rank by the Germans. In 1944, he and thousands of other French collaborators fled to the Reich, seeking to avoid the prosecution that was to befall all collaborators. He was killed on 22 February 1945 while traveling to the town of Sigmaringen, when his car was strafed by Allied fighter planes. (*Bundesarchiv*)

Soldiers entering what had been a *Mikveh* (Jewish bathhouse), which the Germans had turned into a brothel. This photo was taken somewhere in Brittany, most likely in the city of Brest. The confiscation of Jewish property occurred all across occupied Europe. (*Archives nationales*)

Resistance fighters pose for a picture. Notice that most are either carrying the British Lee-Enfield bolt-action, magazine-fed repeating rifle, or the British Sten gun, a submachine gun chambered in 9×19mm. (*Archives nationales*)

Member of the *Garde Mobile*. During the rule of Vichy France, the *Garde Mobile* was referred to simply as the *Garde*. When reformed in 1940, it consisted of 6,000 men. This member is carrying what looks like the MAS-38 submachine gun. (*Archives nationales*)

Members of the Resistance somewhere in a French forest. The Vichy French security forces proved too unreliable to employ effectively against the Resistance. This is why in 1943 the *Milice* was created. (*Archives nationales*)

The *Milice* was a political paramilitary organisation established on 30 January 1943 by the Vichy regime, with the support of Nazi Germany, for the purpose of suppressing the French Resistance during the Second World War. Although nominally led by Vichy Prime Minister Pierre Laval, who served from 1942 to 1944, the organization was effectively directed by its Secretary General, Joseph Darnand. The *Milice* was actively involved in extrajudicial killings and targeted assassinations, and played a significant role in the arrest and deportation of Jews and members of the Resistance within occupied France. When many of its members fled France in 1944, most ended up serving in the French SS 'Charlemagne' Division. (*Archives nationales*)

Milice members guarding suspected Resistance men, some time in 1944. (*Archives nationales*)

A poor-quality photo, but nevertheless an important one given that it depicts members of the French Resistance preparing to blow up a rail line. (*Mary Evans Picture Library*).

Members of the French *Milice* marching. The Franc-Garde, which was the armed wing of the *Milice*, were basically armed with British weapons, like the Lee-Enfield No. 4 Mk I rifle, the Sten gun, which was a relatively inexpensive submachine gun to manufacture, and the Mk-Im Bren light machine gun (shown here). (*Archives nationales*)

An American member of the Office of Strategic Services examines a MAS-38 submachine gun from a member of the *Maquis* of Vercors, 1944. (*Archives nationales*)

French *Milice* parade near the Arc de Triomphe in Paris, 1944. (*Archives nationales*)

August 1944. The *Forces françaises de l'Intérieur* (French Forces of the Interior) seen here after capturing a town from the German garrison. (*Archives nationales*)

The more the French Resistance increased its activities, the greater the repression by German security forces. Here members of the German *Ordnungspolizei* drive through a French town that has been devastated. Notice that the passenger has his Gewehr 98 rifle at the ready, indicating that these policemen expected contact with members of the FFI. (*Bundesarchiv*)

A member of the French *Milice* watches as suspected Resistance members are lined up. He seems to be watching the prisoners while grinning. The Germans have a word for this: *Schadenfreude* – spiteful pleasure. (*Archives nationales*)

Another view from the same incident. Other members of the *Milice* guard suspected Resistance members. (*Archives nationales*)

Above, an Italian-built Re-2002 Ariete fighter-bomber in the employ of the Luftwaffe. In 1944 a special squadron was created to support German anti-partisan operations in France. *Geschwader Bongart* was established in mid-April 1944, primarily from the *III.* and *IV. Gruppen* of *Fliegerzielgeschwader* 2. It employed principally the Fw 190 fighter-bomber and the Re-2002 fighter-bomber. The squadron also contained Ju 88 and Do 17 light bombers. (*Author's collection*)

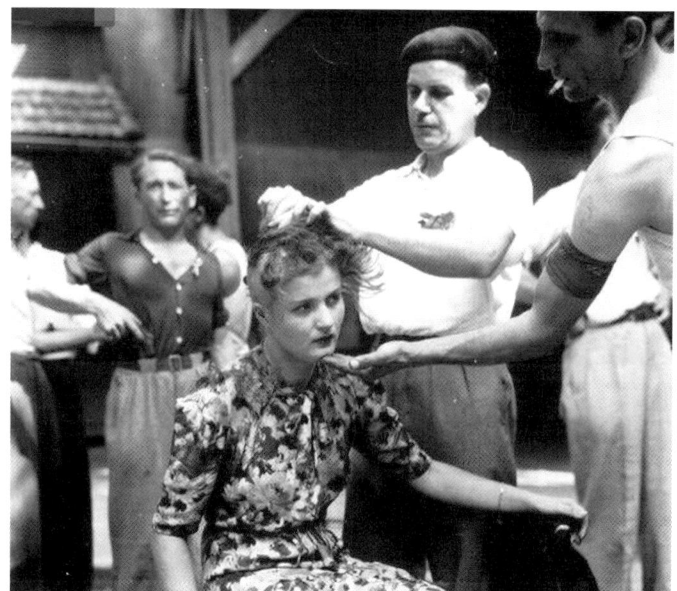

The price of fraternisation. A woman has her hair cut off by men of the Resistance. Quite often the women were brutalized. They would have their hair removed in the street for all to witness. In the background a member of the Resistance witnesses the spectacle while holding a pistol on his waist. (*Archives nationales*)

Here we see women who have had relations with German soldiers being accosted by the French Resistance. The punishment for a French woman who in one way or another, fraternised with the enemy, was to remove her clothing in public, cut off the mane of her head, and parade her through the streets while the crowd taunted and insulted her. Quite often, a swastika was either painted on their forehead or, if their tormentors were particularly vengeful, a swastika was carved into their forehead with a knife. Although brutal, French women fared better than French males who collaborated with the Nazis. Their punishment was often execution. (*Archives nationales*)

Occupation duty for a German soldier was far less hazardous in France than in Russia or the Balkans. Quite often men would go to great lengths to remain on occupation duty. Of course, as the war dragged on and the Resistance increased its operations, the safety that many German soldiers felt in 1940 and 1941 disappeared. (*Archives nationales*)

This was the outcome of a Resistance attack along the road between Souillac and Rouffignac-Saint-Cernin-de-Reilhac. During the war, this road proved to have the highest density of German vehicle ambushes by the Resistance, especially in 1944. (*M. R. Evans Collection*)

Another hamlet is set ablaze, 1944. Although the photograph is not quite clear, we can make out that the men involved are from the SD. They are also using a German Shepherd dog to assist in tracking down partisans. In the early 1930s the German Army rebuilt its military hound training school, located in Brandenburg, near Berlin. There it accommodated and trained 2,000 dogs at any one time. By the start of the Second World War, around 200,000 had been trained. (*M. R. Evans Collection*)

A French Souma S–35 tank in the service of the *Wehrmacht*. The Germans employed dozens and dozens of captured tanks to augment their military, especially the army security forces. These French tanks were used against the partisans all across occupied Europe. (*M. R. Evans Collection*)

The mother of a member of the *Jeunes de l'Europe Nouvelle* (JEN), or Young People of the New Europe, is escorted down the stairs from a French cathedral. Her son had been assassinated by the *Francs-tireurs et partisans français*. The JEN was the youth movement for young Frenchmen who supported the pro-Axis Vichy government. Many members of the JEN would go on to serve in the *Milice*. Initially, the Germans forbade the JEN and the *Milice* to carry weapons – prompting the British SOE to send the following message to Resistance members in France: 'They are unarmed, hit them now! They have nothing to shoot back with.' (*Archives nationales*)

A grainy picture but very rare, showing members of the *Groupes mobiles de réserve* of the *Gendarmerie Nationale*. This force was created by the Vichy government when the effectiveness of the regular police was brought into question. Here a squad of GMR men search a home for a suspected Resistance member. (*Archives nationales*)

16 July 1942. GMR troops and German *Ordnungspolizei* guard buses which have been filled with French Jews. The buses are parked next to the train cars that will take these unfortunate people to transit camps before their final destination: extermination camps in Poland and Germany. (*Archives nationales*)

District, in the city of Augsburg, was also employed in the occupation of the Alsace region in June 1940. Like *Polizei-Bataillon 54*, the *Polizei-Bataillon 74* helped to garrison Strasbourg and the surrounding towns. The *Polizei-Bataillon 55* had been created a month later, in July and had immediately been posted to the city of Colmar and the surrounding region.

Like the police battalions sent to Lorraine, *Polizei-Bataillon 54*, *Polizei-Bataillon 55*, and *Polizei-Bataillon 74* were employed not only in security and other policing duties, but to forcibly expel French Jews and other 'undesirables' on lists made by the SD and *Gestapo* of political opponents and persons thought to be opposed to the new German administration. Eventually, the expulsions from Alsace and Lorraine included an estimated 100,000 French citizens, Jews and non-Jews who had migrated into these two regions after 1918.[14] The region of Alsace was soon handed over to Robert Wagner, the *Gauleiter* (Nazi Party District Leader) of Baden. In October 1940 an additional police battalion, *Polizei Bataillon 51* made its appearance in Alsace. It arrived from Poland and was posted to Saverne (west-northwest of Strasbourg) in Alsace. This battalion remained in Alsace until the spring of 1942, when it was sent to Russia.

Occupation Duty in France, 1940–1941

Although the *Maquis* made life increasingly difficult for the Germans, particularly from 1943–4, occupation duty in France remained choice duty even up until its liberation in 1944. Compared to the dangers of occupation duty in the Balkans, anyone lucky enough to be stationed in France considered himself very fortunate indeed. This goes double for the meat grinder that was the Eastern Front. On average, Hitler was losing 3,000–5,000 men in Russia on a 'quiet' day. Because the German Army occupied the northern part of France beginning in July 1940, and the entire country as of November 1942, complete with German military government and administrative headquarters and forces, there was little need for the *Ordnungspolizei* in the country. Still, a small cadre was kept in occupied France and later, police forces were sent south to help occupy that part of France that had been under the control of the Vichy French government. The following table lists the German police battalions which served in France and the Low Countries from 1940–4. Where the month is known when the battalion or regiment was employed in France, a numerical designation represents the month of arrival. A second numerical designation in the next preceding year (or years) indicates when the unit left. A shaded box means the unit in question was not in France or the Low Countries in that year:[15]

Table 7. German Police Forces in France and the Low Countries, 1940–1944.

Year:	1940	1941	1942	1943	1944
Month:	Month	Month	Month	Month	Month
Battalions					
41	6[16]				
42		8[17]	7		
51	10	5			
54	6[18]				
55	7[19]			8[20]	
62	10[21]	see[22]			2[23]
63	9[24]	10[25]	7[26]	6[27]	
64	6[28]	3[29]	2[30]		
65	5[31]				
66	7[32]		5[33]		
67	5[34]		2[35]		
68	12[36]				
69				8[37]	
74	6[38]				
93	6[39]				
105			5[40]		
112		3[41]	6[42]		
121	1[43]		1[44]		
122	6[45]	3[46]	6[47]		
123	10[48]	10[49]	6[50]		
124	10[51]	1[52]			
254	12[53]	6[54]			
316			7[55]		
323		7[56]			
Regiments					
3			7[57]		
4			6[58]	6	
14				3[59]	3[60]
19					6[61]
28			11[62]	8	2[63]

The incorporation of Alsace and Lorraine into the Nazi Reich created a unique situation during the occupation of France. While the rest of the country was under direct German military control, Alsace and Lorraine were treated as integral parts of Greater Germany. This led to intense Germanisation efforts, including the forced adoption of German customs, language, and laws. The regions also became focal points for Nazi military strategy and collaborationist activities, while the Resistance and persecution of Jews were significant parts of daily life for the people there. The Nazi occupation of Alsace and Lorraine was marked by the complex dynamics of military governance, collaboration, and resistance, ultimately culminating in their liberation by the Allied forces in 1944. In France the Germans kept the equivalent of one to two police regiments at any one time. For example, On 1 October 1940 *Polizei-Bataillon 62* (*Hauptmann der Schutzpolizei* Wilhelm Ney), now under the command of *Major der Polizei* Franz Keller, was sent to France. In November 1940 it was located in La Madeleine (near Lille). In March 1941 it was transferred to the Brittany region and placed under the control of the *Militärbefehlshaber Frankreich*. There it remained deployed between Brittany and Normandy.

Occupation Duty in France, 1942–1944

In July 1942 the German *Orpo* moved the 316th and 323rd *Orpo* Battalions to the Paris area and began forming the 4th Police Regiment. These two battalions now became the 1st and 2nd Police Battalions of the 4th Police Regiment (respectively). In addition, a '3rd Police Battalion' was created by employing a cadre of personnel from the 62nd Reserve Police Battalion, which was located in Dieppe and Pourville, plus additional police recruits from the Reich. This police regiment remained in the Paris region until June 1943 when it was transferred to the *Generalgouvernement* (rump Poland).

Polizei-Regiment 28 'Todt' was 'officially' raised in France in November 1942, however the only battalion that was actually in France in November 1942 was *Reserve-Polizei-Bataillon 62*, while *Polizei-Bataillon 69*, which was supposed to become the *II. Bataillon* of *Polizei-Regiment 28 'Todt'*, was actually still located in Russia. A *III. Bataillon* for this regiment was eventually formed by transferring some personnel from *Reserve-Polizei-Bataillon 62* and *Polizei-Bataillon 69*, with the overwhelming majority of the personnel coming from new police recruits that had been trained by *Polizei-Ausbildungs-Bataillon 'Oranienburg'*. In August 1942 the battalion was designated as the *III. Bataillon* of the forming *Polizei-Regiment 4*, but in November 1942 it became the *I. Bataillon der Polizei-Regiment 28 'Todt'* and performed police duties in Brest (Brittany). Both the *Kommando der Ordnungspolizei Rennes* (KdO Rennes), and *Kommando der*

Ordnungspolizei Paris (KdO Paris) were established in 1940. However, it wasn't until 1943 that a supreme commander of the *Orpo* was created in France. This was the *Befehlshaber der Ordnungspolizei Paris* command, led by *Generalmajor der Polizei* Paul Scheer (15 March 1943 – July 1944). In 1944 several police units took part in anti-partisan operations against French Resistance forces. For example, during the battle for Vercours in July and August 1944, *SS-Polizei-Regiment 19* was part of the German forces employed against the FFI in that battle.

There were two major combat episodes which occurred in 1942. The first happened in August and involved the *4. Kompanie* of *Reserve Polizei-Bataillon 62*. In the summer of 1942, this police company was under the command of *Hauptmann der Schutzpolizei* Eicker and in August 1942, it was stationed in the French coastal town of Dieppe.[64] The *Reserve Polizei-Bataillon 62* was sent to help bolster the defences of the German *302. Infanterie-Division*, which had been holding this part of Adolf Hitler's so-called 'Atlantic Wall' since May 1941. The current commander of *Reserve-Polizei-Bataillon 62* was *Major der Schutzpolizei* Becker. Thus, *Infanterie-Regiment 571* of *302. Infanterie-Division* was holding Dieppe itself, while its two sister regiments (*Infanterie-Regiment 570* and *Infanterie-Regiment 572)* were arrayed on both flanks of *Infanterie-Regiment 571*.[65]

Although *Infanterie-Regiment 571* was up to full strength, it contained a large proportion (20 per cent) of men from former Polish territory that had been annexed by Germany.[66] They had been labelled as '*Volksdeutsche*' (ethnic-Germans) and drafted into the *Heer* (German Army), but few spoke more than a few words of German and fewer still had much desire to fight for a German victory. The German command realised this and knew that *Infanterie-Regiment 571* needed to be 'stiffened' with other units which had a predominance of Reich Germans. In the summer of 1942, the *Wehrmacht* was heavily engaged in Russia. As a result, there were few reinforcements available for the German Army in the West. Every available source of manpower was sought in order to alleviate the crisis.

It was for this reason that *Reserve-Polizei-Battalion 62* had been shifted to the Dieppe area in early 1942. In this way, the *4. Polizei-Kompanie* of this battalion took part in defending Dieppe against the aborted Allied landing in August 1942. The Canadians bore the brunt of the invasion, which was geared to test the defences of the Germans. The plan had called for the Canadians to land and hold Dieppe for one day, but it appears that just about everything went wrong for the invaders. The Canadians suffered dreadful losses. The extent of the employment of this police company was attested to by the fact that after the battle, fifteen of its officers, NCOs and men received the Iron Cross.[67] After the battle of Dieppe, *Reserve-Polizei-Battalion 62* took part in one more battle before its employment in the occupation of southern France. This other engagement was fought against the successful British Commando attack against the German naval base at St. Nazaire. These attacks convinced the OKH that defences in the West needed to be reinforced immediately or at the very least, beginning in 1943.[68]

The largest operation for the German police in France in 1942 was the occupation of territories administered by the Vichy government, in the so-called unoccupied zone. This been administered by the Vichy French government since July 1940. The reason for the invasion was the fear which the Germans had that the Vichy government might be emboldened by the Allied landings in North Africa. There the Vichy military had given up almost without a shot being fired. The Germans believed that Vichy might try to seek a peaceful surrender to the Allies and thus open up southern France to an unopposed invasion. It was also feared that the Vichy forces would join the Allies and thus turn their arms against German forces. This fear was not beyond the realms of possibility and indeed, as it turned out, many Vichy units simply joined the Allies after they surrendered in North Africa.

The Allies might thus land on continental Europe unopposed. On 11 November 1942 the German Army invaded southern France in order to prevent this from happening.[69] In November 1942, *Polizei-Regiment 28* underwent a comprehensive reorganisation under the command of *Oberstleutnant der Schutzpolizei* (Lieutenant-Colonel) Fritz Helmut Kosterbeck. The regiment's *I. Bataillon* and *II. Bataillon* were reconstituted using personnel drawn from the *III. Bataillon* of *Polizei-Regiment 4* and *III. Bataillon* of *Polizei-Regiment 17*, respectively. The *III. Bataillon* was reformed using members of the *Polizei-Sonder-Kompanie 'Todt'*. The principal German *Orpo* unit which took part in the occupation of southern France was *Polizei-Regiment 4* which had been stationed in Paris during the summer but was mobilised for action in the autumn for the invasion of Vichy France. When *SS-Polizei-Regiment 4* left France for Poland in early June 1943, the *Orpo* sent *SS-Polizei-Regiment 28 'Todt'* to southern France in August, to replace *SS-Polizei-Regiment 4*.[70] *Oberst der Schutzpolizei* Bernhard Griese, who had been the former commander of *Polizei-Bataillon 323* (redesignated as *II. Bataillon, SS-Polizei-Regiment 4)* was chosen as the commander of *Polizei-Regiment 28 'Todt'*. *Oberst der Schutzpolizei* Griese had been born on 17 January 1887 and was therefore 56 years old in 1943.[71] *Polizei-Regiment 28 'Todt'* (later, *SS-Polizei-Regiment 28 'Todt'*) was established in November 1942 as a security force for the Todt Organisation operating in the occupied territories, but specifically along the Atlantic coast, building fortifications. The *I. Bataillon* was stationed in Brest from around the end of 1942 to the beginning of 1943. From March 1943 to August 1943, the entire regiment was stationed in the Arnhem area of The Netherlands.

Some historians have been confused about the exact time when *Polizei-Regiment 28 'Todt'* was actually in southern France. The misunderstanding arises from the fact that the regiment was formed piecemeal. But one German document from *19. Armee* dated 25 January 1943 clears up the confusion. This document states that while *Polizei-Regiment 28 'Todt'* was indeed a part of *19. Armee* in January 1943, it only possessed the *I. Polizei-Bataillon* (i.e., *Reserve-Polizei-Bataillon 62*).[72] The *'II. Bataillon'* of *Polizei-Regiment 28 'Todt'* was designated to be *Reserve-Polizei-Bataillon 69*, which in January 1943 was fighting in southern Russia. The demand to finally bring *Polizei-Regiment 28 'Todt'* together finally pushed the withdrawal of *Reserve-Polizei-Bataillon 69* from Russia. It was initially sent to The Netherlands in February 1943. It had been ordered to The Netherlands in order to reorganise and replenish its ranks. It was in The Netherlands that the bulk of *Polizei-Regiment 28 'Todt'* was finally grouped together.[73]

This occurred in March 1943 when *Reserve-Polizei-Bataillon 62* was sent to Holland to join *Reserve-Polizei-Bataillon 69*. There, together with transfers from both battalions, plus new recruits from *Polizei-Ausbildungs-Bataillon Oranienburg* (stationed in the Reich) and *Polizei-Kompanie 'Todt'*, a brand-new *'III. Bataillon'* was created for *Polizei-Regiment 28 'Todt'*. By early August 1943 the regiment (now redesignated as *SS-Polizei-Regiment 28 'Todt'*) was considered fit and ready for service. It was only in August 1943 that the *II. Bataillon* and *III. Bataillon* (until then in Latvia and Ukraine) of *SS-Polizei-Regiment 28*, were attached in February, and joined the *I. Bataillon*, which was originally stationed in Brest. The regiment was then deployed in southern France and stationed in Marseille. From this city, it took part in several operations against the Resistance. Advance elements of the regiment had actually arrived in Marseilles in July 1943, when the entire port facility of that southern coastal city was completely destroyed. This was done in order to prevent their use by a possible Allied landing. In addition, the section of Marseille that was destroyed had been a refuge for criminals, Black Market dealers, runaway Jews, and even German Army deserters. The operation against the port facilities of Marseilles had begun in January 1943 as a large round-up of people in the region of the city surrounding the port. In that month alone the Germans, in cooperation with the Vichy police, rounded up some 40,000 people.[74]

SS-Polizei-Regiment 28 'Todt' was briefly employed in disarming Italian troops in September 1943. The regiment seems to have left Marseille in December 1943, since a record of the OKW (Armed Forces High Command) war diary, dated 14 December 1943, declared: 'Notice of the transfer of SS Police Regiment 28 "Todt" from Marseille to the region of Dijon-Lyon was given'.[75] In March 1943, the regiment was assembled in Arnhem in the Netherlands and transferred to Marseille in southern France in August 1943. In mid-December 1943, *SS-Polizei-Regiment 28 'Todt'* moved to the Vichy and Dijon-Lyon area. Plans had also been made to rename the regiment from *SS-Polizei-Regiment 28 'Todt'* to *'SS-Polizei-Regiment 14'*. However, this plan seems to have been dropped, since enough documentation exists listing *SS-Polizei-Regiment 28 'Todt'* as being in existence as late as March 1945. Most likely some members of the regiment were drafted into the 'new' *SS-Polizei-Regiment 14* that initially at least, was named *SS-Polizeiregiment 28 'Todt'*. According to one German source, the new *I. Polizei-Bataillon* and *III. Polizei-Bataillon* of the reformed *SS-Polizei-Regiment 14* was created by simply re-designating the *I. Polizei-Bataillon* and *III. Polizei-Bataillon* of *SS-Polizei-Regiment 1*. The *II. Polizei-Bataillon* of the regiment was the surviving 'old' *II. Polizei-Bataillon* from *Polizei-Regiment 14*.[76] *Polizei-Regiment 14* was reorganised in southern France.

Establishment of the 13th Reinforced Police Panzer Company

The *13. (verstärkt) Polizei-Panzer-Kompanie* (13th (Reinforced) Police Armoured Company) was established as a strengthened armoured police unit pursuant to an order issued by the *Reichsführer-SS und Chef der Deutschen Polizei*, Heinrich Himmler.[77] The directive originated from the *Reichsministerium des Innern* (Reich Ministry of the Interior) under the *Ordnungspolizei* command structure, designated as *Ordnung der Oberkommando IK (2) 251 Nr. 3/43*, and dated 6 January 1943. Contrary to the standard practice of forming such units at the *Polizeifahrzeugschule Wien* (Police Motor Vehicle School in Vienna), the 13th Company was instead attached directly to *SS-Polizeiregiment 'Griese'*, then stationed along the Atlantic coast of France for coastal security duties. Subsequently, by order of the *Reichsführer-SS* (Order Nr. 3267, dated 15 February 1943), two armoured car platoons – including all vehicles and personnel – were transferred *en masse* from the *7. Polizei-Panzer-Kompanie* (7th Police Armoured Company) to assist in the formation of the 13th Company. These platoons were redeployed from southern Russia, where they had previously operated under *SS-Polizeiregiment*

11. The organisational structure of the newly formed company was as follows:

13. (verstärkt) Polizei-Panzer-Kompanie-
Command Platoon with an associated Supply Train and Workshop Platoon
1st Platoon: 3 × Steyr armoured cars
2nd Platoon: 3 × Steyr armoured cars
3rd Platoon: 6 × Panzer II VK 1601 *Luchs* light reconnaissance tanks
4th Platoon: 4 × Panzer IV Ausf. F1 medium tanks
Flamethrower Armoured Car Platoon: 2 × SdKfz 251 / 16 halftracks

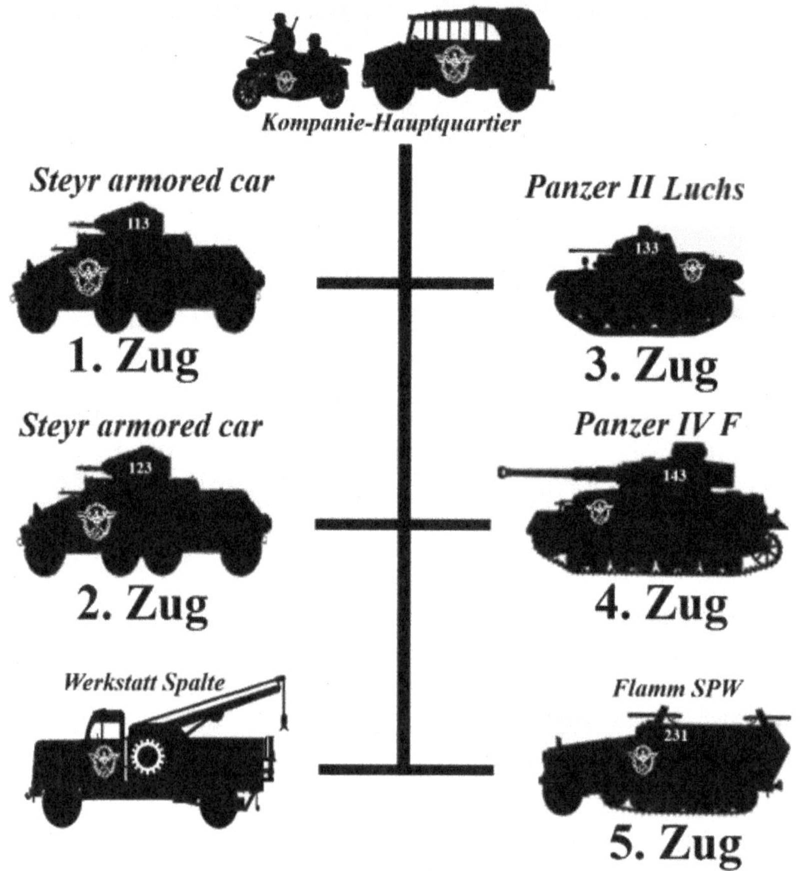

Figure 10. *13. (verstärkt) Polizei-Panzer-Kompanie* in August 1943.

The company's initial base of operations was the villa colony of *'Les Beaumettes'*, near Marseille, where approximately 200 personnel were billeted in eleven small summerhouses. The unit's initial strength totalled six officers, twenty-two non-commissioned officers, and 188 enlisted men. From its formation until 11 July 1943, the 13th Company remained assigned to *SS-Polizeiregiment 'Griese'*, operating along the southern French coast. During this period, the unit participated in the evacuation and systematic destruction of the Marseille harbour area, actions that included the arrest of numerous foreigners and Jews. Later in July 1943, *SS-Polizeiregiment 'Griese'* was reorganised and redesignated as *SS-Polizei-Regiment 14*. Shortly thereafter, it was redeployed to Croatia, concluding the company's initial operational phase in France.

Some time in mid to late July, the company was redeployed to the Balkans, where it was attached to *SS-Polizei-Regiment 14*. There, it participated in operations against partisan forces. For the rest of the war, *Polizei-Panzer-Kompanie 13* remained attached to *SS-Polizei-Regiment 14*. The Allied landings in Sicily in July 1943 temporarily changed the employment of the new regiment. In September it was sent to northern Italy. In that month the regiment was employed in disarming Italian troops along the Adriatic Coast of northern Italy. It appears that from October to November 1943 it was once again operating against the partisan forces in Slovenia.[78] However, in December 1943 *SS-Polizei-Regiment 14* was listed as part of the *II. SS-Panzerkorps* under *14. Armee* in Italy.[79] The regiment operated alongside *Grenadier-Regiment 214* performing road security duty to keep the supply line for *14. Armee* open.

In February and March 1944, the *I. Bataillon, SS-Polizei-Regiment 19*, under the command of *SS-Sturmbannführer und Major of the Schutzpolizei* Richard Maiwald, was deployed to the Haute-Savoie region to secure the rear areas of Operation *Hoch-Savoyen*, a German anti-partisan operation directed against the *Maquis des Glières*. On 19 April 1944, Maiwald was assigned to a regimental command training course and was temporarily succeeded by *Major der Schutzpolizei* Wilhelm Fischer. The *I. Bataillon, SS-Polizei-Regiment 19* replaced the *III. Bataillon, SS-Polizei-Regiment 28 'Todt'* that was on its way to Slovenia. The battalion was distributed as follows:

- *I. Bataillon Hauptquartier*, Annecy
  - *Hauptmann der Schutzpolizei* Schulz
- *1. Kompanie*, Annecy
  - *Oberleutnant der Schutzpolizei* Rassi

- *Polizei-Panzer-Kompanie 13* (no armoured vehicles whatsoever), Annecy
  - *Oberleutnant der Schutzpolizei* Kolmer
- *2. Kompanie*, Annemasse
  - *Hauptmann der Schutzpolizei* Guth
- *3. Kompanie*, Cluses
  - *Hauptmann der Schutzpolizei* Heinrich

In Annecy, the *1. Kompanie* replaced *Gebirgsjäger-Bataillon I./98* in the Galbert district. *Polizei-Panzer-Kompanie 13* (no armoured vehicles at this time), replaced the *12. Kompanie, III. Bataillon, SS-Polizei-Regiment 28 'Todt'* in Saint-François School, while the headquarters staff of *I. Bataillon* established itself in the Hôtel du Mont-Blanc. The first major operation in which *I. Bataillon, SS-Polizei-Regiment 19* took part in ran from 18 to 21 May 1944. The operation was directed by the local *SiPo*-SD. The policemen combed a vast region of the Chablais. The battalion arrested hundreds of people, burned dozens of homes, deported around fifty people and shot just over a dozen members suspected of being *Maquisards*. After the D-Day landings on 6 June, the *Maquisards* increased their operations against German forces, rail and transport facilities and command and control centres. Because of this increased activity, the Germans became more brutal in the manner in which they carried out operations and in executions performed in retaliation for guerrilla attacks. On 5 June, *SS-Polizei-Regiment 19* executed twenty-eight factory workers from the Ugine steelworks in Savoy. On 15 June they razed the village of Puisots, just north of Annecy. Three days later, men from *SS-Polizei-Regiment 19* executed twenty-five *Maquisards* that were being held in jail at Annecy.

Last Operations of the German Police and Withdrawal from France

In May 1944, *II. Bataillon, SS-Polizei-Regiment 19* and *III. Bataillon, SS-Polizei-Regiment 19* that were operating in Lower Styria and Upper Carnolia in Slovenia were withdrawn. They were transferred to France, to the region of the Massif Central, where the *III. Bataillon* stationed itself in Lyon alongside the regimental staff. This battalion worked to reinforce *Sicherungs-Brigade 74* during the battle of Mont Mouchet. In June 1944, the entire regiment was sent to the region of Paris, France. This was done to reinforce German security forces there owing to the growing attacks by the local *Maquis*, who were now emboldened by the Allied landings in Normandy on 6 June 1944. In July 1944 it was reported that the *I. Bataillon* of *SS-Polizei-Regiment 19* was still located in Annecy, France.

The same source states that its commander, as of July 1944 was still *SS-Sturmbannführer und Major of the Schutzpolizei* Richard Maiwald. Back in December 1943, it had been *Major der Schutzpolizei* W. Fischer.[80] In addition, the commander of *SS-Polizei-Regiment 19* at this time was *Oberst der Schutzpolizei* Hubert Kölblinger, although he was later replaced. The commander of the *III. Bataillon, SS-Polizei-Regiment 19* was *SS-Sturmbannführer und Major der Schutzpolizei* Sprengleweski. *Major der Schutzpolizei* Sprengleweski had been the former 'Schulungsleiter' (Principal Police Training Officer) for *Wehrkreis VII*.[81] Later, in 1944, Sprengleweski would lead the *I. Bataillon* of *Polizei-Freiwilligen-Regiment 3 'Serbien'*.[82] In July 1944, *I. Bataillon, SS-Polizei-Regiment 19*, was located in Haute-Savoie. During Operation Bettina, which was directed against the *Maquis* de Vercors, it was made responsible for securing the medical base.

By September 1944, *SS-Polizei-Regiment 19* was led by *Major der Schutzpolizei* Bartscht. The regiment had been quartered in Langres in late August. Then on 3 September *Reichsführer-SS* Heinrich Himmler ordered *SS-Polizei-Regiment 19* moved to Belfort, in order to protect what remained of the Vichy government of Marshal Pétain. On 12 September 1944, however, the Vichy French government soon proceeded further east, towards Sigmaringen in Germany, which it reached in October 1944.[83] *Sicherungs Kampfgruppe Generalleutnant Ottenbacher* (Security Battle Group Lieutenant-General Ottenbacher) was another anti-partisan formation. This ad-hoc battle group was a provisional brigade composed of police and security forces. The security forces were under the command of *Generalleutnant* Otto-Ernst Ottenbacher.[84] The two principal components of this 'provisional brigade' were *SS-Polizei-Regiment 19* and *Sicherungs-Regiment 200*.[85]

Generalleutnant Ottenbacher was a career Army officer who had expertise in fortress and security matters. His career posts had included service as fortress commander of Lötzen in *Wehrkreis V* (5th Military District) in 1941.[86] By September 1944, however, the German *1. Armee* and *19. Armee* were in full flight. *Kampfgruppe Ottenbacher*, along with the remnants of the *716. Infanterie-Division* and several other splinter groups – initially under the *LXIV. Armeekorps* were doing their best to delay the American and French advance towards the provinces of Alsace and Lorraine along the Franco-German border.[87] Towards the end of September 1944 *SS-Polizei-Regiment 19* was detached from *Sicherungs Kampfgruppe Generalleutnant Ottenbacher* and was assigned to the *LXVI. Armeekorps*:

Along the Moselle [River], from Charmes ten miles south to Epinal, the *LXVI. Armeekorps* under *19. Armee* held the river line with a motley collection of *16. Infanterie-Division*, and *Gruppe Ottenbacher* remnants; stragglers from other *kampfgruppen* chopped up in the Dijon salient; two battalions of the 19th SS Police Regiment, and some Luftwaffe and Kriegsmarine 'retreads'.[88]

Kampfgruppe Ottenbacher consisted of *SS-Polizei-Regiment 19, Sicherungs-Regiment 1000 (motorisiert), Sicherungs-Aufklärungs-Abteilung 1000* and *Sicherungs-Regiment 200*. The second regiment, *Sicherungs-Regiment 1000 (mot.)*, was renamed as *Grenadier-Regiment 1212 (motorisiert)* and added to the *189. Infanterie-Division* on 17 December 1944.[89] *Sicherungs-Regiment 1000 (mot.)* had two battalions with three rifle and one Flak company each, as well as an infantry gun company (*13. Kompanie*), an anti-tank company (*14. Kompanie*) and a panzer company (*15. Panzer-Kompanie*). The latter was equipped with French tanks. *Sicherungs-Aufklärungs-Abteilung 1000* had one armoured scout car company. Again, this unit was equipped with a mixture of French and German armoured vehicles. *SS-Polizei-Regiment 19* had three police rifle battalions.

These police battalions had three rifle companies and one heavy weapons company. The heavy weapons companies had one heavy machine gun and one medium mortar platoon each. The regimental headquarters controlled the engineer platoon, anti-tank company, and the attached *13. (schwere) Polizei-Panzer-Kompanie*. From October to November 1944 *SS-Polizei-Regiment 19* served under the *16. Volksgrenadier-Division* (still under *19. Armee*). In January the regiment became a reserve component of *Heeresgruppe G* (Army Group 'G') in the region of Colmar.[90] In March 1945 the unit was still under the same army group. In October 1944 *SS-Polizei-Regiment 19* was attached to the *16. Volksgrenadier-Division* in the vicinity of Bruyères, in Alsace. In December 1944 *SS-Polizei-Regiment 19* was once again transferred to Slovenia, this time with all three of its battalions. In March 1945 it was located in Celje, in *Untersteiermark* (Lower Styria). The *SS-Polizei-Regiment 17*, which had been operating under *Polizei-Kampfgruppe Hannibal* in East Prussia, was transferred in November 1944 to the Slovenska Bistrica area of Slovenia. At the end of March 1945 *SS-Polizei-Regiment 19* moved to Kranj. It was there that *SS-Polizei-Regiment 19* joined *Kampfgruppe von Seeler* (*Oberst* Werner von Seeler), which already contained *SS-Polizei-Regiment 17*.

This battlegroup actually contained around 30,000 men. The principal units were as follows: *SS-Polizei-Regiment 17* (parts), *SS-Polizei-Regiment*

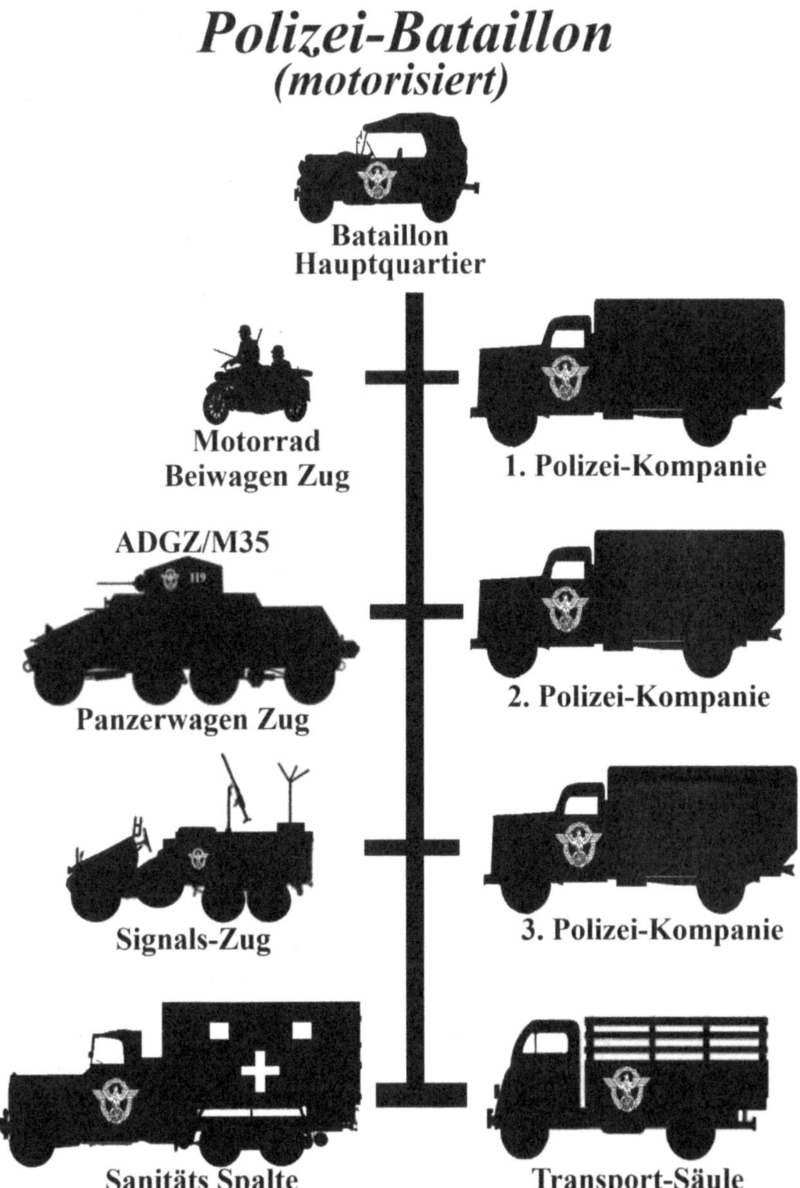

Figure 11. A typical pre-war German motorised police battalion. Many pre-war German police vehicles continued to be employed during the Second World War. Some battalions contained four police companies instead of three.

19, SS-Polizei-Regiment 28 Todt (parts), *Feldgendarmerie-Bataillon 3 (motorisiert), Polizei-Panzer-Kompanie 13, Polizei-Panzer-Kompanie 14, Polizei-Pionier-Kompanie Krainburg, Polizei-Infanterie-Geschütz-Kompanie Alpenland, SS-Ersatz-Regiment 'Prinz Eugen', Russisches-Schutzkorps, Serbisches-Freiwilligen-Korps, Marine-Flak-Abteilung 720 Heeres-Flak-Abteilung 309, Heeres-Flak-Abteilung 310,* one battalion from *Lehr-Regiment Brandenburg.* In addition, the battlegroup contained a few hundred Slovenian Domobrans.

THE *SICHERHEITSDIENST* IN FRANCE: ORIGINS, STRUCTURE, AND OPERATIONS IN OCCUPIED AND VICHY TERRITORIES

Origins and Organisational Framework

The *Sicherheitsdienst des Reichsführers-SS* (SD, Security Service of the *Reichsführer-SS*) originated in the early 1930s. It was formally institutionalised in 1932 under the leadership of Reinhard Heydrich, who was appointed by Heinrich Himmler to lead this nascent organisation. Initially tasked with monitoring ideological loyalty within the National Socialist movement, the SD rapidly evolved into the central intelligence agency of the SS and, by extension, the Third Reich. In 1936, Himmler oversaw the consolidation of the *Geheime Staatspolizei* (*Gestapo*, or Secret State Police) and the *Kriminalpolizei* (*Kripo*, or Criminal Police) into a unified structure known as the *Sicherheitspolizei* (*SiPo*). The *Gestapo* was primarily responsible for political surveillance, repression, and arrest of perceived enemies of the regime, while the *Kripo* continued to investigate conventional criminal offences such as murder and theft. This consolidation marked a critical step in the centralisation of Nazi internal security.

In 1939, these agencies were brought under the umbrella of the newly established RSHA, which functioned as the supreme command structure for all Nazi security and intelligence services. The RSHA, under Heydrich and later Ernst Kaltenbrunner, was divided into seven departments (*Ämter*), each with a distinct functional domain:

- Amt I – Administration and Legal Affairs
- Amt II – Ideological Research
- Amt III – *SD-Inland* (Domestic Intelligence)
- Amt IV – Gestapo (Political Policing and Repression)
- Amt V – *Kripo* (Criminal Police)
- Amt VI – *SD-Ausland* (Foreign Intelligence)
- Amt VII – Archival Work and Ideological Documentation

The SD's intelligence activities were conducted mainly through Amt III, which focused on internal surveillance and public opinion within the Reich, and Amt VI, which oversaw espionage and foreign intelligence in occupied and neutral states. The RSHA's structure reflected the fusion of SS ideology with state authority, aiming to enforce ideological conformity and eliminate all perceived enemies – political, racial, or otherwise. The SD's organisation extended into occupied territories through a hierarchical system. At the top were *SD-Oberabschnitte* (main districts), aligned with SS regional commands. Beneath these were *SD-Abschnitte* (sub-districts) at the provincial and urban levels, which in turn oversaw local *Außenstellen* (outposts). These offices were often co-located with *Gestapo* and *Kripo* units and worked in close collaboration, especially in matters of repression, counter-intelligence, and population control.

While not a law enforcement agency in the conventional sense, the SD functioned as the ideological watchdog of the Nazi regime. Its members – predominantly SS officers – were frequently university-educated and trained in fields such as law, history, and linguistics, making them effective instruments of totalitarian control. In occupied territories, SD personnel often operated as part of *Einsatzgruppen*, mobile killing units responsible for mass executions, particularly in Eastern Europe. These actions foreshadowed the SD's pivotal role in implementing the Holocaust, especially in identifying and facilitating the deportation of Jewish populations.

The *Sicherheitsdienst* in France: Operations in Occupied and Vichy Zones

Following the French defeat in 1940, the SD played a central role in German counterinsurgency and intelligence operations across both the Occupied Zone (northern and western France) and the nominally sovereign Vichy Zone (southern France) until its occupation in

November 1942. In the Occupied Zone, the SD operated as an integral component of the German security administration, alongside the *Gestapo* (RSHA Amt IV), *Kripo* (Amt V), and the MBF, the German military command. SD regional offices were established in major cities such as Paris, Lille, and Dijon.

The SD's primary mission in France involved intelligence-gathering, surveillance, and ideological enforcement. Its agents focused on identifying and neutralising resistance movements – particularly Gaullist networks, Communist partisans, and members of the FTP. The SD also closely monitored perceived ideological enemies, including Jews, Freemasons, clergy, and liberal intellectuals. Interrogations were often conducted in tandem with the *Gestapo*, with whom the SD shared both administrative infrastructure and field operations. In addition to counterinsurgency work, the SD coordinated with *Einsatzkommandos* and *Sicherheitskommandos* on operations of mass repression, especially that targeting Jewish communities. The SD was deeply implicated in orchestrating and executing mass deportations, including the notorious Vel d'Hiv Round-up (July 1942), in which over 13,000 Jews were arrested and interned in inhumane conditions before deportation to extermination camps.

In the Vichy Zone, until the German occupation in November 1942 (Operation *Anton*), SD activity was necessarily more covert due to the formal sovereignty of the Vichy regime. After the full occupation of Vichy France, the SD was able to operate more openly, establishing offices and expanding its network of collaborators. Surveillance intensified, targeting Spanish Republicans, Jewish refugees, foreign diplomats, and suspected Allied sympathisers. The SD also extended its coordination with French fascist militias, such as the *Milice*, especially in campaigns of anti-Resistance terror in 1943–4.

The SD: Legacy and Implications

The SD's operations in France exemplify the fusion of intelligence, repression, and ideological policing that characterised Nazi occupation policy. In contrast to more conventional military or administrative organs, the SD functioned as a political weapon – tasked not only with gathering information but with shaping behaviour, enforcing conformity, and exterminating dissent. Its role in deportations, repression of the Resistance, and ideological surveillance renders it a central actor in the machinery of occupation and genocide. Understanding the SD's structure and function in France not only illuminates the mechanics of Nazi control but also underscores the vital interplay between local collaboration, totalitarian ideology, and institutionalised violence. It stands as a stark reminder of the bureaucratic and psychological architecture underpinning occupation regimes.

German Security Apparatus in Occupied France: Structure, Roles, and Key Figures

1. Organisational Framework

Following France's defeat in 1940, Nazi Germany imposed a multilayered security apparatus in the occupied and Vichy zones. Alongside the *Wehrmacht*, the SS and several police and intelligence organisations worked to suppress resistance, control civilian populations, and orchestrate the persecution of Jews. Heinrich Himmler, in his dual role as *Reichsführer-SS* and head of the German Interior Ministry, established a security hierarchy merging ideological policing, surveillance, and paramilitary roles. This centralisation was symbolised by the RSHA, which integrated:

- *Gestapo* – political repression and mass arrests (RSHA Amt IV).
- *Kripo* – policing non-political crimes (RSHA Amt V).
- SD – ideological intelligence: Amt III (domestic) and Amt VI (foreign espionage).

This concentration of power enabled the SS to enforce Nazi ideology across both occupied and Vichy France.

2. Waffen-SS and Ordnungspolizei in France

Uniting elements of military and police oversight, the *Waffen-SS* and *Orpo* contributed to security and repression:

- *Waffen-SS* divisions, such as 'Das Reich', frequently operated in France both as combat units and in anti-partisan and reprisal actions – most infamously at Oradour-sur-Glane where 642 civilians were massacred.
- A *Waffen-SS* battalion from the *17. SS Panzergrenadier Division 'Götz von Berlichingen'* massacred 124 civilians in the village of Maillé on 25 August 1944.

- The *Orpo* were employed in occupation duty all across Europe. They supported *Wehrmacht* operations, patrolled occupied zones, guarded vital infrastructure, and participated in mass round-ups and took part in anti-partisan operations.

3. Core Security Agencies

Gestapo (RSHA Amt IV): Operated in tandem with the SD to identify and dismantle resistance networks. They led surveillance campaigns targeting Jews, Freemasons, clergy, and partisans, often collaborating with both German and Vichy police.

Sicherheitsdienst (RSHA Amt III & VI): Functioned as the SS-run intelligence service, infiltrating underground groups, maintaining lists of suspected resistant individuals and Jews, and coordinating persecution with state authorities. In both Occupied and Vichy Zones, SD agents shared facilities and operations with the *Gestapo*.

4. Operations in Occupied and Vichy Zones

Occupied Zone:

SD and *Gestapo* offices were established in major cities – Paris, Lyon, Lille, Dijon – under the overall leadership of the *Befehlshaber der Sicherheitspolizei und des SD* (BdS). Central headquarters was located at 84 Avenue Foch in Paris, with torture chambers operating in the basement. Their duties included:

- Intelligence-gathering on Resistance networks and Jews.
- Arrest, interrogation, deportation.
- Coordinated mass actions such as the Vel d'Hiv Round-up (July 1942) and the rue Sainte-Catherine raid (February 1943) in Lyon, where 86 Jews were detained.

Vichy Zone

Until Operation *Anton* in November 1942, operations were more covert, relying on liaison with Vichy's *Service de surveillance du territoire*. The SD infiltrated French pro-German networks, monitored refugees, Spanish Republicans, and opposition elements. Post-occupation, SD offices opened openly, intensifying surveillance and deportations.

5. Prominent SS and Police Officers in France

Table 8. Prominent SS and Police Officers in France.

Officer	Rank & Role	Notes
Klaus Barbie	*SS-Hauptsturmführer, Gestapo* chief in Lyon (1942–4)	Arrest, torture, execution of Jean Moulin and 13,000+ Jews; dubbed 'Butcher of Lyon'
Rudolf Böhmler	*SS-Sturmbannführer*, SD counter-espionage	Focused on SOE networks; largely undocumented post-war
Theodor Dannecker	*SS-Hauptsturmführer, Judenreferent*	Organiser of 60,000+ deportations, including Vel d'Hiv; he was a key Eichmann deputy
Herbert Hagen	*SS-Sturmbannführer*, staff chief to Oberg in Paris	Coordinated deportations; convicted in 1980, served 4 years
Hermann Herold	Senior police official, GFP / *SiPo*-SS in Poitiers	Oversaw police merger and repression in central France
Hans Lipps	*SS-Obersturmführer, Gestapo* Bordeaux	Repression of Resistance & Jews; evaded prosecution
Kurt Lischka	*SS-Obersturmführer*, KdS Paris (Jan 1942–Sept 1943)	Oversaw deportations (~73,000 Jews); convicted 1980, served limited time
Carl (Karl) Oberg	*SS-Brigadeführer, Höhere SS und Polizeiführer Frankreich* (1942–4)	Oversaw anti-Jewish policy including Vel d'Hiv; post-war sentenced but released 1962.

6. Principal SD Posts in France

The main station posts of the *Sicherheitspolizei* and SD were as follows:[1]

Beauftträger des Befehlshaber der Sicherheitspolizei und des SD beim Militärbefehlshaber in Belgien und Nordfrankreich (Brussels)
SS-Obersturmbannführer Karl Hasselbacher (June – September 1940)[2]
SS-Standartenführer Constantin Canaris (October 1940 – 26 November 1941)
SS-Obersturmbannführer Ernst Ehlers (December 1941 – January 1944)
SS-Standartenführer Constantin Canaris (1 February – 15 September 1944)
Kommandeur der Sicherheitspolizei und des SD Wallonien
SS-Obersturmbannführer Eduard Strauch (31 May – Oktober 1944)
Unofficial SD Representative in France
SS-Sturmbannführer Helmut Knochen (May 1940 – April 1942)
Befehlshaber der Sicherheitspolizei und des SD im Bereich des Militärbefehlshabers für Frankreich in Paris
SS-Gruppenführer und Generalleutnant der Polizei Max Thomas (27 July 1940 – 30 September 1941)

SS-Brigadeführer Walter Bierkamp (30 September 1941 – 5 June 1942)
SS-Standartenführer Helmut Knochen (6 June 1942 – 2 September 1944)
SS-Obersturmbannführer Franz Stossberg (2 – 30 September 1944)
SS-Obersturmbannführer Friedrich Suhr (30 September – December 1944)
Kommandeur der Sicherheitspolizei und des SD Paris[3]
SS-Obersturmbannführer Kurt Lischka (January 1942 – September 1943)
SS-Obersturmbannführer Hans Henschke (Oktober 1943 – August 1944)
SS-Obersturmbannführer Friedrich Suhr (January – 30 November 1944)
Kommandeur der Sicherheitspolizei und des SD Saint-Quentin
Dr. Hans Joachim Ludwig Otto Peters
Karl Westphal
Emmanuel Wickenden
Günter Sadzik
Kommandeur der Sicherheitspolizei und des SD Châlons-sur-Marne
SS-Hauptsturmführer Modest Graf von Korff (July 1942 – May 1943)
SS-Sturmbannführer Dr. Karl Lüdcke (24 July 1943 – 28 August 1944)
Kommandeur der Sicherheitspolizei und des SD Nancy
SS-Sturmbannführer Horst Ellissen (1941–3)
SS-Sturmbannführer Rudolf Schmaling (1943 – November 1943)
SS-Sturmbannführer Franz Hoth (November 1943–4)
Kommandeur der Sicherheitspolizei und des SD Rouen
Sturmbannführer Werner Rolf Mühler (1 April 1941 – October 1942)
SS-Obersturmbannführer Bruno Müller (May–November 1944)
Kommandeur der Sicherheitspolizei und des SD Dijon
SS-Sturmbannführer Friedrich Mußgay (August 1940 – May 1941)[4]
SS-Sturmbannführer Anton Meier
SS-Sturmbannführer Wilhelm Hult
Kommandeur der Sicherheitspolizei und des SD Vichy
SS-Hauptsturmführer Hugo Geissler (killed by FFI on 12 June 1944)
SS-Sturmbannführer Karl Boemelburg
Kommandeur der Sicherheitspolizei und des SD Nice (subordinate to KdS Vichy)
SS-Hauptsturmführer Schulz
SS-Hauptsturmführer Dr. Gerhard Keil (September 1943 – 1944)
Kommandeur der Sicherheitspolizei und des SD Limoges
SS-Hauptsturmführer Hans Nicolai Jessen (November 1942 – May 1943)
SS-Sturmbannführer August Meier (May 1943 – 1944)
Kommandeur der Sicherheitspolizei und des SD Lyon
SS-Sturmbannführer Werner Rolf Mühler (12 November 1942 – April 1943)
SS-Hauptsturmführer Fritz Hollert (April – 3 July 1943)
SS Obersturmbannführer Dr. Werner Knab (3 July 1943 – August 1944)
Kommandeur der Sicherheitspolizei und des SD Marseille
SS-Obersturmbannführer Werner Rolf Mühler (January 1943 – June 1944)
SS-Obersturmbannführer Friedrich Wilhelm Nölle (1944)

Kommandeur der Sicherheitspolizei und des SD Montpellier
SS-Obersturmbannführer Dr. Hellmut Tanzmann (November 1942)
Kommandeur der Sicherheitspolizei und des SD Toulouse
SS-Sturmbannführer Dr. Rudolf Bilfinger (June – November 1943)
SS-Sturmbannführer Friedrich Suhr (November – December 1943)
Kommandeur der Sicherheitspolizei und des SD Rennes
SS-Sturmbannführer Dr. Hermann Heerdt (1 June 1942 – March 1943)
SS-Sturmbannführer Hartmut Adolf Pulmer (March 1943 – 3 August 1944)
Kommandeur der Sicherheitspolizei und des SD Angers
SS-Hauptsturmführer Hans-Dietrich Ernst (June 1942 – August 1944)

The initial commander of the *SD-Aussenstelle Rennes* was *SS-Sturmbannführer* Dr. Rudolf Meiners, who had extended jurisdiction over Brittany beginning 1943 onward. The headquarters was actually located in Angers, not Rennes, though Rennes had an *SD-Aussenstelle* (SD branch office). Within Brittany, especially in Rennes, SD/*SiPo* operations were usually headed by *SS-Hauptsturmführer* Herbert Olschowy, who operated out of the Rennes SD post. This post was heavily involved in anti-Resistance operations, arrests, and deportations.

Kommandeur der Sicherheitspolizei und des SD Poitiers
Dr. Hermann Herold (June 1942 – September 1944)
Kommandeur der Sicherheitspolizei und des SD Bordeaux
SS-Sturmbannführer Herbert Martin Hagen (August 1940 – May 1942)
SS-Hauptsturmführer Modest Graf von Korff (July 1942 – May 1943)
Hans Luther (June 1943 – October 1943)
SS-Sturmbannführer Dr. Walther Machule (6 November 1943 – 1944)
SS-Sturmbannführer Dr. Josef John (1944)
Kommandeur der Sicherheitspolizei und des SD Orleans
SS-Sturmbannführer Karl Westphal
SS-Hauptsturmführer Fritz Merdsche
Befehlshaber der Sicherheitspolizei und des SD Westmark (Metz)
SS-Brigadeführer Anton Dunckern (July 1940 – June 1944)
Kommandeur der Sicherheitspolizei und des SD Metz
SS-Obersturmbannführer Herbert Zimmermann (July – November 1944)
Befehlshaber der Sicherheitspolizei und des SD Elsass (Straßburg)
SS-Obergruppenführer Gustav Adolf Scheel (August 1940 – January 1941)
SS-Oberführer Hans Fischer (November 1941 – December 1943)
SS-Standartenführer Erich Isselhorst (January 1944 – 10 December 1944)

7. *Einsatzkommando*

In occupied France, these were mobile units of Nazi repression which operated from 1940 to 1944. During the German occupation of France, multiple *Einsatzkommandos* – mobile field units often referred to as 'flying columns' – were deployed to combat Resistance activities and enforce Nazi authority. These units operated across various regions, reporting to the *Kommandeur der Sicherheitspolizei und des SD* (KdS) for their respective sectors, under the ultimate supervision of the RSHA in Berlin. Though their structure and size varied, their core functions included intelligence gathering, targeted arrests, and direct repression – sometimes amounting to war crimes.

1. *Einsatzkommando Marseille*
    Commander: *SS-Obersturmbannführer* Werner Rolf Mühler (January 1943 – June 1944)
    Based in the port city of Marseille, this unit carried out extensive surveillance and repression of both Resistance networks and civilian populations. Under Mühler's command, *Einsatzkommando Marseille* spearheaded the razing of the Old Quarter, and orchestrated mass arrests, particularly targeting Jews and suspected resisters. Their actions were instrumental in consolidating German control during this critical period.

2. *Einsatzkommando Rennes*
    Jurisdiction: Brittany region, subordinate to KdS Angers or KdS Bretagne
    Active from 1941, commanded initially by *SS-Sturmbannführer* Dr. Hermann Heerdt, later by *SS-Obersturmbannführer* Hartmut Adolf Pulmer, with deputy officers like *SS-Untersturmführer* Hans Krüger and Helmut Walter.
    Comprised around seventy officers and fifteen civilian secretaries, this *Einsatzkommando* focused on intelligence gathering and the suppression of *Maquis* (rural Resistance) groups.
    Operated through Section IV, led by *SS-Sturmbannführer* Fritz Barnekow (~30 agents), which conducted war crimes during summer 1944 counter-insurgency operations against the *Maquis* of Morbihan and Côtes-du-Nord. It also established the *Selbstschutzpolizei*, a collaborationist auxiliary force, and deployed a *Rollkommando* – a rapid-response unit under Adolf Breuer – to reinforce operations in volatile areas.

3. *Einsatzkommando Paris*
    Operating under SS leadership, particularly Helmut Knochen, this unit served as a principal organ of intelligence and counter-Resistance activity within the capital. It coordinated with French collaborators to dismantle urban networks, conduct arrests, and implement racial and ideological policies, facilitating broader repression in Île-de-France.

4. *Einsatzkommando Orléans*
    Commander: *SS-Sturmbannführer* Dr. Walter Kehrer
    Functioned under the KdS Paris authority to monitor and suppress the Resistance in central France. The unit played a direct role in

apprehending and executing individuals perceived as threats, serving as a regional node of the *Gestapo* and SD apparatus.

5.   *Einsatzkommando Nancy*
Commander: *SS-Sturmbannführer* Wilhelm Schneider
Responsible for surveillance and anti-Resistance activity in northeastern France. The unit collaborated closely with the SD and other security agencies, executing arrests and reprisals against civilians and partisan forces.

6.   *Einsatzkommando Le Mans*
Commander: *SS-Hauptsturmführer* Eugen Reusing
Active across the Sarthe department and surrounding areas, this unit coordinated with the *Feldgendarmerie* and *Wehrmacht*. It executed punitive measures – including mass arrests and executions – against those labelled enemies of the Reich, reflecting the SD's wider role in occupation-era atrocities.

7.   *SD-Außenstelle* Chalon-sur-Saône
1941–3 Commander: *SS-Untersturmführer* Heinz Röthke
From 1943: Hans Krüger (demoted to *SS-Untersturmführer*), under KdS Dijon led by *SS-Sturmbannführer* Dr. Albert Rapp
This outpost served the Burgundy – Franche-Comté region, engaging in surveillance and enforcement. Krüger, transferred after loose disclosure of atrocities in Poland, continued to facilitate war crimes and liaison work from Dijon.

These *Einsatzkommandos* operated with tactical flexibility and brutal efficiency. They enforced Nazi ideological conformity and responded swiftly to partisan threats, often leading local repression and leveraging collaboration with French auxiliary police. Their tactics included torture, summary executions, deportation, and destruction of civilian infrastructure.[5]

Though these units were disbanded or absorbed into other security apparatuses during France's liberation in 1944, their legacy underscores the mobile, decentralised nature of Germany's approach to counterinsurgency and racial persecution. Post-war trials revealed both individual accountability and broader questions of collaboration, complicity, and institutional memory in France. By integrating localised *Einsatzkommandos* into a broader security framework, the Nazi regime achieved tailored, region-specific responses to Resistance threats. The legacy of these units is reflected not only in the physical harm done, but in their role as exemplars of state-sanctioned tactical violence. For historians, they offer compelling case studies on how ideology, bureaucracy, and military innovation combined to facilitate occupation repression and shaped the contours of wartime France.

Conclusions

The German security forces in France constituted a cohesive, hierarchical machinery blending ideological control, police authority, military enforcement, and judicial powers – centred in the RSHA under SS command. This system enabled systematic suppression of resistance and coordinated persecution of Jews, both through overt reprisals and clandestine coordination with Vichy. Prominent figures like Barbie, Dannecker, and Oberg wielded extraordinary influence, instigating atrocities and deportations whose effects reverberate in collective memory and ongoing historical discourse. Understanding this apparatus is critical to comprehending how state terror was operationalised across the Occupied and Vichy Zones.

Chapter 9

THE HOLOCAUST IN FRANCE

Introduction

The implementation of the Holocaust in France and the Low Countries represents a complex convergence of Nazi ideological imperatives, occupation policies, and varying degrees of local complicity and resistance. Following the military conquests of 1940, Nazi Germany imposed differentiated administrative regimes across Western Europe, shaping the trajectory and efficacy of anti-Jewish policies in each territory. In the Netherlands, a German civilian administration under Arthur Seyss-Inquart facilitated the swift enforcement of radical anti-Semitic legislation, resulting in the registration, segregation, and eventual deportation of over 100,000 Jews – more than 75 per cent of the prewar Jewish population – most of whom were murdered in extermination camps.[1]

Belgium and northern France were placed under German military rule, while unoccupied southern France operated under the nominally sovereign Vichy regime. Despite its ostensibly autonomous status, Vichy voluntarily implemented anti-Semitic laws and actively collaborated with the German authorities in the identification, internment, and deportation of Jews, with foreign Jews bearing the brunt of these measures. The Holocaust in France, like elsewhere in Western Europe, unfolded in phases: legal disenfranchisement, economic expropriation, mandatory registration, internment, and ultimately deportation to death camps – primarily Auschwitz. While orchestrated by German SS and *Gestapo* units, these policies were deeply reliant on the cooperation of local bureaucracies, police forces, and in some instances, civilian collaborators.

France's unique internal division – between the German-occupied northern zone and the collaborationist Vichy regime in the south – produced a fragmented but ultimately complicit framework in which over 75,000 Jews were deported, with fewer than 3,000 survivors. In contrast, the Netherlands experienced the highest proportion of Jewish victims in Western Europe, largely due to the highly efficient Dutch civil administration and limited grassroots resistance. These comparative cases underscore the reality that the 'Final Solution' was not a monolithic or purely German enterprise but was shaped and enabled by the specific political, social, and administrative contexts of each occupied state.

The Holocaust in France: The Early Phase (1940–1941)

Following the defeat of France and the armistice of June 1940, the *Militärbefehlshaber in Frankreich* was established in Paris to oversee the Occupied Zone, which included Paris and the industrialised north. In alignment with Nazi racial ideology and strategic objectives, the MBF initiated a series of anti-Semitic policies. These included the registration and identification of Jews, the imposition of curfews and professional bans, internment of foreign Jews, and the confiscation or 'Aryanisation' of Jewish property. Even in this early stage, French police and administrative bodies actively facilitated these policies.

In September 1940, German authorities mandated a census of Jews in the Occupied Zone. Conducted by French police and local municipal authorities, this census identified approximately 150,000 Jews, many of them recent immigrants or stateless persons from Eastern Europe. On 27 September 1940, the first German anti-Semitic ordinance formally defined Jewish identity using racial criteria. This legal framework enabled the systematic exclusion of Jews from public and professional life – especially in law, medicine, publishing, and education. Jewish-owned businesses were required to identify themselves and were subsequently confiscated or transferred to non-Jewish ownership under duress and at significantly undervalued rates. By the end of 1941, approximately nineteen trains carrying Jews had departed France for camps in the East. This number increased dramatically: to 104 trains in 1942, 257 in 1943, and 326 in the first eight months of 1944.

La Rafle du billet vert, 14 May 1941

La Rafle du billet vert, or the Green Ticket Round-up, took place in Paris on 14 May 1941, under the joint authority of the German occupation forces and the Vichy French police. It marked a critical early step in the implementation of anti-Jewish measures in France, preceding the more widely known mass round-ups of 1942, such as the Vel d'Hiv round-up. By early 1941, Germany was preparing the logistics of the 'Final Solution' but had not yet launched mass deportations from

Western Europe. In occupied France, the Vichy regime had already introduced anti-Semitic statutes and cooperated with German authorities in identifying and isolating Jews, particularly foreign Jews (those without French citizenship). The round-up was meticulously organised and executed by French police forces under the direction of Theodor Dannecker, the SS officer in charge of Jewish affairs in France, and with the collaboration of René Bousquet, secretary-general of the Vichy police. Around 6,694 foreign Jewish men aged between 18 and 55, primarily from Poland, Romania, the Soviet Union, and other Eastern European countries, were targeted.

Days prior to the round-up, the French prefecture issued summonses in the form of green-coloured tickets (hence the name *billet vert*), which ordered recipients to present themselves at specific locations under the pretence of 'examination of their situation'. These tickets deceptively stated that the purpose was administrative review of immigration status and work permits. No mention of arrest or detention was made. On 14 May 1941 over 3,700 men responded to the summons in good faith and voluntarily reported to designated schools and gymnasiums in Paris. Upon arrival, they were immediately arrested, held in temporary detention centres, and then transferred to internment camps in France, most notably at Beaune-la-Rolande, Pithiviers, and Drancy (established as a transit camp in August 1941). The detained men were kept under harsh conditions. There was widespread overcrowding and inadequate sanitation. They were not immediately deported, as systematic deportations of Jews from France had not yet begun. However, these men would become among the first French-based Jews deported to Auschwitz in 1942, once the deportation infrastructure was established. The Green Ticket Round-up is significant for several reasons. The operation was entirely carried out by the French police without direct German presence during the arrests, illustrating the early and active collaboration of Vichy France in Nazi racial policies.

This operation served as a testing ground for future mass arrests and deportations, such as the Vel d'Hiv round-up in July 1942, which targeted entire Jewish families. The operation exemplified the Vichy regime's prioritisation of foreign Jews as more 'disposable', often in an attempt to demonstrate loyalty to Germany and preserve native French Jews – at least initially. The use of official summons was purposely under false pretences, and established a pattern of bureaucratic manipulation and deceit, later employed in other round-ups across Europe. In subsequent months, interned Jews faced worsening conditions and eventual deportation. Many of those arrested during *la Rafle du billet vert* perished in Auschwitz, especially after the first convoys of Jews began leaving France in March 1942. The round-up set a precedent and demonstrated that large-scale arrests could be conducted with minimal public resistance, emboldening both Vichy and Nazi authorities. The Green Ticket Round-up of May 1941 represents a turning point in the Holocaust in France. It was not only a precursor to later, more massive deportations, but also a concrete example of how collaborationist governments actively participated in the persecution and eventual extermination of Jews. Its deceptive tactics, targeted population, and methodical implementation reflected the growing alignment between Vichy France and the Nazi project of racial cleansing, even before the 'Final Solution' had been fully operationalised

The Holocaust in France: The Latter Phase (1942–1944)

Although initial deportation proposals by military officials such as General Otto von Stülpnagel were motivated by concerns over reprisals and partisan violence rather than ideological extermination, the shift in 1942 toward full-scale genocide in France was driven by the increased involvement of the RSHA. From spring 1942 onwards, SS and *Gestapo* units took operational control over anti-Jewish measures, with key figures such as Theodor Dannecker and Helmut Knochen directing deportation efforts. The transition from internment to extermination was marked by the coordination of French and German authorities in logistical and police operations. Crucially, both the French National Police and the Vichy-run police in the unoccupied zone contributed manpower and infrastructure to the machinery of deportation. This culminated in the Vel' d'Hiv Round-up, the largest mass arrest of Jews on French soil.

The Rafle du Vélodrome d'Hiver

On 16–17 July 1942, one of the most infamous episodes of the Holocaust in Western Europe unfolded in the heart of Paris. Codenamed *Opération Vent printanier* ('Operation Spring Breeze'), the *Rafle du Vélodrome d'Hiver* – commonly referred to as the Vel' d'Hiv round-up – was a mass arrest of Jews carried out by the French police under orders from the collaborationist Vichy regime. The operation resulted in the detention of 13,152 Jews, including 3,118 men, 5,919 women, and 4,115 children, the vast majority of whom were later deported to Auschwitz. Fewer than 800 of them survived the war. What sets this round-up apart is the almost complete absence of direct German involvement during the arrest phase. Instead, the Vel' d'Hiv operation was orchestrated and executed by approximately 9,000 French personnel, including municipal police officers, gendarmes, plainclothes detectives, cadets from the Paris Police Academy, and members of the *Gardes Mobiles* (mobile police units).

Arrest squads were organised into three- to four-man teams and dispatched throughout the capital to apprehend Jewish residents according to pre-prepared lists compiled by French authorities. In addition, several hundred volunteers from the *Parti Populaire Français* (PPF) – a fascist and collaborationist political organisation led by Jacques Doriot – assisted in the operation, proudly donning armbands and participating under the ideological banner of anti-Semitism and loyalty to the Nazi cause. The round-up was the product of coordination between key Vichy and German officials, including René Bousquet (Secretary General of the Vichy National Police), Louis Darquier de Pellepoix (Commissioner for Jewish Affairs), and SS representatives: *SS-Hauptsturmführer* Theodor Dannecker and *SS-Standartenführer* Helmut Knochen, both important and high-ranking members of the German security apparatus in France. While German agents planned the broader deportation strategy in line with the evolving directives of the 'Final Solution', the actual arrests in Paris were entrusted fully to the French police – underscoring the degree of Vichy collaboration and the internalisation of Nazi racial ideology within French administrative structures.

Those arrested were initially confined at the Vélodrome d'Hiver, an indoor cycling stadium located in Paris's 15th arrondissement, near the Eiffel Tower. The Vel' d'Hiv, completely unsuitable for mass detention, quickly became a scene of human misery. Over 13,000 individuals, including entire families with small children, were crammed into the arena under appalling and inhumane conditions. The facility had no beds, no sanitary facilities, and minimal access to food or water. The glass ceiling and sealed ventilation created suffocating daytime heat, while the nights brought a cold, damp chill. Many detainees fell ill; others succumbed to despair. No humanitarian provisions were made for the children, who constituted nearly a third of those interned. After several days in these conditions, detainees were transferred to Drancy and other internment camps, such as Beaune-la-Rolande and Pithiviers. Drancy, located in the northern suburbs of Paris, served as the principal transit camp for Jews being deported from France to extermination camps in the East – primarily Auschwitz-Birkenau. From the summer of 1942 onward, convoys left Drancy regularly. Of the more than 13,000 arrested during the Vel' d'Hiv round-up, the vast majority were deported to Auschwitz, where they were murdered shortly after arrival.

The Vel' d'Hiv round-up stands as the single largest mass arrest of Jews on French soil during the Second World War and has become emblematic of the active collaboration of the Vichy regime in the Nazi extermination project. Unlike similar round-ups across Nazi-occupied Europe that were typically led by German forces, this operation was entirely French in its execution. It reveals the chilling efficiency and ideological compliance of Vichy France in the Nazi programme of racial annihilation. The episode also reflects the Vichy regime's policy of sacrificing foreign-born Jews first, in a cynical attempt to curry favour with Berlin and spare native French Jews – an illusion that ultimately collapsed as the deportations expanded to include all Jews regardless of nationality. The use of French police forces, civilian volunteers, and administrative machinery illustrates the bureaucratic normalisation of genocide, in which ordinary civil servants and law enforcement officers became key instruments of extermination. The *Rafle du Vélodrome d'Hiver* is therefore more than a tragic chapter in French history; it is a powerful case study in state-sponsored complicity, the perversion of legal and administrative structures, and the moral collapse of a regime that actively chose collaboration over sovereignty. It exemplifies how the machinery of the Holocaust depended not solely on German planning, but on the enthusiastic participation of local governments, institutions, and individuals who facilitated the Final Solution on their own soil.

The Collaborationist Role of the Vichy Regime in France

The Vichy regime, established following France's defeat by Nazi Germany in June 1940, represented not merely a government of national accommodation but one that actively participated in the racial and ideological policies of the Third Reich. Under the guise of national regeneration, or the *Révolution nationale*, the regime pursued a reactionary vision rooted in authoritarianism, xenophobia, and anti-Semitism. Integral to this vision was Vichy's voluntary and systematic participation in the persecution of Jews, even in the absence of German coercion.[2]

One of the earliest indications of this alignment was the enactment of the *Statut des Juifs* in October 1940. This legislation, drafted and imposed by Vichy without German prompting, defined Jewish identity in racial terms and excluded Jews from public service, the professions, education, and cultural life.[3] A second statute in June 1941 extended these exclusions and laid the groundwork for the Aryanization of Jewish property. French authorities compiled comprehensive registries of Jewish residents, implemented discriminatory quotas, and seized thousands of businesses and homes, transferring them to non-Jewish hands – often at below market value.[4]

The regime's complicity deepened with the increasing integration of French police into the Nazi machinery of deportation. Beginning in 1941, French law enforcement agencies actively assisted the German SS and *Gestapo* in arresting Jews, often conducting operations autonomously. The most notorious example was the Vel' d'Hiv round-up on 16–17 July 1942.[5]

This operation, part of the broader *Opération Vent printanier*, was coordinated by Jean Leguay, then a high-ranking Vichy police official, under the supervision of René Bousquet, Secretary-General of the National Police. Though Bousquet later attempted to rehabilitate his reputation after the war, archival evidence and testimony confirmed his central role in facilitating the round-up and deportation of Jews, including minors.[6] He was eventually indicted for crimes against humanity but was assassinated in 1993 before facing trial. Another central figure in Vichy collaboration was Pierre Laval, who served as both Deputy Prime Minister and later as Prime Minister under Pétain. Laval was not merely a passive facilitator but a zealous collaborator who, in a speech on 22 July 1942, infamously stated that he wished for the success of German arms and supported the deportation of Jewish children alongside their parents.[7] His actions reveal the depth of ideological alignment between senior Vichy officials and Nazi goals, far beyond what was required or requested by the occupiers.

While some apologists later framed Vichy's collaboration as a pragmatic effort to preserve a measure of autonomy under occupation, modern scholarship, particularly the work of Robert O. Paxton, has decisively refuted this claim. Paxton's groundbreaking analysis demonstrated that Vichy's anti-Semitic policies were internally generated and enthusiastically enforced, not merely imposed by Berlin.[8] Similarly, Henry Rousso's concept of the *Vichy syndrome* has explored how post-war France struggled to confront this legacy, often through denial, minimisation, or mythologisation.[9] Between 1942 and 1944, more than 75,000 Jews were deported from France, with the overwhelming majority murdered in extermination camps.[10] These deportations were made possible not only by German planning but by the meticulous records, administrative efficiency, and active participation of French state institutions under the Vichy regime. The result was not only the decimation of France's Jewish population but also a lasting moral stain on the Republic's history. The Vichy government's collaboration in the Holocaust remains a foundational example of how state bureaucracies can become agents of genocide through a combination of ideology, opportunism, and authoritarian governance.

Assistance from the French, Belgian, and Dutch Resistance

While collaboration with Nazi occupiers tragically marked much of Western Europe, Resistance movements across France, Belgium, and the Netherlands played a crucial, albeit perilous, role in efforts to protect Jewish populations from deportation and extermination. These clandestine activities, conducted by diverse partisan groups, religious organisations, and civil society actors, constituted vital counterpoints to the machinery of genocide imposed by the Nazis and their local collaborators. In France, numerous Resistance networks and underground groups actively engaged in hiding Jews, facilitating their escape, and providing forged identity documents to shield them from arrest. The French Resistance, an amalgamation of communist, Gaullist, and other political factions, frequently coordinated with religious institutions – most notably branches of the Catholic Church – which supplied shelter and false papers, enabling thousands of Jews to evade capture.

Despite the omnipresent threat of arrest, torture, and execution by both German occupiers and the Vichy regime's police forces, these acts of solidarity and defiance saved countless lives. Such efforts were often localised and depended heavily on individual courage and community support networks, illustrating the complex social fabric of occupied France.[11]

Similarly, in Belgium, which fell under German occupation in May 1940, Jewish communities endured systematic persecution in accordance with Nazi racial policies. Belgian Jews faced the same exclusionary laws and discriminatory decrees imposed throughout Western Europe. By the time the Nazis began mass deportations in 1942, many Belgian Jews had either fled the country or gone into hiding, relying in part on the burgeoning underground resistance.[12] Unlike the Vichy regime in France, the Belgian government under King Leopold III adopted a more ambivalent and cautious stance toward German demands, though collaborationist elements – most prominently the Rexist Party led by Léon Degrelle – actively supported Nazi objectives, including the identification and deportation of Jews.[13]

The deportation process in Belgium was marked by the central role of the Mechelen Transit Camp (also known as Malines), established by the Nazis as a holding facility where Jews and other victims were assembled before being transported primarily to Auschwitz and Sobibor extermination camps. Belgian authorities, including the gendarmerie and local police forces, frequently cooperated with German security services by providing intelligence, assisting in arrests, and facilitating the logistical apparatus of deportation. Nonetheless, there were documented instances of Belgian police officers who resisted or refused to comply with orders to arrest Jews, reflecting a degree of individual moral opposition within the occupying administrative apparatus.[14]

One of the most significant deportation operations occurred in August 1943 in the Brussels region, during which approximately 2,500 Jews were rounded up by German forces and transported to Mechelen before their eventual deportation eastward. The Rexist militia played a notorious role in these actions, actively collaborating with Nazi authorities to apprehend Jewish individuals. The Belgian collaborationist regime's provision of detailed lists of Jewish residents greatly facilitated Nazi efforts to identify and capture Jews, contributing to the grim statistic that roughly 90 per cent of Belgian Jews deported to extermination camps perished.[15]

Parallel to the mechanisms of persecution, the Belgian Resistance emerged as a vital counterforce to Nazi genocide. This heterogeneous movement comprised communist partisans, monarchist sympathisers, and other groups who established extensive networks of safe houses and escape routes. These underground channels enabled many Jews to evade capture by smuggling them out of occupied Belgium, often towards neutral countries or safer zones. Resistance operatives also provided false documentation, food, and shelter, risking their own lives in defiance of the occupiers and their collaborators.[16]

The Dutch Resistance similarly engaged in efforts to rescue Jews and others targeted by the Nazis. Although the Netherlands suffered one of the highest percentages of Jewish victims in Western Europe – due in part to the efficient Nazi administrative apparatus and limited initial resistance – the bravery of Dutch underground groups and sympathetic civilians played a critical role in saving lives. These groups often coordinated clandestine hiding places, forged papers, and escape routes that, despite pervasive risks, provided refuge to thousands.[17]

In conclusion, while the collaborationist governments and police forces in France, Belgium, and the Netherlands abetted the Holocaust through active participation in arrests and deportations, the resistance movements in these countries represented vital sources of opposition and humanitarian aid. The efforts of these groups underscore the complex dynamics of occupation, where complicity and courage existed in stark juxtaposition. The clandestine networks of rescue and protection were instrumental in preserving segments of the Jewish populations, thereby challenging the totalising scope of Nazi extermination policies in Western Europe.

An Overview of *Ha Shoah* in France, Belgium, Holland and Luxembourg

The Holocaust, a term synonymous with the systemic annihilation of Jews and other minorities deemed undesirable by the Nazi regime, remains one of the most horrific and deliberate genocides in human history. Spanning from 1940 to 1945, the Nazi regime sought not only to segregate and exploit but ultimately to exterminate European Jewry and other groups they deemed racially inferior. In countries like France, Belgium, Luxembourg, and the Netherlands, the process of apprehending, deporting, and murdering Jews unfolded with a chilling bureaucratic efficiency. Between 1940 and 1944, tens of thousands of Jews were forcibly rounded up, transported to concentration and extermination camps, and subsequently murdered in the most brutal and dehumanising manner. In France, the deportations and the impact which they had cannot be underestimated. The process of the persecution of the Jews in France began soon after the Nazi occupation in 1940.

France's Jewish population was both native-born and comprised of refugees who had fled the escalating anti-Semitic violence in Eastern Europe. Approximately 76,000 Jews were deported from France between 1942 and 1944, with two primary categories of victims: around 25,000 French-born Jews and roughly 51,000 foreign Jews, many of whom had sought refuge from Germany, Austria, Poland, and other Eastern European nations. The vast majority of these deported Jews were sent to Auschwitz, Sobibor, Majdanek, and Theresienstadt, some of the most notorious death camps and ghettos. Despite initial hopes of survival for many who were deported, the survival rate for French Jews was devastatingly low. Of the 76,000 Jews deported from France, fewer than 2,500–3,000 returned. The majority were murdered in the extermination camps, a tragic testament to the ruthlessness of the Nazi regime's 'Final Solution'.

In Belgium as in France, a tragic fate awaited the Jewish population. Belgium, like France, became a site of systematic persecution following the German occupation in 1940. The total number of Jews deported from Belgium was approximately 25,000 – the majority of whom were foreign-born refugees fleeing Nazi persecution in Germany, Austria, and Eastern Europe. A significantly smaller percentage were Belgian-born Jews. Belgium's Jews were primarily deported to Auschwitz and

Sobibor, where they faced immediate execution upon arrival. A smaller proportion was sent to Theresienstadt, but the survival rates were similarly catastrophic. Roughly 10 per cent of Belgian Jews – around 2,500–3,000 individuals – survived the *ha Shoah*, with the remaining 90 per cent perishing in the gas chambers, forced labour, and the brutal conditions of the concentration camps.

For the Jewish community in the Netherlands, the period of Nazi occupation was also a tragic tale of loss on a grand scale. The Netherlands saw one of the highest rates of deportation in Western Europe. The total number of Dutch Jews deported between 1942 and 1944 was approximately 107,000 – a staggering number when considering the pre-war population of Jews in the Netherlands was around 140,000. Most of the Jews deported from the Netherlands were sent to Auschwitz and Sobibor, two of the most infamous extermination camps. The survival rate for Dutch Jews was even more appalling than that of France or Belgium. By the end of the war, only about 5,000–6,000 Dutch Jews had survived the camps, an incredibly small percentage of the total deported. Many of those who managed to survive did so through the efforts of brave Dutch citizens, Resistance groups, and underground networks that hid Jews in rural homes and churches. Despite these efforts, the overwhelming majority of Dutch Jews were murdered in Nazi concentration and extermination camps.

Although Luxembourg is a small country, the fate of the Jews there was equally devastating. Luxembourg, with a Jewish population of around 3,500 before the Nazi occupation, faced a tragic fate during the Holocaust. A significant portion of Luxembourg's Jewish community was made up of immigrants and refugees from Germany, Austria, and Poland. After the German invasion in 1940, the Nazi regime commenced a systematic process of identifying and deporting Luxembourg's Jews. From October 1941 until June 1943, approximately 1,300 Jews were deported from Luxembourg, primarily to the Łódź Ghetto, Theresienstadt, Auschwitz, and Majdanek. Most of these individuals were taken from the Fünfbrunnen transit camp in Luxembourg, a holding site where Jews were temporarily detained before being transported to the death camps. The survival rate for Jews deported from Luxembourg was staggeringly low. Only about fifty individuals survived the Holocaust, meaning that over 95 per cent of those deported perished, primarily in Auschwitz and other extermination camps. Some Jews managed to escape or flee the country to France, Portugal, or Switzerland, and they represent the small group of Luxembourg Jews who survived the war. By 1944, following the mass deportations, Luxembourg was declared '*Judenrein*' (cleansed of Jews) by the German authorities.

The final period of round-ups in the latter part of the war (1944–5), marked the final stages of the Holocaust in Western Europe as the Nazi regime desperately sought to eradicate any remaining Jewish populations before the Allied forces liberated the region. In France, the final mass deportations occurred between 1944 and August 1944, primarily from the Drancy transit camp. Approximately 11,000–12,000 Jews were sent to Auschwitz and other camps during this period. In Belgium, the final deportations took place in early 1944, with about 500–700 Jews deported, but the majority of mass deportations had occurred earlier in 1942 and 1943. The Netherlands continued deportations until September 1944, when the Westerbork transit camp was liberated. Luxembourg's final deportations in 1944 saw another 700–800 Jews taken from the country, leaving a relatively small number of survivors, many of whom had fled before the full scale of the Nazi terror had been unleashed.

The total number of Jews deported from Nazi-occupied countries in Western Europe, including France, Belgium, Luxembourg, and the Netherlands, is estimated to be around 1.1 million. The vast majority of these individuals were murdered upon arrival at extermination camps. This figure does not account for the millions of Jews from Eastern Europe – such as Poland and the Soviet Union – who were similarly targeted and exterminated in the same period. The systematic deportation and genocide of Jews from countries like France, Belgium, Luxembourg, and the Netherlands were key components of the Nazis' 'Final Solution', which ultimately led to the deaths of approximately six million Jews across Europe. Despite the courageous efforts of resistance movements and individuals who risked their lives to save Jews, the scale of the Nazi killing machine, coupled with the active collaboration of local authorities in the occupied countries, made it possible for the Nazis to carry out this atrocity with unprecedented efficiency. The Holocaust in these Western European nations stands as a profound reminder of the dangers of unchecked hate, the power of authoritarian regimes, and the importance of remembering the victims of these atrocities. The stories of survival, resistance, and collaboration continue to serve as critical lessons in humanity's ongoing struggle against intolerance and bigotry. Sadly, most people tend to have a short memory. Perhaps this is why history so often repeats itself.

Chapter 10

MAJOR GERMAN ANTI-PARTISAN OPERATIONS

By 1943, the activities of the French Resistance were escalating in both scale and intensity, particularly in anticipation of an Allied invasion. This growing threat led the German military and their French collaborators, including the Vichy regime and the *Milice*, to launch a series of violent and often indiscriminate anti-partisan operations aimed at dismantling the Resistance movement and terrorising the civilian population into submission. These operations were also designed to prevent the Resistance from disrupting German military strategies and logistics, particularly in the lead-up to Operation Overlord, the Allied invasion of Europe. The major operations undertaken in 1943 were *Unternehmen Ventôse*, and *Unternehmen Frühling*.

As 1943 gave way to 1944, the French Resistance, emboldened by the imminent prospect of an Allied invasion, further intensified its activities in anticipation of the liberation of France. The growing Resistance movement, particularly in rural and occupied regions, posed a significant challenge to the German military apparatus, which had already been contending with partisan activity in various European territories. In response, the German *Wehrmacht* and SS initiated a series of coordinated anti-partisan operations. The ensuing military campaigns, often marked by indiscriminate violence and atrocities, were central to the broader German strategy of maintaining control over occupied France during the final months of the war.

Unternehmen Frühling (April 1943)
Unternehmen Frühling (Operation Spring), launched in April 1943, targeted the *Maquis* – the rural, often mountainous, guerrilla groups that had been forming in the south and central regions of France. The

Maquis had become increasingly active by 1943, engaging in sabotage and ambushes against German supply convoys and garrisons. The operation was a joint effort between the *Heer*, *Waffen-SS* and the Vichy militia, which had become a crucial ally in anti-partisan operations. The German operation was conducted in the operational region of *LXXXVI. Armeekorps*. The primary objective of Operation Spring was to disband the *Maquis* by surrounding and encircling their hideouts, making escape impossible. The operation involved the deployment of SS battalions from the *2. SS-Panzer-Division 'Das Reich'*, supported by the local collaborationist French militia forces and auxiliary police.

The *'Das Reich'* SS panzer division had been stationed in the Toulouse region, where it had been replenishing and reorganising itself after months of combat on the Russian Front. The German forces in this drive made use of reconnaissance planes and extensive patrols to locate Resistance groups, while the *Milice*, which had been established in January 1943, facilitated searches in rural villages suspected of harbouring partisans. These Frenchmen often acted as guides and translators for the German forces involved in an operation. Though the operation did manage to capture a number of Resistance fighters and destroy some *Maquis* strongholds, the *Maquis'* decentralised structure meant that many units managed to escape, regroup, and continue their activities in the region.

Unternehmen Korporal

Unternehmen Korporal (Operation Corporal) was a major German anti-Resistance offensive in the *Maquis* de l'Ain and Haut-Jura region of southeastern France. Specifically, the operation took place near the Swiss border. This area is part of the Rhône-Alpes region (today called Auvergne-Rhône-Alpes), and specifically, the Jura Mountains area, where a large partisan force was said to be operating. The principal towns that were targeted by the German drive included Belley, Hauteville, Nantua and Oyonnax. This anti-partisan operation ran from 5 to 13 February 1944, and involved roughly 2,500 German army, police, SD, *Gestapo*, and *Milice* troops. The force was under the overall command of *Generalleutnant* Karl Pflaum's *157. Reserve-Division* headquarters. This was the largest operation to date in the area, marking the first time the *Wehrmacht* committed full army units rather than leaving anti-Partisan work to police forces. The German *kampfgruppe* (combat group, or task force) included elements of *Reserve-Grenadier-Regiment 157* (four reserve mountain training battalions) from *157. Reserve-Division*. The battalions contained around 600 men each. For artillery support, two reserve mountain artillery batteries (75mm and 150mm howitzers) from *Reserve-Artillerie-Regiment 7* were also employed.

On 4 February 1944, amid a memorial service for recently fallen Resistance fighters, a *Maquis* patrol intercepted a car driven by a collaborator. The Resistance seized this local French *Gestapo* leader, whose *nom-de-guerre* was 'Houizot'. The pro-Nazi Frenchman was taken to a Resistance camp which was located at Pré Carré farm. When he was searched, the Resistance found a map listing the location and the names of the entire local pro-German informer network. This included every collaborator in the Ain-Haut-Jura area. Armed with this vital piece of information, the *Maquis* were planning to wipe out the pro-Nazi informer network in this region. Around this time, the Germans surrounded suspected *Maquis* hideouts, employing infantry, artillery, some armour, and even air support from the recently established *Geschwader Bongart*. Deep snow hampered the movement of the German forces and the *Milice*, but the snow also exposed guerrilla tracks. The Germans employed air support, requesting that the farm be strafed. The air raid forced the *Maquis* to take cover in the nearby woods. While the air raid was underway and the Resistance men were trying to find cover in the nearby woods, a collaborator entered the farm and freed Houizot.

On 8 February, around 300 troops attacked a *Maquis* headquarters located at *la Montagne* farm. One Resistance fighter, named Julien Roche, volunteered to stay behind to cover the retreat of the other partisans. In the ensuing firefight, Roche was killed. Altogether nine Resistance fighters died trying to escape from the farm, while only eleven managed to escape. In reprisal for their support of the Resistance and for providing shelter to the partisans in their farm, the Berne brothers were arrested and subjected to torture. Subsequently, the brothers were executed by the *Gestapo*. Their sister, Irène, was not killed, but was deported to a concentration camp in Germany, while the family farm was deliberately destroyed by fire. In this battle, the Germans lost two men killed and one wounded. Houizot informed his *Gestapo* friends that the entire informer network in the area had been compromised. This did not sit well with Houizot's German handler, who sarcastically asked him why he needed to travel around the countryside with such sensitive information? Houizot did not reply, but simply nodded his head in agreement that what he had done was quite foolish. Now the *Gestapo* went about warning its informers that their lives were in danger. The *Milice* were tasked with going to each informer, and letting them know of their situation. The local *Milice* commander took the opportunity to imply that the only way to be safe now for any informer who had been discovered, was to join either the female branch of the *Milice* or the *Milice* action groups (if you were a man). This scare tactic usually worked.

The threat of being assassinated if you were discovered to be aiding the Germans was real. For example, between September and December 1943 – just a mere four-month period – no less than 709 assassinations and executions were carried out by the Resistance against known collaborators. According to statistics published by the Vichy government, 230 gendarmes, 147 members of the *Garde Mobile* (of which nineteen were officers), 152 police officers, thirty members of the *Milice*, and 150 civilians.[1] The Resistance court established in Lyon, for example, adjudicated around 1,800 cases between 1940 and 1944, involving Vichy French officials and collaborators. The most famous person executed by order of this secret court was the well-known French reporter, Henri Beraud. Thus, a good number of the exposed informers opted to join the *Milice*. At least in the *Milice* you were given a gun, and the men of the *Milice* tended to travel in groups to avoid assassination.

As *Unternehmen Korporal* developed, *Gestapo* officers accompanying the German soldiers entered Nantua and Oynnax three days later, on 11 February. In these towns they proceeded to arrest fifty-seven men – thirty from Nantua and twenty-seven from Oyonnax. The *Milice* and *Gestapo* had entered these two localities with a list of suspected Resistance fighters. The men who were apprehended were first interrogated and tortured, then sent by train to Mauthausen concentration camp. By 13 February, the operation had inflicted major losses on the Resistance. Forty Resistance fighters were killed. The Germans also arrested 339 people, of which 287 were eventually deported to camps in Germany. During the operation, about ninety-nine farms and homes were purposely burned to the ground. *Unternehmen Korporal* was a harsh, large-scale *Wehrmacht*-led drive to crush local Resistance in the Ain–Haut-Jura by combining infantry, artillery, air, and *Milice* units. Its success in disrupting fixed *Maquis* camps came at the cost of severe civilian suffering, mass arrests, deportations, and destruction of property. Yet, its long-term effect was to push the Resistance toward more agile and resilient forms of resistance. From then on, the *Maquis* in this region kept on the move, often staying in one place no more than one or two days.

Unternehmen Frühling II (7–18 April 1944)[2]
Unternehmen Frühling II (Operation Spring II), conducted between 7 and 18 April 1944, was a large-scale German anti-partisan operation

in eastern France, directed primarily against elements of the French Resistance, particularly the *Maquis* operating in the Ain department and the southern Jura region. The operation was undertaken as part of a broader German strategy to suppress growing Resistance activity throughout France in the lead-up to the Allied invasion. The *Wehrmacht*, supported by units of the SS, German police, and collaborationist forces including the *Milice* and Vichy police, initiated the assault after encircling the region for some time. Despite prior efforts by Vichy-aligned forces to control the area, they had proven incapable of subduing the *Maquis*, whose numbers and confidence had grown considerably. The Ain and Haute-Savoie departments, located in the Auvergne-Rhône-Alpes region near the Swiss border, held strategic value due to their proximity to escape routes into neutral Switzerland and their rugged, forested terrain, which favoured guerrilla operations. The 157th Reserve Division played a central role in the offensive, deploying several thousand troops to target Resistance camps and sympathetic villages.

In response to the operation, the *Maquisards* adopted a strategy of dispersion, avoiding direct confrontation and instead forming small, mobile units to evade capture. Despite this, the German forces achieved significant short-term success: over 900 individuals were arrested, 148 executed, and 204 Resistance camps destroyed. Entire villages – Racouze, Chougeat, La Rivoire, Vernon, and Sièges – were burned in punitive reprisals for acts of sabotage, particularly against rail infrastructure. Civilian losses were heavy, with 199 arrested, 149 deported, and forty-four were killed. In total, approximately seventy buildings were destroyed during the operation. Although *Unternehmen Frühling II* succeeded in temporarily disrupting *Maquis* activity, its brutal nature alienated the local population and further fuelled anti-German sentiment. German commanders also drew key tactical conclusions: notably, that collaborationist forces, including the Vichy police and even the *Milice*, were largely unreliable in mountainous terrain and combat conditions. Conversely, it was observed that when confronted by a well-coordinated, numerically superior *Wehrmacht* force, the FFI could not effectively resist in conventional terms. Ultimately, heavy snowfall forced a halt to the operation.

Unternehmen Treffenfeld

In the wake of *Unternehmen Frühling II*, the German military initiated *Unternehmen Treffenfeld*, a large-scale counterinsurgency operation targeting the *Maquis du Mont Mouchet*. Situated at the junction of the Lozère, Cantal, and Haute-Loire departments in south-central France,

Mont Mouchet had emerged as a major stronghold of the French Resistance. Its symbolic and strategic significance was comparable to that of the *Maquis* stronghold in the Vercors region. The primary aim of Treffenfeld, conducted in June 1944, was to dismantle the growing concentration of Resistance fighters who had assembled in anticipation of Allied landings in Normandy. Although distinct from earlier operations, it followed the logic of preceding efforts such as *Unternehmen Frühling*, which sought to suppress other prominent resistance movements, notably the *Maquis de l'Ain et du Haut-Jura*. The FFI in that area had begun organising a 'Free Zone' in support of the anticipated Allied advance. They would achieve this by recapturing the towns of Oyonnax and Nantua, which had been taken by FFI forces.

Another goal was to set free German soldiers that had been captured by the *Maquis*. The operation was launched from 10–14 June 1944. Approximately 9,000–10,000 German troops took part, including *Wehrmacht* infantry, SS units, several *Feldgendarmerie* companies, *Luftwaffe* ground forces belonging to *IV. Luftwaffen-Feld-Korps*, supported by the French *Milice* and the Vichy paramilitary police, the GMR. The *Maquis* suffered heavy casualties but managed to delay the Germans with fierce resistance. Eventually, Mont Mouchet was overrun, but the Resistance fighters retreated into surrounding regions and continued guerrilla warfare. The units employed were the following:

Gebirgs-Jäger-Ersatz-Regiment 1 der 157. Reserve-Division.
Freiwilligen (Kosaken) Stamm-Regiment 5 der Freiwilligen-Stamm-Division
with:
    Kosaken Reiter Abteilung 403
        Kosaken Reiter Abteilung II/454
        Kosaken Reiter Abteilung III/454
Feldgendarmerie-Trupp 64
Wachkompanie der Luftwaffen-Feld-Korps IV
Radfahr-Kompanie der Luftwaffen-Feld-Korps IV
SD Posten in Bourg-en-Bresse (Ain)
SD Posten in Oyonnax (Ain)
SD Posten in Saint-Claude (Jura)

The *Maquis* had approximately 2,700 to 3,000 fighters in the area. However, many only lightly armed, but highly motivated. Mont Mouchet was captured after several days of fighting. The *Maquis* base, camps, and supplies were destroyed or seized. The Germans and their French collaborationist forces inflicted heavy casualties on the Resistance. Around 150–200 *Maquisards* were killed. Dozens were captured, tortured, and executed. Civilians suspected of aiding the Resistance were killed, deported, or subjected to reprisals. A massacre at Dortan occurred, where 35–36 civilians were killed. This was perpetrated by men from *Freiwilligen (Kosaken) Stamm-Regiment 5*.

The Germans reported 450 deaths, including both Resistance fighters and civilians. The FFI acknowledged eighty-five killed and eighty wounded. The operation led to widespread displacement, with many civilians fleeing the region due to the destruction and reprisals. This operation exemplified the brutal tactics employed by the Germans to suppress the Resistance in France. The atrocities committed during this operation, particularly the Dortan massacre, remain a sombre chapter in the history of the French Resistance. From 12 to 22 July 1944, the three Cossack cavalry battalions of *Freiwilligen-Stamm-Regiment 5 (Freiwilligen-Stamm-Division)* were responsible for the massacre in Dortan, a village that was completely burned down. Thirty-six people were killed, which was interspersed with rape and torture. In total, 278 buildings were burned in the following villages and towns: one in Saint-Rémy, five in Valresson, sixty-seven in Chevignat and Roissiat, forty-seven in Verjon, forty-five in Cuisiat, eighty-two in Pressiat, and thirty-one in Poisoux.

In spite of this apparent German success, the *Maquis* in the area were not destroyed. Many fighters escaped using knowledge of the terrain and regrouped later. German forces did not eliminate Resistance activity in the region, which resumed within weeks. The Resistance successfully delayed and harassed Axis units, tying down troops that could have been used elsewhere. The operation increased local civilian support for the *Maquis* due to brutal reprisals by Axis troops. Although *Unternehmen Treffenfeld* was a tactical victory for the Germans, it was a strategic failure because the *Maquis* regained strength over the summer of 1944. As a result, the French partisans played a critical role in harassing retreating German troops after the Allied landings in southern France – Operation Dragoon, launched in August 1944.

Battle of Mont Mouchet

The Germans conducted another anti-partisan operation against the French *Maquis* between 2 to 11 June 1944. This operation was launched on Mont Mouchet, in the Auvergne region. This area was a stronghold of the *Maquis*. The operation against the *Maquis du Mont Mouchet* was a significant engagement, resulting in the deaths of approximately 125 Resistance fighters and 100 civilians, with many others wounded or captured. The Germans involved were from the *Jesser Brigade*. The *Jesser Brigade* (also known as *Kampfgruppe Jesser*, *Brigade Jesser*, or *Division Jesser*) was a mobile infantry unit formed in June 1944 under the command of *Generalmajor* Kurt von Jesser. In reality the formation was *Sicherungs-Brigade 74*, which Jesser led from June to August 1944. The brigade was specifically established to suppress and eliminate French Resistance groups, particularly the *Maquis*, in the Auvergne and Limousin regions. The *Sicherungs-Brigade 74* was a composite force drawn from various *Wehrmacht*, SS, and police units, including:

- *Sicherungs-Regiment 1000*
- *Aufklärungs-Abteilung 1000*
- *III. Bataillon der SS-Polizei-Regiment 19*
- A battalion from the *Volga Tatar Legion*
- A battalion from the *Azerbaijan Legion*
- *Artillerie-Regiment 28 (189. Reserve-Division)*
- *Feldgendarmerie* motorised detachments
- *Flak* units
- *Luftwaffe* squadrons from Aulnat airbase

These units were organised into several *Kampfgruppen* (combat groups), each led by a German officer:

- *Kampfgruppe Hellmuth Abel*
- *Kampfgruppe Johann Enss*
- *Kampfgruppe Rittmeister Coelle*

The brigade's headquarters was located in Royat, near Clermont-Ferrand, and it operated primarily in the Cantal, Puy-de-Dôme, and Aveyron departments. Initial German reconnaissance and skirmishes occurred from 2–9 June 1944. The main German assault on Mont Mouchet took place from 10–11 June 1944. The *Maquis* withdrew from the area following intense fighting and bombardment on 11 June. The battle was part of German efforts to eliminate large concentrations of Resistance fighters who might support Allied landings. The Resistance force, numbering around 2,700–3,000 fighters, had concentrated in the Mont Mouchet massif, spanning Lozère, Cantal, and Haute-Loire. They faced approximately 3,000 to 4,000 Axis troops in the first phase, with more reinforcements arriving later, including *Osttruppen*, *Milice*, and *Wehrmacht* troops. The operation resulted in heavy casualties for the Resistance, with approximately 238 fighters killed and 180 wounded, as well as about 100 hostages executed by the Germans. *Sicherungs-Brigade 74* also conducted operations in Murat, where they executed reprisals against civilians following Resistance attacks. On 12 June, a German detachment, accompanied by militiamen of the *Milice*, arrived in Murat, executing four men and arresting thirteen others. The following day, Resistance fighters ambushed German forces, killing ten and wounding fifteen. In retaliation, twenty-five hostages were executed near Soubizergues on 14 June 1944.

Unternehmen Bettina
The Topography of the Vercors Region
The Vercors area has been described as being shaped like a giant arrowhead, 45km (30 miles) long by 30km (20 miles) wide. Its foothills are supplied with water from four rivers near the alpine area that spreads east to Italy and Switzerland. The Massif is part of the Prealps, located in the Auvergne-Rhône-Alpes region. It straddles the departments of Isère and Drôme. The closest major city is Grenoble, to the northeast. The massif forms a kind of natural fortress above the Rhône Valley and the city of Grenoble. It's primarily a limestone plateau that rises abruptly from the surrounding valleys. Altitudes vary from around 400m in the lowlands to over 2,300m at the highest points. The Grand Veymont is the highest peak: 2,341m (7,680ft). The edges of the plateau are marked by sheer cliffs – especially on the east, above Grenoble. Deep gorges and canyons (e.g. *Gorges de la Bourne*) cut through the massif, carved by rivers and glacial erosion. These cliffs made the area strategically isolated, which is why it was a stronghold for Resistance fighters (the *Maquis du Vercors*) in the Second World War. The interior has dense forests, alpine meadows, and karstic terrain – full of sinkholes, caves, and underground rivers. The *Plateau du Vercors* is often snow-covered in winter and lush in summer. Mountain roads like *Col de Rousset, Col de la Bataille,* and *Route des Grands Goulets* lead into the massif. Towns like *Villard-de-Lans, Lans-en-Vercors,* and *La Chapelle-en-Vercors* serve as gateways.

The Creation of the République du Vercors
It was in this highly defensible region that the *Maquis*, emboldened by the Allied landing in Normandy on 6 June 1944, established the *République du Vercors* (Vercors Republic). This area therefore, represented a large region of the German rear area that was not under German control. Because of this threat, it didn't take the Germans long in trying to organise an anti-partisan drive against it. In addition to threatening the rear of German forces operating in southern France, what prompted a

stronger reaction by the Germans against the activities of the FFI in the Vercors area were also the massive airdrops of weapons that the Allies began to drop all over occupied France.

The first such daylight airdrop of weapons and supplies, designated Operation Zebra, took place on 25 June 1944. In this operation, 180 B-17 bombers of the United States Army Air Force, supported by fighter escorts, dropped 2,160 containers of weapons and ammunition to agents of the SOE and members of the Resistance across the regions of Ain, Jura, Haute-Vienne, and Vercors. The success of this mission prompted a subsequent and more extensive airdrop by Allied forces, known as Operation Cadillac, which was executed on 14 July 1944. Operation Cadillac was performed by the 100th Bomb Group of the USAAF when 349 bombers (mostly B-17s escorted by 534 fighters), dropped 3,791 containers full of weapons and munitions. If this were to continue unabated and unchallenged, then the FFI forces would become more powerful than they already were. Therefore, it was important for the Germans to attack the larger concentrations of *Maquis* forces. This is what prompted Operation Bettina.

Unternehmen Bettina was launched in mid-July 1944. It involved about 10,000 German troops, including men from the Brandenburg commando unit, which landed in gliders. The operation was led by *Generalleutnant* Karl Pflaum, commander of the German *157. Reserve-Division*. The Germans deployed around 9,000 troops for this operation from the following forces:

- Two Grenadier battalions: *Reserve-Grenadier-Bataillon 179* and *Reserve-Grenadier-Bataillon 199* of *Reserve-Grenadier-Regiment 157 (157. Reserve-Division)*.
- Four mountain infantry (*Gebirgsjäger*) battalions: *Reserve-Gebirgsjäger-Bataillon I. /98, Reserve-Gebirgsjäger-Bataillon II. /98, Reserve-Gebirgsjäger-Bataillon 99, Reserve-Gebirgsjäger-Bataillon 100* of *Reserve-Gebirgsjäger-Regiment 1* (regimental commander: *Oberst* Franz Schwehr).
- Two artillery batteries from *Reserve-Gebirgsjäger-Artillerie-Abteilung 79* from *Reserve-Artillerie-Regiment 7*.
- Three *Ost* (Eastern European) battalions made up of non-German conscripts from the USSR: *Ost-Bataillon 406, Nordkaukasisches Infanterie-Bataillon 836*, and *Ost-Bataillon 654*.
- There were 400 men which came in on gliders. The glider attack included some 200 men from the *Fallschirm-Bewährungstruppe*, along with several French volunteers from the *SiPo*-SD post in Lyon and two *Ostlegionnaire-Kompanien* (Russian, Ukrainian and Caucasian

volunteers) from the *7. und 8. Kompanie der Brandenburg-Legionnaire-Lehr-Bataillon*, that belonged to *Lehr-Regiment-Brandenburg*. These men were brought in twenty DFS230 gliders, and two of the larger Gotha Go 242B gliders. The twenty-two gliders were from *I./1. Luftlandegeschwader*, which was referred to as *Fallschirm-Bataillon Jungwirth*. This initial glider assault was followed by some 200 elite commandos which were landed at the partially-built airstrip near Vassieux. Together, these 400 men formed *Fallschirm-Kampfgruppe-Schäfer*. The commandos were members of *Streifkorps Südfrankreich*, which had been organised from the *Brandenburg-Legionnaire-Lehr-Bataillon*.

- Artillery and air support, which was provided by two fighter-bomber squadrons under *Luftwaffe Geschwader Bongart*.
- A police unit: *I. Bataillon der SS Polizei-Regiment 19*.
- A security battalion: *I. Bataillon der Sicherungs-Regiment 200*.

One unique and devastating element of the assault was the use of twenty-two gliders, which silently dropped German commandos into the heart of Vercors, particularly Vassieux-en-Vercors, surprising the Resistance. The force that was brought in by gliders towed by Junkers Ju 88 light bombers were men from the *Brandenburgers* – the ground force of the *Abwehr* (German Army intelligence). The field units sent in by glider were commando units This commando group had its beginnings with the Brandenburg unit, *Streifkorps Südfrankreich*. In the spring of 1944, a specialised Brandenburger unit formed specifically for employment in southern France.

The operation began on 21 July 1944. The *Maquis* numbered about 4,000 men, many of whom were poorly armed and lacking heavy weapons. The French partisans emboldened by the Allied landings in Normandy, established a 'republic of Vercors'. This 'republic' was a self-proclaimed Allied zone in the interior of the German lines. There was no secret to it, since FFI units expected General De Gaulle to send Free French reinforcements from North Africa. Thus, the Germans were aware of the heavy, blatant FFI presence there. In July 1944, the Vercors resistance formally declared itself as a 'Free French Republic' and began organising militarily under traditional army structures to anticipate Allied support, several battalions were created and employed in the defence of Vercors. These units were not French Army regulars. The designation of the units had been created by the FFI in name only. The FFI had named their partisan battalions as *Chasseurs Alpins* simply to honour the French Army alpine troops. The order of battle for the French at the Battle of Vercors was as follows:

6e Bataillon de Chasseurs Alpins-
Led by commandant Costa de Beauregard (alias 'Durieu'). The area of operation was the northern part of the Vercors (Autrans, Méaudre, Villard-de-Lans). It was composed of *Maquisards* who had knowledge of the local terrain and experience in alpine climbing.

11e Bataillon de Chasseurs Alpins-
Led by Major Jean Prévost (aka 'Capitaine Goderville') and other officers. This battalion became the nucleus of the Vercors 'army'; many local fighters identified themselves under the 11e BCA banner.

12e Bataillon de Chasseurs Alpins-
Led by Commandant Philippe (real name Pierre Ullmann). Officially created on 13 July 1944, days before the German assault. The problem during the battle was that it was still forming and equipping when the fighting began. As a result, it was not committed fully and only saw limited service under fire.

14e Bataillon de Chasseurs Alpins-
Commanded by Captain Bourdeau (also known as Fayard). This unit was positioned along the western and southwestern edges of the Lente Forest.

11e régiment de Cuirassiers-
Reconstituted as a *Maquis* cavalry/mechanised unit, though it had little armour. It was stationed at Vassieux-en-Vercors, a key target of the German glider assault on 21 July 1944. The *11e régiment de Cuirassiers* was led by Captain Jean Geyer, also known by his resistance pseudonym 'Thivollet'. Under his command, the regiment was reconstituted by the French Forces of the Interior (FFI) and played a significant role in the defence of the Vercors Plateau against the German offensive in July 1944. However, Geyer was a career military officer and this reconstituted regiment was mostly composed of young *Maquisards* who resented Geyer's elitist bearing.[3]

On the morning of 21 July, German troops began their attack in earnest against the FFI in Vercors. The greatest defeat of the French partisans had begun. At 9:30 am, Colonel Huet, received the following message: 'Planes approaching from the south, Colonel'. 'They can't be from Algiers,' thought Huet, 'otherwise we would have been notified.' 'They must be German', he replied. The first German planes over Vassieux were the Fw 190 fighter-bombers and the Dornier Do 217 light bombers. Approximately 400 French troops had been working at Vassieux that morning. The runway, designed to accommodate larger shipments of arms was almost completed. The runway not only allowed more supplies to be flown in, but also more Allied troops. Who were these glider troops who played a vital role in Operation Bettina?

In the spring of 1944, a specialised Brandenburger unit was created specifically for employment in southern France. The men selected came from various Brandenburger units: primarily the *Legionnaire Bataillon* of *Lehr Regiment Brandenburg* and the bulk of the *7. Kompanie* and *8. Kompanie, II. Bataillon, 3. Regiment Brandenburg*. The *Legionnaire Bataillon* contained two companies of volunteers from the Soviet Union. The *1. Kompanie* was nicknamed 'Weiss' (White), and contained Belarusian volunteers, with a sprinkling of Ukrainians. The *1. Kompanie*, was nicknamed 'Schwarz' (Black), and contained Soviet citizens from the Caucasus region and Central Asia, including Azerbaijanis, Armenians, and men from Turkestan. The *7. Kompanie, II. Bataillon, 3. Regiment Brandenburg* contained many Italian volunteers with a sprinkling of Germans, while the *8. Kompanie, II. Bataillon, 3. Regiment Brandenburg* consisted mostly of Spaniards, but also had some Germans in its ranks.

The first Brandenburgers to form *Streifkorps Südfrankreich* were the Spaniards of *8. Kompanie*. From them, an *Einsatzgruppe Pyrenären* was formed for duty along the Spanish-French frontier. This group contained fifty Spaniards under the command of an *Oberleutnant* Demetrio. *Einsatzgruppe Pyrenären* was subordinate to *Streifkorps Biscaya*, which in turn, reported to *Streifkorps Südfrankreich*. Exactly how many Soviet citizens joined *Streifkorps Südfrankreich* is not known, although it is

Figure 12. On the morning of 21 July 1944 FFI troops stationed in and around Vassieux were treated to this spectacle in the sky. Junkers Ju 88 light bombers towing gliders carrying assault troops, while Focke-Wulf Fw 190 F fighter-bombers performed escort duty.

known that it was a significant number. French accounts of a German assault in the Vercors area tell of a German-Russian glider assault force that landed as part of a greater operation. Descriptions of these men leave almost no room for doubt that these 'Russian commandos' belonged to *Hauptmann* Alexander Aux's *Legionnaire Bataillon* of the *Lehr-Regiment Brandenburg*. Additional evidence supporting this theory is the fact that the Vercors area, which bordered the French-Italian and French-Swiss frontiers, was the jurisdictional operation zone for *Streifkorps Südfrankreich*.

Because the planes were coming from the direction of the Mediterranean coast, the people initially thought they were Allied planes. Someone yelled, 'It's the Yanks! It's the Yanks!', but quickly saw the black Balkan Cross of the German *Luftwaffe* and changed that to, 'Run! It's the Boche!' Too late – the German fighters and light bombers were already making their descent in the attack formation. Moments later the first rounds of 20mm cannon fire and the explosions of the bombs rocked the town of Vassieux. The DFS 230 gliders carrying *Streifkorps Südfrankreich* did not take long following the German support planes, with the great majority of the gliders landing in Vassieux, and ironically, on the uncompleted runway. The runway was quickly overrun by the fierce assault. Many French survivors of this assault described these paratroopers as husky men, speaking what was almost certainly Russian or one of its dialects. They were described as having a coarse and chiselled appearance, which was typical of many Eastern Europeans.

The objective of the landing at Vassieux was two-fold. First, the Germans would secure the runway and deny its use to the *Maquis*. Bombing from the air was no guarantee of preventing its use, so the only sure-fire way of preventing its use was to capture the airfield and then destroy it. Second, the German glider troops were to set up a buffer to prevent FFI forces, which were being pushed from the north, from escaping to the southwest. Simultaneously, German ground troops advanced from all sides, including the Drôme valley and Grenoble, surrounding the plateau.

Elements of the German *9. Panzer-Division* were driving up from the south and southeast. Soon the only escape route for the French would be Vassieux. The precision and swiftness of the glider assault caught the French off guard. Within minutes, the FFI lost more than 100 men at Vassieux. Approximately 250–300 glider troops landed at Vassieux. Soon the French command realised that it could not hold out against the German attack. Elements of *Gebirgsjäger-Ersatz-Regiment 1* and *Reserve-Grenadier-Regiment 157 (157. Reserve-Division)*, plus *Kampfgruppe Zabel (9. Panzer-Division)* were advancing from the north, east and south, respectively. In addition, those German forces were supported by *I. Bataillon der SS-Polizei-Regiment 19*, around 200 men of the *Feldgendarmerie*, and the SD command stationed in Grenoble.

The DFS 230 gliders and the two Gotha Go 242 gliders that took part in the operation did not take long from the point that the tow line was loosened to the final moments when the gliders landed on the plateau. Ironically, the partially completed airfield that the FFI had been building in order to receive heavier weaponry, served as the perfect glider site. Some French survivors of the battle described many of these assault troops as being well built and speaking what sounded like Russian. First, the German objective by making an air landing at Vassieux was twofold. First, the Germans would secure the runway and deny its use to the French by preventing any further air drops. Second, the German glider troops were to set up a buffer to prevent FFI forces, which were now in the process of being pushed south from Grenoble and St. Nizier, from escaping the trap by withdrawing south or southeast.

The Lente Forest lay northwest of Vassieux. The locality of Font d'Urle lay just south of the forest. It was there that the FFI had its forming *14e Bataillon de Chasseurs Alpins* (14th Mountain Battalion). It was this unit which was closest to Vassieux and therefore was the ideal unit to come to the aid of FFI forces there. From the south, *Kampfgruppe Zabel* was moving north. It was composed of a motorised battalion from *Panzergrenadier-Regiment 10 (9. Panzer Division)*. The Lente Forest lay northwest of Vassieux. The locality of Font d'Urle lay just south of the forest. It was there that the FFI had its forming *14e Bataillon de Chasseurs Alpins* (14th Mountain Battalion). It was this unit which was closest to Vassieux and therefore was the ideal unit to come to the aid of FFI forces there. From the south, *Kampfgruppe Zabel* was moving north.

Kampfgruppe Zabel was composed of a motorised battalion from *Panzergrenadier-Regiment 10 (9. Panzer Division)*. The other battalion which formed part of *Kampfgruppe Zabel* was *Marschbataillon Müller* from *352. Infanterie-Division*. From the north, elements of *157. Reserve-Division* were driving south and east. Soon the French command realised that the Germans were in the process of a major anti-partisan operation in the region which included close to 10,000 men.

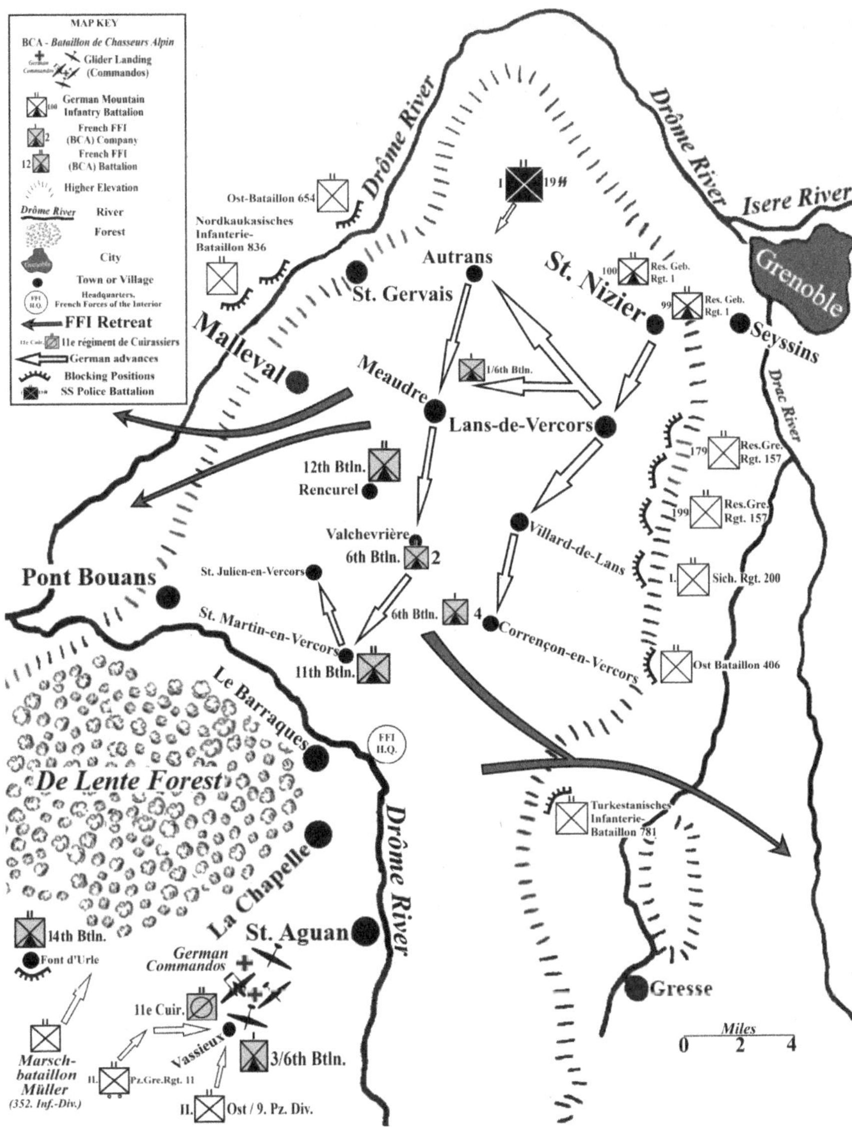

Figure 13. *Unternehmen Bettina.* The battle for the Vercors, July 1944.

At the start of the battle, soon after Vassieux was captured, the decision was made to try and retake the town from the glider troops. A French patrol was sent out in the early afternoon to try and obtain information about which would be the best attack vector in order to capture the town. The patrol quickly came into heavy enemy fire. The

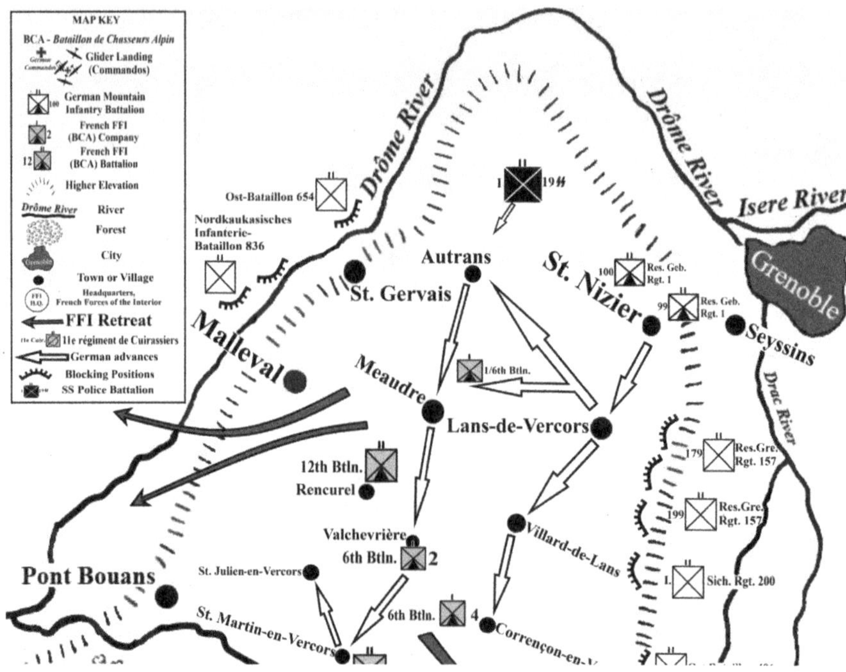

Figure 14. The first half of the Vercors map.

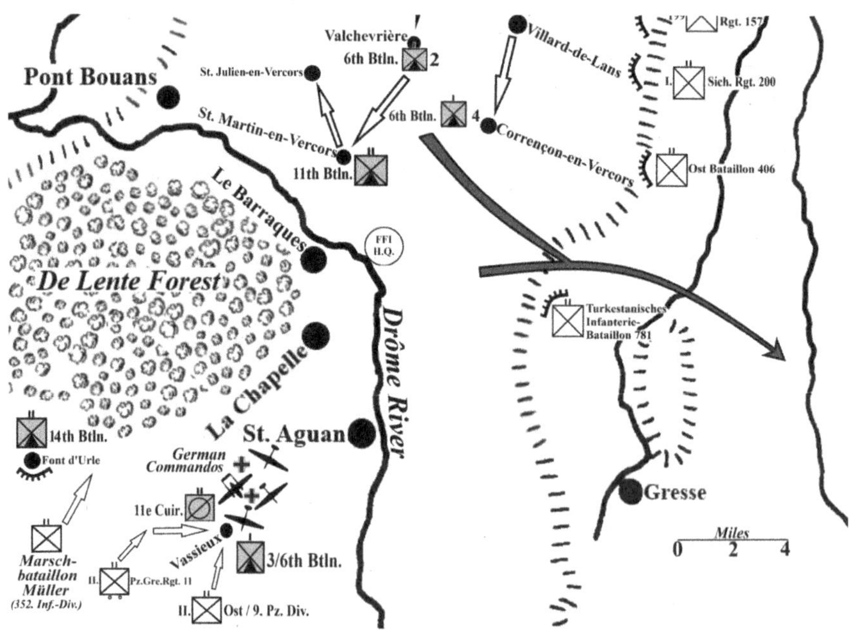

Figure 15. The second half of the Vercors map.

glider troops had apparently been equipped with heavy machine guns and light mortars. The attack was temporarily postponed until the evening. Later that night, the *Maquis* tried to retake the town. To aid the attackers, it was raining steadily, further obstructing the field of view of the defenders in town. The French assault was so aggressive, that the attacking troops actually managed to reach the buildings at the outskirts of Vassieux. However, an American OSS officer inexplicably ordered a retreat just as the FFI troops entered the edge of the town. His after-action report claimed that the French forces had been driven off by heavy automatic weapons fire. To this day, questions keep being asked about why the assault was called off at a moment when the FFI troops had actually reached the edge of town.

On Saturday, 22 July 1944, just one day after the glider assault, the sky over Vassiuex was once again covered with dozens of planes. This time they were Junkers Ju 52 transport planes, bringing in additional

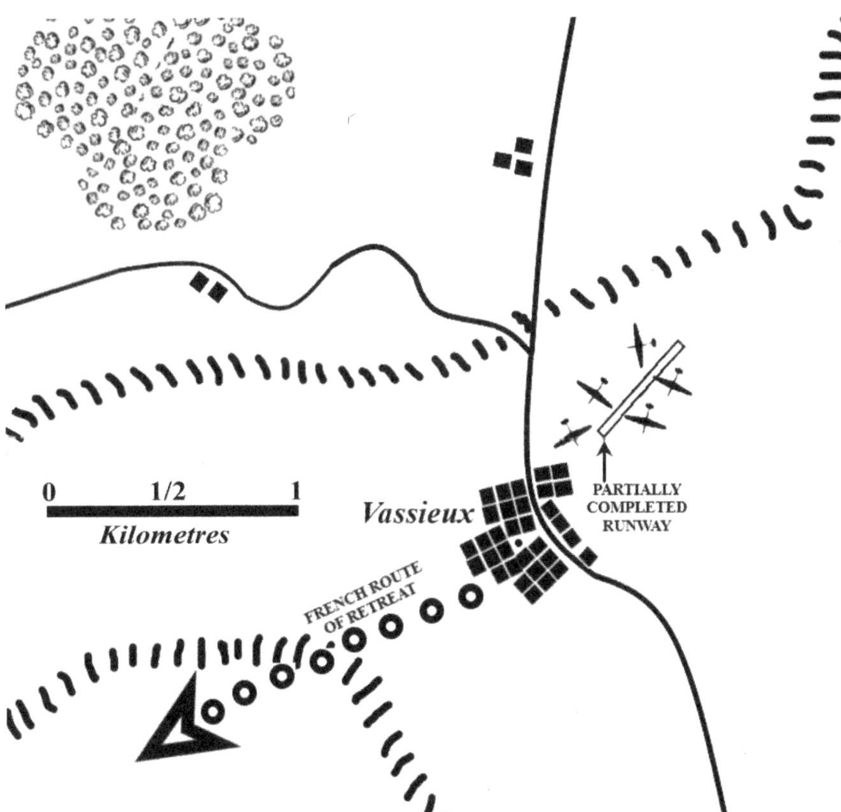

Figure 16. Detailed view of Vassieux and the surrounding area.

German troops by taking advantage of the partially completed airfield. The French fighters watched in horror, as the 'Auntie Jus' landed on the vert airfield which they had been working hard to complete. 4 The pressure against the FFI forces defending the Vercors continued to increase as three battalions attacking form the south (two of them from *9. Panzer-Division*) pressed their attack. From the north several battalions of troops from *157. Reserve-Division* (soon to be redesignated as *157. Gebirgs-Division*) pressed south. Slowly but surely, these German forces began to tighten the noose around the FFI troops in the Vercors. Despite fierce resistance, the *Maquis* were overwhelmed. Two days after the German glider assault (23 July) their commander, François Huet, ordered his forces to disband into smaller groups in order to escape and continue the fight elsewhere. After 23 July the role of the *Maquis* was to evade capture or death. Axis losses included sixty-seven *Franc-Gardes* of the *Milice* killed, German losses were sixty-five killed, 133 wounded, and eighteen missing. The *Maquis* lost 639 men killed, with about 150 captured. In addition, the partisans captured were all executed in the following days.

The civilian toll was also tragic. Some seventy-two civilians were killed in Vassieux-en-Vercors, including some who were simply executed. Another twenty-five wounded *Maquis*, plus the medical staff including nurses and even a priest, were executed in *Grotte de la Luire*, a cave that was being used as a field hospital. In total, some 201 civilians were murdered and 500 houses were destroyed. Although the operation was a tactical German victory, it didn't achieve total suppression of the Resistance. Many *Maquis* fighters survived and continued their efforts. When the Allies landed in southern France (Operation Dragoon) on 15 August 1944, and Grenoble was liberated on 22 August, the surviving *Maquis* rejoined the fight. The Battle of Vercors has since become a symbol of French resistance and sacrifice during the Second World War. The glider assault on Vassieux-en-Vercors is remembered as one of the few such operations by Germany during the war.

Luftwaffe support for anti-partisan operations

Geschwader Bongart was established in mid-April 1944, primarily from the *III.* and *IV. Gruppen* of *Fliegerzielgeschwader 2* (2nd Aviation Target Squadron), which had been constituted in February of the same year under the command of *Luftflotte III*. Initially, *Fliegerzielgeschwader 2* was intended to support anti-aircraft training operations through target towing missions. The unit was now equipped predominantly with the Italian manufactured Reggiane Re.2002 Ariete fighter-bomber. These planes had been delivered from the Reggiane and Caproni production

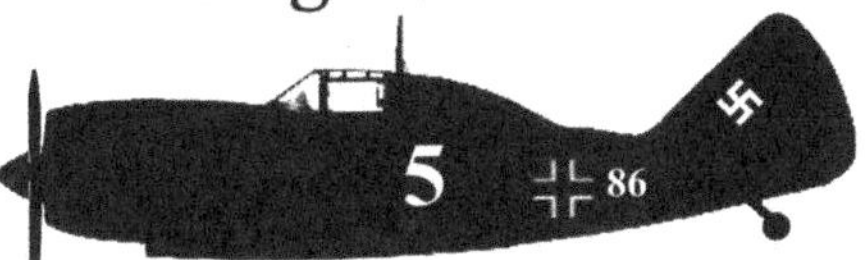

Figure 17. The various aircraft employed by *Geschwader Bongart*.

facilities in Italy. As the activities of the French Resistance intensified in central and southern France beginning in the autumn of 1943, the German command decided to reassign two squadrons from *Luftflotte III* specifically to support operations against the growing partisan threat. Hermann-Josef Freiherr von dem Bongart was appointed to command this new air group. On 15 April 1944, he was ordered to transfer the two squadrons to Bourges, where preparations began for dedicated anti-partisan operations under the designation *Geschwader Bongart*.

The unit's headquarters was established in Charleville, approximately 100km east of Paris, concurrently with the formation of *I. Gruppe*. Elements of the unit were formed throughout April 1944. From June to September 1944, *Geschwader Bongart* conducted operations from several airfields, including Lyon-Bron, Bourges, Valence, Clermont-Ferrand, and Avord (approximately 20km east-southeast of Bourges). Active operations commenced in late May 1944 and continued until mid-August 1944, with missions concentrated in central and southeastern France. One of the unit's most significant engagements occurred in July 1944, during a major German offensive against an estimated 4,000–5,000 Resistance fighters concentrated on the Vercors Plateau.

Daily Operational Summary of Unternehmen Bettina (Operation Bettina)

21 July 1944:

Luftflotte III reported the initiation of a combined army-air force operation in the region east of Valence. Aircraft from *Geschwader Bongart* provided air cover for twenty-two gliders, which landed on the Vercors Massif south of Grenoble. A German battle group established a defensive hedgehog position in Vassieux-en-Vercors, although the day's objectives were not fully achieved due to strong partisan resistance. Re. 2002 fighter-bombers and other *Luftwaffe* aircraft dropped approximately 7.5 tons of ordnance. Additional support was provided by fourteen aircraft from *Jagdfliegerführer Süd* (Fighter Pilot Leader South), with *Geschwader Bongart* conducting forty-four sorties.

22 July 1944:

Another 7.5 tons of bombs were dropped on French Forces of the Interior (FFI) positions in Vercors. Air operations extended east of Valence, where bombing destroyed a road approximately 8km north of Die. Supplies were delivered to Vassieux-en-Vercors, where German forces were consolidating. Concurrently, mopping-up operations occurred in Bouganeuf, Ussel, Limoges, and Châteauroux. *Geschwader Bongart* flew sixty-eight sorties, while *Jagdfliegerführer Süd* conducted seventeen sorties in support of the *157. Reserve-Division*. Missions included air cover, direct support, and logistical resupply.

23 July 1944:
The *Luftwaffe* deployed ten tons of high-explosive bombs in the Vercors sector. According to *Luftflotte III*, the operation was proceeding in line with expectations. German forces reached Vassieux-en-Vercors, approximately 100km southeast of Resistance-held areas. *Geschwader Bongart* flew sixty-three sorties, while *Jagdfliegerführer Süd* flew six.

24 July 1944:
Combat operations against the Resistance on the Vercors Plateau continued. *Geschwader Bongart* executed twenty sorties, sixteen of which were direct attack missions and four for supply and medical evacuation purposes.

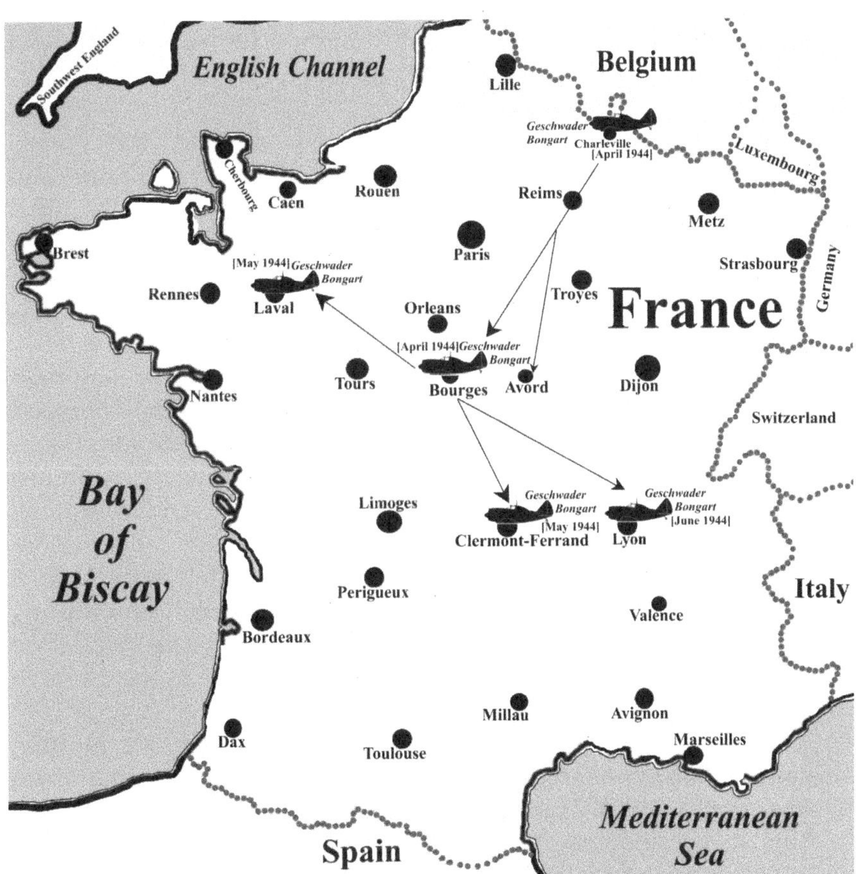

Figure 18. The staging bases and dates where the squadrons of *Geschwader Bongart* were located in 1944.

25 July 1944:

Geschwader Bongart flew thirty-two sorties targeting Resistance positions. *Luftflotte III* reported a collapse in Resistance activity by the end of the day, following intensive fighting. German forces-initiated mop-up operations across the plateau.

26 July 1944:

The final day of the Vercors campaign saw eighteen sorties flown by *Geschwader Bongart* in support of the *157. Reserve-Division* and *Kampfgruppe Schäfer* (force created from *Streifkorps Südfrankreich*, a *Brandenburg* formation). The operation concluded successfully, with numerous Resistance fighters reported killed and substantial quantities of weapons and ammunition seized. Meanwhile, Valence Airfield – a base of operations for *Geschwader Bongart* – was attacked by Allied aircraft, resulting in the destruction of five Junkers Ju 88s and one Dornier Do 17. *Luftflotte III* speculated that these air raids were intended to disrupt *Geschwader Bongart*'s anti-partisan operations.

The German Withdrawal

Following the significant losses sustained in June, the French Resistance temporarily refrained from large-scale operations and focused on reorganising its forces. As previously noted, with only a few exceptions, there were no major massacres for approximately two months after mid-June. However, this relative lull did not signify an end to the German campaign against the Resistance. On the contrary, violent practices by German troops became increasingly systematic. Hostage-taking in so-called 'bandit villages', and the summary execution of captured Resistance members were commonplace. After June/July 1944, it became almost impossible for the *Maquisards* to surrender. Capitulation was rarely a viable option, as it almost inevitably led to their death at the hands of their German captors. Consequently, they either continued fighting, knowing that surrender was out of the question, or went into hiding. Nevertheless, by August 1944, Resistance activity resumed with greater intensity, prompting renewed and often brutal reprisals from German forces – an escalation that must be understood within the broader context of the German military's withdrawal from France.

After the devastating German assault on the Vercors in July, surviving *Maquisards* regrouped and participated in hit-and-run attacks on retreating German forces moving through the Rhône Valley in August. These attacks were critical in tying down German forces and preventing orderly retreats. In central France (including Corrèze,

Haute-Vienne, and Cantal) the Resistance launched numerous attacks, including ambushes of convoys, destruction of roads and railways, and blocking key routes such as the N89 and Route Nationale 20. The impact of these actions disrupted German supply lines and slowed down withdrawals, forcing German troops into less defensible and more exposed positions where they became vulnerable to both Resistance and Allied attacks. Though largely symbolic in military terms, on 24–25 August Resistance fighters in Lyon, including those from the FTP and the MUR, launched coordinated attacks on German positions and administrative buildings. These actions contributed to the German retreat and helped prepare the city for the arrival of Free French and Allied forces.

Resistance units attacked German convoys retreating through cities like Tours, Blois, and Orléans in the Loire Valley. They blew up bridges, derailed trains, and laid mines, often in coordination with advancing American units. The towns of Souillac and Rouffignac-Saint-Cernin-de-Reilhac are both located in southwestern France, within the historical region of Périgord, now part of the Nouvelle-Aquitaine administrative region. The main route in June 1944 connecting Souillac and Rouffignac-Saint-Cernin-de-Reilhac was the D 703 (formerly RN 703), which runs roughly east-west through the Dordogne Valley and passes directly through both towns. Souillac is located in the Vézère Valley. The road between Souillac and Rouffignac-Saint-Cernin-de-Reilhac proved to have the highest density of German vehicle ambushes by the Resistance, especially in August 1944. As the Germans began a full withdrawal from France in August, several major Resistance attacks were carried out by the FFI and *Maquis* groups in southern and central France. Following the Allied landings of southern France on 15 August, FFI fighters in the Rhône-Saône corridor carried out a series of roadblocks, ambushes, and demolitions in the Rhône and Saône Valley. In addition, the Resistance blew up rail and bridges to slow the retreat of the German *19. Armee*. These actions complemented American advances, helping the US Seventh and French First Armies move rapidly toward Dijon by severing German supply and communication lines.

Following this Resistance offensive, on the night of 21–22 August, German troops began to withdraw from Grenoble. Before they withdrew, the Nazis blew up several key bridges that could be used by Allied forces. *Maquis* groups from surrounding massifs – some supported by parachuted detachments – immediately launched operations to secure the city. They occupied strategic points and assisted the arriving US 36th Infantry Division in securing Grenoble by midday, capturing the town just hours after the German departure.

After the brutal suppression of the Vercors uprising in July, the surviving *Maquis* took to guerilla warfare in early August. Beginning around 8 August, they carried out several raids on retreating German detachments, reportedly killing around twenty-seven German soldiers. By 22 August, *Maquis* forces from Vercors participated in the liberation of Grenoble and marched victoriously into the city.

Between 18–25 August, FTP and FFI units in Paris instigated a widespread uprising against German occupiers. The Paris Police turned on Vichy authorities on 19 August, enabling resistance attacks on German positions across the city. On 23 August, Madeleine Riffaud and FTP operatives led an assault on a German armoured train trapped in the Buttes-Chaumont tunnel, resulting in thirty-five German soldiers killed and over eighty taken prisoner. By 25 August, with FFI help and advancing Free French divisions, the commander of the *325. Sicherungs-Division, General der Infanterie* Dietrich von Choltitz and the last commander of the Paris garrison, surrendered. These operations slowed down German withdrawals, damaged morale, and prevented the destruction of infrastructure (like bridges) that the Germans often tried to demolish during retreat. It also reduced the ability of the *Wehrmacht* to reinforce critical positions that would facilitate the withdrawal of the German Army from France. These guerrilla attacks also helped pave the way for Allied advances, often directly coordinating with American and Free French troops. The Resistance's activity also signalled the re-establishment of French sovereignty, preparing liberated zones for Allied occupation and provisional French governance.

Chapter 11

CONCLUSIONS: BETWEEN OCCUPATION AND LIBERATION: MEMORY, MORALITY, AND THE MEANING OF RESISTANCE

This study has examined, in granular detail, the mechanisms through which the German occupation regime sought to dominate France between 1940 and 1944, and the evolving responses of the French Resistance and segments of French society to this domination. What emerges is a complex and deeply layered portrait of occupation, collaboration, and resistance – marked by administrative sophistication, ideological extremism, and moral ambiguity.

The Architecture of Occupation and the Gradual Erosion of French Sovereignty

At the heart of the German presence in France was a carefully stratified system of control. The German Military Administration, governed initially by the German Armistice Commission and later supplanted by increasingly radical elements from the SS and SD, imposed a logic of domination premised on both coercion and co-optation. German officials such as Otto von Stülpnagel, and later Carl-Heinrich von Stülpnagel and Wilhelm Keitel, presided over a machinery of occupation that blended administrative bureaucracy with ideological enforcement. The GFP, initially subordinated to the *Wehrmacht*, evolved into a key instrument in the repression of dissidence, especially following the end of army control and the expansion of SS authority. As explored in this volume's analysis of Senior Secret Field Police Superintendent 'West', the GFP's counterinsurgency operations were both systematic and brutal, reflecting the broader German doctrine of *Schrecklichkeit* – governance through terror.

Parallel to the German apparatus, the Vichy regime – especially under the leadership of Pierre Laval and collaborators such as Joseph Darnand – accelerated the erosion of French sovereignty. Through judicial tools like the Section spéciale, and paramilitary repression by entities such as La Milice and the Police Nationale, Vichy not only administered German directives but frequently outpaced them in zeal. The regime's voluntary participation in round-ups such as the *Rafle du Vélodrome d'Hiver* and the Green Ticket Round-up underscores the internalisation of Nazi objectives by Vichy elites.

Collaborationist Militias and the Expansion of Internal Repression

This study has further illustrated how repression was increasingly decentralised through the proliferation of independent, pro-German militias. These included ideological and regional groups such as *La Brigade nord-africaine*, *La Phalange Raciste*, *Le Corps Franc Français*, and the *Bezen Perrot Groupe*. Some, like the *Hauskapelle Bordeaux* and *Le Mouvement National Antiterroriste de Lyon*, acted with relative autonomy, creating localised zones of terror where civilian populations were subjected to arbitrary justice, torture, and summary execution. Figures such as Henry LaFont blurred the lines between ideological collaboration and criminal enterprise, reinforcing how occupation bred opportunism alongside fanaticism. The activities of the *Carlingue* (French *Gestapo*) offer a case study in the criminalisation of collaboration, with their use of torture, blackmail, and extortion carried out in the name of counterinsurgency.

The Resistance: From Fragmentation to Strategic Coordination

In contrast, the Resistance – initially divided by ideology, region, and operational capacity – underwent a remarkable transformation. Early movements such as the FTP emerged in response to repression, often operating independently. However, with the increasing militarisation of the occupation and the introduction of compulsory labour (STO), the Resistance began to absorb *réfractaires* – young men fleeing forced labour – who formed the nucleus of the *Maquis* networks. The coordination of these groups, through structures like the MUR and later the FFI, was catalysed by Allied support. Operations by the SOE Free French Section and the OSS, including missions such as Operation Jedburgh, provided arms, training, and organisational cohesion. The role of arms deliveries and clandestine supply drops was particularly crucial in the run-up to D-Day, as it allowed the Resistance to transition from sabotage to quasi-conventional warfare. Chapters detailing major French Resistance operations (1940–4) and Resistance zones illustrate how the Resistance's strategic role evolved in tandem with Allied planning. Sabotage of railways, attacks on German logistics, and the seizure of liberated zones (as in the *République du Vercors*) made clear that the Resistance had become more than a moral symbol – it was a strategic force multiplier.

German Counterinsurgency and the Routinisation of Terror

The response from the Nazi security apparatus was brutal and unrelenting. Chapters on major anti-partisan operations in 1943 and 1944, including *Unternehmen Bettina*, demonstrate how the *Wehrmacht* and SS, often in cooperation with the *Luftwaffe* and local collaborators, adopted tactics honed in the East: mass reprisals, hostage executions, village liquidations, and scorched-earth campaigns. These efforts were aimed not only at punishing Resistance actions but at severing the social bonds between fighters and civilians. In territories like Alsace-Lorraine, the integration of German police structures and the enforcement of Germanisation policies further demonstrate the ideological dimension of repression, culminating in the forced conscription of local youth into the *Wehrmacht* (*Malgré-nous*). The SD's operations in both occupied and Vichy zones, detailed in this volume, reveal a systematic effort to penetrate Resistance networks and erode civilian morale through psychological warfare, blackmail, and informant networks.

The Holocaust, Vichy, and the Limits of Sovereignty

Nowhere was the collaboration between Vichy and Nazi Germany more devastating than in the orchestration of the Holocaust in France. Beginning with the early round-ups of foreign Jews in 1941 and intensifying after 1942, the French state became a willing participant in genocide. The bureaucratic efficiency with which Jews were arrested, interned, and deported – often without direct German involvement – speaks to the moral collapse of the Vichy apparatus. The broader implications of this are addressed in comparative chapters covering *ha Shoah* in France, Belgium, Holland, and Luxembourg, offering a transnational view of complicity.

Legacies of Resistance and Repression

Ultimately, as explored in the final chapters on the fall of Vichy and the withdrawal of the German police, the occupation's infrastructure of repression proved unsustainable under the pressure of Allied advance and internal revolt. Yet the physical collapse of the regime did not bring immediate moral clarity. The post-war reckoning with collaboration was uneven, often politicised, and marked by selective memory.[1] Key figures were prosecuted, but many others reintegrated quietly into the structures of the Fourth Republic. The Resistance, by contrast, left a legacy both inspirational and contested. It helped to restore national honour, legitimise the provisional government under de Gaulle, and lay the groundwork for post-war reconstruction. But its mythologisation often came at the cost of obscuring the diversity of its participants and the limits of its reach. Women, foreign fighters, communists, and colonial subjects all played indispensable roles, yet their stories were often marginalised in the dominant narrative of a unified, republican resistance.

Final Reflections

In synthesising the administrative, military, and human dimensions of occupation and resistance, this study has sought to move beyond simplistic binaries of heroism and betrayal. Instead, it has emphasised the structural foundations of repression, the agency of actors on all sides, and the contingent nature of moral decision-making under totalitarian rule. The occupation of France was not merely a German, and to a lesser degree, Italian project – it was co-produced by local collaborators, shaped by strategic exigencies, and contested at every level by acts of defiance, large and small. What emerges is a portrait of France in extremis: a society fractured by war, ideology, and survival, yet capable – through the actions of its *resistants* – of reclaiming its dignity. The French Resistance, though born fractured, in isolation and anonymity, ultimately helped define the character of modern France. Its legacy is not only one of liberation but of a fundamental moral reckoning with the choices individuals and nations make under the weight of tyranny.

MAJOR STATION POSTS OF THE *SICHERHEITSDIENST* IN FRANCE AND THE LOW COUNTRIES, 1940–1944

BdS Frankreich in Paris [France]
SS-Standartenführer Helmut Knochen (May 1940–September 1944)
SS-Obersturmbannführer Friedrich Suhr (from November 1944)
> *KdS Angers*
> *KdS Bordeaux*
> *KdS Châlons-sur-Marne*

SS-Hauptsturmführer Modest Graf von Korff (July 1942–May 1943)
SS-Sturmbannführer und Regierungsrat Dr Karl Lüdcke (24 July 1943–28 August 1944)
> *KdS Dijon*
> *KdS Lyon*
> *KdS Limoges*
> *KdS Montpellier*
> *KdS Nancy*
> *KdS Orléans*
> *KdS Paris*
> *KdS Poitiers*
> *KdS Rouen*

SS-Obersturmbannführer Bruno Müller (May 1944–November 1944)
> *KdS Saint-Quentin*
> *KdS Toulouse*
> *KdS Vichy*

Befehlshaber der Sicherheitspolizei und des SD Belgien und Nordfrankreich (Brüssel)- [Belgium & Northern France]
SS-Standartenführer Dr. Constantine Canaris
SS-Obersturmbannführer Karl Friedrich Georg Haselbacher
SS-Obersturmbannführer Ernst Ehlers
SS-Standartenführer Dr Constantin Canaris
    KdS Wallonien
SS-Obersturmbannführer Eduard Strauch (31 May 1944–October 1944)

BdS Westmark (Metz) [annexed eastern France]
SS-Brigadeführer Anton Dunckern (July 1940–June 1944)
    KdS Metz
SS-Obersturmbannführer Herbert Zimmermann (1944)

BdS Elsass (Straßburg) [annexed eastern France]
SS-Obergruppenführer Gustav Adolf Scheel (August 1940–January 1941)
SS-Oberführer Hans Fischer (November 1941–December 1943)
SS-Standartenführer Erich Isselhorst (January 1944–10 December 1944)

BdS Niederlande [the Netherlands]
SS-Brigadeführer und Generalmajor der Polizei Hans Nockemann (May 1940–July 1940)
SS-Gruppenführer Wilhelm Harster (15 July 1940–29 August 1943
SS-Gruppenführer Erich Naumann (September 1943–July 1944)
SS-Oberführer Karl Eberhard Schöngarth (from September 1944)

Appendix II

THE GERMAN MILITARY ADMINISTRATIVE DISTRICTS IN FRANCE

June 1941 Order of Battle[1]

Kommandant von Großraum Paris (Paris)
Generalleutnant Ernst Schaumburg (31 July 1940 – 30 April 1943)
Landesschützenregiment 94
       Landesschützenbataillon 425 (3 Kp.) (Pantin)
       Landesschützenbataillon 541 (6 Kp.) (Asnières)
Secret Field Police Groups:
GFP-11
GFP-550
GFP-603
GFP-610
GFP-649
Established on 21 June 1941:
GFP-733
GFP-734
GFP-735
Gendarmerie (rural police) units:
Feldgendarmerie-Trupp 584
Feldgendarmerie-Trupp 757
Feldgendarmerie-Trupp 785
Feldgendarmerie-Trupp 796
Feldgendarmerie-Trupp 896,
Feldgendarmerie-Trupp 903,
Feldgendarmerie-Trupp 923,
Feldgendarmerie-Trupp 933

3. Feldgendarmerie -Ersatz-Kompanie
Stalag 111 (Drancy)
Stalag 220 (St. Denis)

 Feldkommandantur 584 (St. Maurice/Paris-Ost)
 Oberst Max von Mertens
  Kreiskommandantur 785 (Nogent-Sur-Marne)

 Feldkommandantur 757 (Neuilly/Paris-West)
 Generalmajor Johannes Hochbaum
  Kreiskommandantur 786 (Montrouge)
  Kreiskommandantur 896 (Asnières)

Militärverwaltung in Nordwestfrankreich
Militärverwaltungsbezirk A – (St. Germaine en-Laye)
Generalmajor Gustav von Bartenwerffer
Landesschützenregiment 44
Landesschützenregiment 66
GFP-312
GFP-540
GFP-633
GFP-701
Stalag 204 (Amiens)
Stalag 151 (Montagris)
Stalag 153 (Chartres)
Stalag 191 (Laon)
Stalag 200 (Verneuil)

Feldkommandantur 515 – (St. Hellier, Jersey, Channel Islands)

 Feldkommandantur 517 – (Rouen)
  Kreiskommandantur 567 – (Dieppe)
  Kreiskommandantur 637 – (Le Havre)
  Kreiskommandantur 667 – (Rouen)
  Kreiskommandantur 792 – (Forges-le-Eaux)

Feldkommandantur 580 – (Amiens)
  Kreiskommandantur 626 – (Abbeville)
  Kreiskommandantur 638 – (Beauvais)
  Kreiskommandantur 644 – (Albert)
  Kreiskommandantur 686 – (Senlis)
  Kreiskommandantur 736 – (Montdidier)
  Kreiskommandantur 800 – (Amiens)
  Kreiskommandantur 804 – (Compiègne)

Feldkommandantur 589 – (Orléans)
        Kreiskommandantur 542 – (Montargis)
        Kreiskommandantur 544 – (Orléans)
        Kreiskommandantur 577 – (Romorantin)
        Kreiskommandantur 641 – (Vendôme)

Feldkommandantur 602 – (Laon)
        Kreiskommandantur 527 – (Soissones)
        Kreiskommandantur 645 – (St. Quintin)
        Kreiskommandantur 797 – (Vervins)
        Kreiskommandantur 882 – (Laon)

Feldkommandantur 668 – (Bourges)
        Kreiskommandantur 731 – (Vierzon-Ville)
        Kreiskommandantur 776 – (Bourges)

Feldkommandantur 680 – (Melun)
        Kreiskommandantur 543 – (Meaux)
        Kreiskommandantur 781 – (Fontainebleau)
        Kreiskommandantur 894 – (Provins)

Feldkommandantur 684 – (Charleville)
        Kreiskommandantur 612 – (Sedan)
        Kreiskommandantur 704 – (Mézières)
        Kreiskommandantur 747 – (Vouziers)
        Kreiskommandantur 791 – (Rethel)

Feldkommandantur 722 – (St. Lô)
        Kreiskommandantur 583 – (Cherbourg)
        Kreiskommandantur 741 – (Avranches)
        Kreiskommandantur 802 – (Coutances)
        Kreiskommandantur 883 – (St. Lô)

Feldkommandantur 723 – (Caen)
        Kreiskommandantur 763 – (Vire)
        Kreiskommandantur 774 – (Lisieux)
        Kreiskommandantur 789 – (Bayeux)
        Kreiskommandantur 884 – (Caen)

Feldkommandantur 751 – (Chartres)
        Kreiskommandantur 742 – (Dreux)
        Kreiskommandantur 762 – (Châteaudun)
        Kreiskommandantur 805 – (Chartres)

Feldkommandantur 753 – (Evreux)
>> *Kreiskommandantur 743* – (Bernay)
>> *Kreiskommandantur 770* – (Les Andelys)
>> *Kreiskommandantur 801* – (Evreux)

Feldkommandantur 754 – (Alencon)
>> *Kreiskommandantur 545* – (Alencon)
>> *Kreiskommandantur 773* – (Argentan)

Feldkommandantur 758 – (Versailles)
>> *Kreiskommandantur 738* – (St. Germaine)
>> *Kreiskommandantur 761* – (Enghien)
>> *Kreiskommandantur 780* – (Corbeil)
>> *Kreiskommandantur 895* – (Rambouillet)

Militärverwaltung in Westfrankreich
Militärverwaltungsbezirk B (Angers) –
Generalleutnant Karl-Ulrich Neumann-Neurode (July 1940 – 8 July 1942)
Landesschützenregiment 64 (Angers)
>> *Landesschützenbataillon 845* (6 Kp.) (Angers)
>> *Landesschützenbataillon 904* (4 Kp.) (Tours)
>> *Landesschützenbataillon 582* (3 Kp.) (Saumur)
>> *Landesschützenbataillon 678* (3 Kp.) (Saumur)
>> *Landesschützenbataillon 459* (6 Kp.) (Rennes)
>> *Landesschützenbataillon 454* (4 Kp.) (Le Mans)
>> *Landesschützenbataillon 641* (6 Kp.) (Le Mans)
>> *Landesschützenbataillon 733* (4 Kp.) (Laval)
>> *Landesschützenbataillon 691* (6 Kp.) (Laval)
>> *Landesschützenbataillon 658* (4 Kp.) (La Roche)
>> *Landesschützenbataillon 903* (4 Kp.) (Niort)
>> *Landesschützenbataillon 480* (3 Kp.) (Luçon)
>> *Landesschützenbataillon 605* (4 Kp.) (Poitiers)
>> *Landesschützenbataillon 579* (3 Kp.) (Poitiers)
Landesschützenregiment 65 (Pontivy)
>> *Landesschützenbataillon 453* (4 Kp.) (Vannes)
>> *Landesschützenbataillon 745* (6 Kp.) (Vannes)
>> *Landesschützenbataillon 455* (4 Kp.) (St.Nazaire)
>> *Landesschützenbataillon 677* (3 Kp.) (Rennes)
>> *Landesschützenbataillon 746* (6 Kp.) (Rennes)
>> *Landesschützenbataillon 279* (3 Kp.) (St.Brieuc)
>> *Landesschützenbataillon 389* (3 Kp.) (St.Brieuc)
>> *Landesschützenbataillon 388* (3 Kp.) (Quimper)
>> *Landesschützenbataillon 452* (4 Kp.) (Quimper)
Abwehrstelle GFP Gruppe Angers
GFP-632 (Angers)
GFP-30 (Rennes)

Abwehrstelle GFP Gruppe Rennes
Abwehrstelle GFP Gruppe Brest
Oberfeldzeugstab Westfrankreich
Truppenübungsplatz Camp du Ruchard
Truppenübungsplatz Meucon
Truppenübungsplatz Coetquidon
Truppenübungsplatz Auvours
Frontleitstelle (Front Control Office) *Tours*
Feldnachrichten-Kommandantur 7 (Poitiers)
Feldnachrichten-Kommandantur 26
Feldnachrichten-Kommandantur 22 (St.Brieuc)
      Farbare Rundfunksender D zu Funk 22
      Fernsprechbau-Kompanie 15
Kriegsgefangen Bezirk Kommandant L
      Stalag 181 (Saumur)
      Stalag 133 (Rennes)
      Stalag 132 (Laval)
      Stalag 232 (Luçon)
      Stalag 230 (Poitiers)

Feldkommandantur 518 (Nantes)
      Kreiskommandantur 788 (Nantes)
      Kreiskommandantur 504 (Châteaulin)
      Kreiskommandantur 502 (St.Nazaire)

Feldkommandantur 588 (Tours)
      Kreiskommandantur 595 (Angers)
      Kreiskommandantur 793 (Cholet)
      Kreiskommandantur 607 (Saumur)
      Kreiskommandantur 768 (Segre)
      Kreiskommandantur 609 (Ambose)
      Kreiskommandantur 506 (Chinon)

Feldkommandantur 748 (Rennes)
      Kreiskommandantur 806 (Rennes)
      Kreiskommandantur 729 (Faugères)
      Kreiskommandantur 511 (St.Malo)
      Kreiskommandantur 665 (St.Brieuc)
      Kreiskommandantur 759 (Dinan)
      Kreiskommandantur 799 (Kannion)
      Kreiskommandantur 514 (Quingamp)

Feldkommandantur 750 (Vannes)
      Kreiskommandantur 790 (Vannes)
      Kreiskommandantur 735 (Lorient)
      Kreiskommandantur 592 (Pontivy)

Feldkommandantur 752 (Quimper)
      Kreiskommandantur 740 (Quipmer)
      Kreiskommandantur 623 (Brest)
      Kreiskommandantur 733 (Châteaulin)
      Kreiskommandantur 807 (Morlaix)

Feldkommandantur 755 (Le Mans)
      Kreiskommandantur 582 (Le Mans)
      Kreiskommandantur 794 (La Flèche)
      Kreiskommandantur 547 (Mamers)

Feldkommandantur 756 (Laval)
      Kreiskommandantur 586 (Laval)
      Kreiskommandantur 775 (Mayenne)

Feldkommandantur 605 (La Roché)
      Kreiskommandantur 796 (La Roche)
      Kreiskommandantur 505 (Fontenay)
      Kreiskommandantur 597 (Les Sables)
      Kreiskommandantur 564 (Niort)
      Kreiskommandantur 803 (Bressuire)
      Kreiskommandantur 655 (Parthenay)

Feldkommandantur 677 (Poitiers)
      Kreiskommandantur 736 (Poitiers)
      Kreiskommandantur 739 (Civray)
      Kreiskommandantur 651 (Châtellerault)

Militärverwaltung in Ostfrankreich
Militärverwaltungsbezirk C (Dijon)
Generalleutnant Edward Freiherr von Rotberg
Stalag 121 – (Epinal)
Stalag 122 – (Dijon)
Stalag 124 – (Auxerre)
Stalag 142 – (Besancon)
Stalag 161 – (Nancy)
Stalag 141 – (Vesoul)
Stalag 194 – (Nancy)
GFP-7 (Dijon)
GFP-627 (Troyes)
Landesschützenregiment 34 (Dijon)
Landesschützenregiment 95 (Vesoul)
Landesschützenbataillon 385
Landesschützenbataillon 768
Landesschützenbataillon 889

Feldkommandantur 509 (Auxerre)
        Kreiskommandantur 624 (Avallon)
        Kreiskommandantur 728 (Sens)
        Kreiskommandantur 745 (Auxerre)

Feldkommandantur 516 (Chaumont)
        Kreiskommandantur 563 (Chaumont)
        Kreiskommandantur 649 (Langres)
        Kreiskommandantur 888 (St. Dizier)
        Landesschützenbataillon 654 (Chaumont)

Feldkommandantur 531 (Troyes)
        Kreiskommandantur 533 (Troyes)
        Kreiskommandantur 634 (Bor-sur-Aube)
        Kreiskommandantur 734 (Nogent sur Seine)

Feldkommandantur 550 (Epinal)
        Kreiskommandantur 622 (Epinal)
        Kreiskommandantur 660 (Neufchâteau)
        Kreiskommandantur 711 (Saint-Dié) (Saint-Dié-des-Vosges)

Feldkommandantur 560 (Besancon)
        Kreiskommandantur 552 (Dôle)
        Kreiskommandantur 660 (Pontarlier)
        Kreiskommandantur 656 (Besancon)
        Kreiskommandantur 661 (Vesoul)
        Kreiskommandantur 767 (Montbéliard)
        Kreiskommandantur 554 (Belfort)
        Kreiskommandantur 760 (Lure)
        Kreiskommandantur 890 (Gex)
        Kreiskommandantur 889 (Grey)
Landesschützenbataillon 418 (Besancon)

Feldkommandantur 568 (Nevers)
        Kreiskommandantur 726 (Château de Chinon)
        Kreiskommandantur 727 (Clamecy)
        Kreiskommandantur 776 (Burges)
        Kreiskommandantur 891 (Nevers)

Feldkommandantur 590 (Bar-le-Duc)
        Kreiskommandantur 627 (Verdun)
        Kreiskommandantur 629 (Comercy)

Feldkommandantur 591 (Nancy)
        Kreiskommandantur 553 (Nancy)
        Kreiskommandantur 594 (Lunéville)

Kreiskommandantur 596 (Briey)
Kreiskommandantur 892 (Longwy)

Feldkommandantur 608 (St. Menehould)[2]
    Kreiskommandantur 795 (St. Menehould)
    Kreiskommandantur 706 (Vitry-le-François)
    Kreiskommandantur 769 (Reims)
    Kreiskommandantur 695 (Epernay)[3]
    Kreiskommandantur 893 (Dijon)
    Kreiskommandantur 737 (Montbard)

Feldkommandantur 669 (Autun)[4]
    Kreiskommandantur 555 (Moulons)
    Kreiskommandantur 559 (Autun)
    Kreiskommandantur 562 (Chalon-sur-Saône)
    Kreiskommandantur 620 (Beaune)
    Kreiskommandantur 658 (Parey-le-Monial)

Militärverwaltung in Südwestfrankreich
Militärverwaltungsbezirk Bordeaux (Bordeaux)
Generalleutnant Moritz von Faber du Faur

Militärbefehlshaber in Belgien und Nordfrankreich[5]
Militärverwaltungs Bezirk D (Brussels)
General der Infanterie Alexander von Falkenhausen

During the Second World War, the *Militärverwaltung* (MV), or military administration, functioned as the German occupation authority for Belgium and the former French départements of Nord and Pas-de-Calais. It was established in early June 1940, shortly after Belgium's surrender, and operated under the command of *Militärbefehlshaber* in Belgium and Northern France, *General der Infanterie* Alexander von Falkenhausen. The MV reported directly to the *Oberkommando des Heeres* (OKH), the Supreme High Command of the German Army. The administrative structure of the MV was organised into two primary divisions, coordinated through a central Presidium Office responsible for principal matters. The first division, the *Kommandostab*, headed by *Major* Bodo von Harbou, managed military command functions within the occupied territory, including counterintelligence operations. It also oversaw a range of police forces such as the *Feldgendarmerie* and the GFP. The second division, known as the *Verwaltungsstab* and led by *SS-Brigadeführer* (later promoted to *SS-Gruppenführer*) Eggert Reeder, who was tasked with the general civil administration of occupied Belgium and Northern France. This division was further subdivided into two major branches. One of these, the *Verwaltungsabteilung*, under the leadership of Harry von Craushaar, was responsible for policy areas including culture, public health, education, justice, finance, and internal security, managing these through a number of subordinate groups (*Gruppen*).

General Alexander von Falkenhausen held the position of Military Commander in Belgium and Northern France from 22 May 1940 until 15 July 1944. His headquarters was located in Brussels and comprised a total of 1,102 personnel, including 110 officers, 346 officials, 144 non-commissioned officers, and 502 enlisted men, in addition to 164 civilian staff. As military governor, von Falkenhausen was entrusted with the administration of the German military occupation in Belgium and the regions of Northern France situated east of the Somme River, specifically the départements of Nord and Pas-de-Calais. His responsibilities encompassed oversight of the civil administration, police, and internal security, as well as the management of political affairs within the occupied zone. A central aspect of his mandate involved the systematic requisitioning of goods and resources from the occupied territories to support the German war effort and the internal economy of the Reich. Importantly, the *Militärbefehlshaber* (Military Commander) operated independently of the Commander-in-Chief West and *Heeresgruppe D*, reporting instead directly to the *Oberquartiermeister beim OKH* (Quartermaster General at the Army High Command). Nevertheless, overall operational command of German forces in northwestern Europe remained vested in the Commander-in-Chief West. General von Falkenhausen had direct control of the following forces:

Grenzwach-Regiment Clüver (14x companies in three battalions), stationed in Brussels.
Polizei-Bataillon 62 (motorisiert)
1. Feldgendarmerie-Ersatz-Kompanie (Zellick)
2. Feldgendarmerie-Ersatz-Kompanie (Zellick)
Three military field police platoons that were located in Antwerp, Hasselt and Mons.
Landesschützenbataillon 484 (8 Kp.)
Landesschützenbataillon 525 (1 Kp.)
Landesschützenbataillon 651 (4 Kp.)
Landesschützenbataillon 770 (4 Kp.)
Landesschützenbataillon 771 (4 Kp.)
Landesschützenbataillon 773 (4 Kp.)
Landesschützenbataillon 774 (3 Kp.)
Landesschützenbataillon 785 (3 Kp.)

Oberfeldkommandantur 672 (Brussels)
Feldkommandantur 681 (Hasselt)
    Ortskommandantur I/643 (Brussels)
        Kreiskommandantur 689 (Nivelles)
        Kreiskommandantur 913 (Löwen)
Landesschützen Bataillon 774 (3 Kp.)
Landesschützen Bataillon 775 (4 Kp.)
GFP 530 (Brussels)

Feldkommandantur 520 (Antwerp)
Ortskommandantur I/702 (Antwerp)
        Landesschützenbataillon 115 (Brussels)
        Landesschützenbataillon 525 (2 Kp.)
        Landesschützenbataillon 625 (3 Kp.)
        Landesschützenbataillon 657 (4 Kp.)
        Landesschützenbataillon 735 (3 Kp.)
        Landesschützenbataillon 736 (3 Kp.)

Oberfeldkommandantur 570 (Gent)
    Ortskommandantur I/690 (Gent)
    Ortskommandantur I/798 (Ypres)
        Kreiskommandantur 630 (Audenarde)
        Kreiskommandantur 654 (St. Nikolas)
        Kreiskommandantur 708 (Alast)
Landesschützen-Regiment 115 (Brussels)
    Landesschützenbataillon 627 (3 Kp.)
    Landesschützenbataillon 737 (4 Kp.)

Feldkommandantur 578 (Brügge)
        Kreiskommandantur 510 (Brügge)
        Kreiskommandantur 632 (Ypres)
        Kreiskommandantur 652 (Courtai)
        Kreiskommandantur 663 (Roulers)

Oberfeldkommandantur 520 (Mons)
    Ortskommandantur I/750 (Mons)
        Kreiskommandantur 814 (Zoumas)
        Kreiskommandantur 816 (Monds)
        Kreiskommandantur 688 (Chareroi)
Landesschützenbataillon 485 (9 Kp.)
    Feldkommandantur 682 (Namur)
        Ortskommandantur I/942 (Namur)
            Kreiskommandantur 613 (Dinant)
Landesschützenregiment 22 (Namur)
    Landesschützenbataillon 526 (3 Kp.)

Landesschützenbataillon 550 (3 Kp.)
Landesschützenbataillon 835 (3 Kp.)

Oberfeldkommandantur 589 (Lüttich)
   Ortskommandantur I/940 (Lüttich)
      Kreiskommandantur 687 (Huy)
      Kreiskommandantur 691 (Verviers)
Landesschützen-Regiment 22 (Namur)
   Landesschützenbataillon 626 (3 Kp.)
   Landesschützenbataillon 837 (3 Kp.)

   Feldkommandantur 598 (Arlon)
      Kreiskommandantur 636 (Neufchateau)
      Kreiskommandantur 701 (Bastogne)

Oberfeldkommandantur 670 (Lille)
   Ortskommandantur I/699 (Calais)
   Ortskommandantur I/707 (LeTouque)
      Kreiskommandantur 772 (St. Omer)
      Kreiskommandantur 635 (Bethune)
      Kreiskommandantur 639 (Arras)
      Kreiskommandantur 713 (Boulogne)
      Kreiskommandantur 771 (Montreuil)
Landesschützenregiment 22 (Namur)
   Landesschützenbataillon 484
   Landesschützenbataillon 651[6]

   Feldkommandantur 678 (Lille)
   Feldkommandantur 642 (Avesnes-le-Comte)
   Feldkommandantur 692 (Cambrai) FK 705 (Valenciennes)
   Feldkommandantur 714 (Dunkirk)
   Feldkommandantur 715 (Donai)
      Ortskommandantur I/914 (Lille)
Landesschützenregiment 35 (Lille)
   Landesschützenbataillon 908 (4 Kp.)
   Landesschützenbataillon 863 (4 Kp.)
   Landesschützenbataillon 712 (6 Kp.)

THE OFFICES OF THE PARIS *SICHERHEITSDIENST*

When the SD established itself in Paris, its various departments required more than one office. Therefore, during the war the *Gestapo*, SD and *SiPo* operated from multiple addresses in Paris during the German occupation (1940–4). These offices depended on function-intelligence, administration, interrogation, and detention. The main *Gestapo*/SD Headquarters in Paris was 84 Avenue Foch (in the 16th *arrondissement*). It was used for administration, intelligence gathering, and interrogation/torture of suspected Resistance members. During the war, this address was in the most fashionable neighbourhood in Paris. It is located near the Eifel tower as well as the *Arc de Triomphe*. Today, homes on Avenue Foch still run into the millions of Euros. The basement of 84 Avenue Foch housed several jail cells. It was there that people whom the SD had arrested were placed. The basement also housed the interrogation room, which could better be described as a torture room.

Another key *Gestapo* administrative office was located at 11 Rue des Saussaies (8th *arrondissement*). This office was located near the French Ministry of the Interior (Place Beauvau). *SS-Obergruppenführer und General der Polizei* Reinhard Heydrich, who up until June 1942 was head of the RHSA, reportedly stayed here at times; Adolf Eichmann may have also visited during planning of the deportations of Jews from France. Another infamous address which was part of the SD apparatus in Paris was 93 Rue Lauriston (16th arrondissement). This address housed the headquarters of the *Gestapo Français* – also known as the Bonny-Lafont gang. The office housed collaborators and petty criminals who were recruited by Lafont from his time in prison. These worked in conjunction with *Gestapo* officers.

Quite often they would take part in raids, where they would announce themselves with the words, *'Police allemande!'* this office was used for interrogation, torture, extortion, and the persecution of Jews and Resistance fighters. Given that these buildings had a limited capacity to house prisoners, the SD established themselves at *Fresnes Prison* (located southeast of Paris). It was not a *Gestapo* office, but a main detention centre for prisoners of the *Gestapo* and SD. Many people arrested by the *Gestapo* were sent here after interrogation. It was known for horrific conditions and frequent deportations from here to German camps. Although the Drancy internment camp (located northeast suburb of Paris), was run by the French police, it was nevertheless supervised by the Germans. This camp also coordinated with the *Gestapo* and *SiPo*. This camp was used as the main transit camp for Jews being deported to Auschwitz and other extermination camps.

NOTES

Author's Note

1 The estimated number of Germans killed in France by the Resistance
was as follows: around 350 were killed in 1940, 800 in 1941, 2,500 in
1942, 7,000 in 1943 and 14,000 between 1 January and 6 June 1944. This
totalled some 24,650 Germans killed from August 1940 to 6 June 1944.
From 7 June to 30 September 1944 a further 10,000 Germans were killed
by the Resistance and 32,000 were wounded.

Introduction

1 Jacques Benoist-Méchin, *Sixty Days That Shook the West: The Fall of
France, 1940*, ed. and pref. Cyril Falls, trans. Peter Wiles (New York: G.
P. Putnam's Sons, 1963), pp. 357–62.
2 Gaël Eismann, *Hôtel Majestic: Ordre et sécurité en France occupée 1940-1944*
(Paris: CNRS Éditions, 2010), pp. 89–90.
3 Guy Sajer, *The Forgotten Soldier* (New York: Harper & Row, 1971),
pp. 41–52.

Chapter 1: Organisation of the German Military Government in France

1 US National Archives and Records Administration (NARA), *T-78,
Records of the German Army High Command (OKH), Roll 516: Personnel
Documents, 1943–1944*, personnel file of General der Artillerie Oskar
Vogl.
2 H. R. Kedward, *In Search of the Maquis: Rural Resistance in Southern
France, 1942-1944* (Oxford: Clarendon Press, 1993), pp. 2–3.
3 Archives Nationales (France), AJ 40/865, Folder 13, Letter from the
Chairman of the Reich Defence Ministerial Council, Hermann Göring, to
the Military Commander of France, 3 February 1941.
4 Richard Overy, Gerhard Otto, and Johannes Houwink ten Cate, eds.,
Die 'Neuordnung' Europas: NS-Wirtschaftspolitik in den besetzten Gebieten
(Berlin: Metropol, 1997), pp. 109–12.
5 Archives nationales (Pierrefitte-sur-Seine), *AJ/41/1563 à 2131: Délégation
française auprès de la commission allemande d'armistice (D.F.C.A.A. ou
D.F.A.) et délégation économique (D.E.).*

6   Helga Bories-Sawala, *Franzosen im 'Reichseinsatz': Deportation, Zwangsarbeit, Alltag. Erfahrungen und Erinnerungen von Kriegsgefangenen und Zivilarbeitern*, vol. 1 (Frankfurt am Main, 1996), pp. 263–6.

7   Loi n°869 du 4 septembre 1942 relative à l'utilisation et à l'orientation de la main-d'œuvre, quoted in Bernd Zielinski, *Staatskollaboration: Vichy und der Arbeitskräfteeinsatz im Dritten Reich*, Theorie und Geschichte der Bürgerlichen Gesellschaft 11 (Münster: Westfälisches Dampfboot, 1995), p. 120.

8   Archives nationales (Pierrefitte-sur-Seine), *AJ/41/1101 à 1343: Section militaire de liaison de Vichy (S.M.L.), groupes de liaison, détachements de liaison et sections françaises de liaison (S.F.L.) (zone sud)*.

9   In this particular case, the term *Francs-tireurs* is referring to all French underground forces. However, during the German occupation of France, two significant resistance movements used the name *Franc-Tireur*. The first was founded in Lyon in 1940. The second, known as the *Francs-Tireurs et Partisans* (FTP), served as the armed wing of the French Communist Party (PCF) and only began active resistance after Germany invaded the Soviet Union in 1941.

10 US National Archives and Records Administration (NARA), *T-501, Roll 266, Befehlshaber des Rückwärtigen Heeresgebietes, 1940-1942*.

11 Ibid.

12 Stefan Martens, ed., *Frankreich und Belgien unter deutscher Besatzung 1940–1944: Die Bestände des Bundesarchiv-Militärarchivs Freiburg* (Stuttgart: Franz Steiner Verlag, 2002), pp. 83–92.

13 Wolfgang Benz, Gerhard Otto, and Johannes Houwink ten Cate, eds, *Die Bürokratie der Okkupation: Strukturen der Herrschaft und Verwaltung im besetzten Europa* (Berlin: Metropol, 1998), pp. 77–84.

14 Bundesarchiv-Militärarchiv (BA-MA), Freiburg, RW 35, *Militärbefehlshaber Frankreich*, Befehl vom 21. Oktober 1941; Roderick Kedward, *Occupied France: Collaboration and Resistance 1940–1944* (Oxford: Blackwell, 1991), pp. 103–6.

15 AN AJ40/965, dr. 5. *Liste der Feldkommandanten und Oberfeldkommandanten, 15.6.1944 im Heeresgebiet Südfrankreich*, and BA-MA RH 3/v. 206 [OKH] Qu. 4. *Kommandantenverzeichnis der dem Militär Befehlshaber in Frankreich. Stand 31.7.1944*.

16 Mayr was taken prisoner by the *Maquis* on 20 August 1944.

17 *Generalmajor* Brodowski was killed by the French partisans on 20 October 1944.

18 Borgmann assumed this post of 15 February 1944.

19 *Generalmajor* Walter Gleininger committed suicide by a self-inflicted gunshot to the head on 21 August 1944.

20 The FFI attacked Guéret on 8 June 1944, liberating the town and took numerous prisoners, including Reinhard Biebricher. But the day after, elements of the *2. SS-Panzer-Division 'Das Reich'* pushed out the FFI from the town and freed several Germans, including Biebricher.

21 Colonel Metger was captured by the FFI on 22 August 1944.

22 Colonel Kirsten was replaced by *Oberst* Willy Stenz beginning 5 August 1944.
23 BA-MA Frieburg, RW 35/28 *Militar Befehlshaber in Frankreich.*
24 Hans Umbreit, *Der Militärbefehlshaber in Frankreich 1940–1944,* Wehrwissenschaftliche Forschungen (Boppard am Rhein: Harald Boldt Verlag, 1968), pp. 67–8.
25 Then, *Oberstleutnant* Wilhelm Hof assumed command of *Oberfeldkommandantur 564.*
26 Mayr was taken prisoner by the *Maquis* on 20 August 1944.
27 Hühnermann held this post from 10 April to 10 June 1944.
28 This was an elevated command from the original headquarters which in 1940 was *Kreiskommandantur 761.* In 1940 this KK command was located in the town of Enghien-les-Bains, in the region of *Militär Verwaltungs Bezirk A.*
29 Doepping held this post from 25 July to 5 September 1944.
30 *Oberst* Ludwig Dischler held this position from February to August 1944. Before Dischler, you had the following officers in command of *Feldkommandantur 734: Oberstleutnant* Emmer (December 1942–1943), *Oberst* Georg Reinhard (1943–January 1944).
31 Stenz was posted to this command at the end of June 1944.
32 Wolpert assumed this post on 25 June 1944.
33 He assumed this command in April 1944.
34 Bundesarchiv, RH 36 - Kommandanturen der Militärverwaltungen der Wehrmacht.
35 Held this command from 10 April to 12 August 1944.
36 Bundesarchiv, RH 36 - Kommandanturen der Militärverwaltungen der Wehrmacht.
37 Niall MacGalloway, *The Italian Occupation of South-Eastern France, 1940-1943* (PhD diss., University of St Andrews, 2015), pp. 129–32.

Chapter 2: The Secret Field Police in France

1 US National Archives and Records Administration (NARA), *T-501, Records of the German Military Command in Belgium and Northern France,* Roll 108, Frame 000264.
2 From June 1941 until January 1942, Ernst Rassow was *Leiter der Geheime Feldpolizei Ost* (Leader of the Secret Field Police in the East).
3 Dr. Hermann Herold eventually became commander of the *SiPo*/SD in Poitiers.
4 The position of the Paris GFP command was to be left under the command of *Feldpolizeidirektor* Vogel.
5 Wilhelm Krichbaum, *Geheime Feldpolizei (Secret Field Police),* vol. I, XE 019650, SR 380-320-10 (Baltimore: General Staff, US Army G-2 Central Records Facility, 1948), pp. 54–6.
6 CIA - Ci Intermediate Interrogation Report (Ci-iir) No. 57. INTERMEDIATE INTERROGATION REPORT (CI-IIR) No 57 Prisoner: Obst/Lt DERNBACH, Friedrich Leiter III-F Ast ANGERS, S France.

Chapter 3: The SS Enters the Picture

1 Bundesarchiv Berlin-Lichterfelde (formerly Berlin Document Center), *Series 6400: SS Officers' Service Records, Roll 219-B: Röthke, Heinz.*

2 *SS-Dienstalterliste der Schutzstaffel der NSDAP: SS-Obergruppenführer bis SS-Standartenführer. Stand vom 30. Januar 1942.* Edited by SS-Personalhauptamt. Berlin: Reichsdruckerei, 1942.

3 Admiral Wilhelm Canaris was a staunch anti-Nazi. Throughout the war he did his very best to impede Hitler's plans. For example, on 23 October 1940 Adolf Hitler met with the Spanish dictator, Francisco Franco. The meeting was to be held at the Franco-Spanish border town of Hendaye. The subject of the meeting was to try and convince Franco to join the Axis as an active participant. Canaris contacted Franco's foreign minister, Ramón Serrano Suñer, ahead of the meeting, and warned him that joining Nazi Germany in the war would bring about the fall of the Franco regime. Based on that warning, Franco declined Hitler's offer. At the meeting between the dictators, Hitler only managed to get Franco to allow a Spanish volunteer division to be formed to fight alongside the Germans in Russia, but Franco absolutely refused to join the Axis. Afterwards Hitler commented that in the future, he would rather have root canal work than to have to negotiate with Franco ever again. Canaris' treachery only began to surface in February 1944, when he was dismissed. He was implicated in the failed 20 July bomb plot to kill Hitler, and was executed on 9 April 1945.

Chapter 4: The Vichy French Government and Security Forces

1 Marcel Yonque, *La guerre 1939-1945. Saint-Mihiel et la Meuse. Les combats. L'occupation. La libération* (Saint-Mihiel: Éditions Sphères, 2000), pp. 65–7.

2 Not formally a minister, but critical.

3 Marcel Déat was one of only two leading French collaborators to avoid prosecution and death. In April 1945 he travelled with his family to northern Italy, where he took his wife's surname. He lived undiscovered in Milan and Turin and was even assisted by the Catholic Church. He died of natural causes in 1955. The other French collaborator of significant note, was Louis-Ferdinand Céline – the famous writer and Nazi sympathiser. Céline fled to Germany and then Denmark after the war. He was sentenced in absentia by a French court but returned to France in the 1950s, after a general amnesty.

4 Pierre Philippe Lambert and Gérard Le Marec, *Vichy 1940-1944: Organisations, Mouvements et Unités de l'État Français* (Paris: Jacques Grancher, 1992), p. 47.

5 Yann Stephan, *Policing France During the German Occupation*, Chicago: University of Illinois Press, 1992, p. 45.

6 Lambert and Le Marec, *Vichy 1940-1944*, p. 56.

7 Stephan, *A Broken Sword*, p. 16.

8 René Rémond, *Frankreich im 20. Jahrhundert: 1918 bis 1958* (Stuttgart: Kohlhammer, 1994), 401-404.

9   In the unoccupied zone, the Vichy French *Gendarmerie* were allowed rifles and heavier-calibre weapons, but in the German-occupied zone, they could only carry a pistol.

10 It should be noted that these SS divisions evolved significantly in both structure and nomenclature over the course of the war, especially between 1941–3, as they transitioned from motorised infantry to fully-fledged panzer (armoured) divisions. For example, the SS *'Leibstandarte SS Adolf Hitler'* division was officially redesignated *1. SS-Panzergrenadier-Division LSSAH* in October 1943, and later it became the *1. SS-Panzer-Division LSSAH* in March 1944. Likewise, the 'Reich' SS division became *2. SS-Panzergrenadier-Division 'Das Reich'* in October 1943. In mid-1944 it was redesignated as *2. SS-Panzer-Division 'Das Reich'*. Finally, the SS division *'Totenkopf'* was renamed *3. SS-Panzergrenadier-Division 'Totenkopf'* in October 1943. Later still, in 1944, it was renamed as *3. SS-Panzer-Division 'Totenkopf'*.

11 *Befehl von General Adolf Heusinger vom 10.12.40. Oberbefehlshaber der Bodentruppen Generalstab, Abteilung Operationen, Nr. 711/40, streng geheim.*

Chapter 5: Independent Pro-German Militias

1   In June 1942, Joseph Darnand was petitioning the Germans to allow the SOL to operate in occupied France.

2   David Littlejohn, *Foreign Legions of the Third Reich*, vol. 1 (San Jose: R. James Bender Publishing, 1979), p. 174.

3   Philippe Burrin, *France Under the Germans: Collaboration and Compromise* (New York: The New Press, 1996), p. 441.

4   Stephan, *A Broken Sword*, p. 37.

5   Burrin, *France Under the Germans*, p. 443.

6   Littlejohn, *Foreign Legions of the Third Reich*, vol. 1, p. 176.

7   Ibid.

8   Ibid., p. 277.

9   Ian Ousby, *Occupation: The Ordeal of France 1940-1944* (London: John Murray, 1997), p. 304.

10 Jean-Pierre Sourd, *True Believers: Spanish Volunteers in the Heer and Waffen-SS, 1944–1945* (New York: Europa Books, 2004), p. 50.

11 Stephan, *A Broken Sword*, p. 84.

12 Serge Jacquemard, *La bande Bonny-Lafont* (Paris: Fleuve Noir, 1992), pp. 55–62.

13 Stephan, *A Broken Sword*, 55.

14 Jean-Pierre Sourd Donnat, "The French "Selbstschutzpolizei", 1943–1944," *Axis Europa Magazine*, no. 15 (Autumn 1998), p. 3.

15 The province had been ceded by France after the Franco-Prussian War of 1870.

16 Hans Keller (born 29 September 1907) was later transferred to Norway. Bundesarchiv - Hans Keller / Rep. 057-01 Nr. P 1600 k 022 Registratursignatur: B Rep. 057-01 Nr. 1 AR (RSHA) 22/65.

17 Stephan, *A Broken Sword*, p. 47.

18 *SS-Dienstalterliste der Schutzstaffel der NSDAP: SS-Obergruppenführer bis SS-Standartenführer. Stand vom 30. Januar 1942*, ed. SS-Personalhauptamt (Berlin: Reichsdruckerei, 1942), p. 16.

19 Yaacov Lozowick, *Hitler's Bureaucrats: The Nazi Security Police and the Banality of Evil* (New York: Continuum Press, 2000), p. 186.

20 Sourd, *True Believers*, p. 46.

21 Bundesarchiv Freiburg, RH 26-1002, Verband 803: Regiment 3 Brandenburg, Panzergrenadier-Division 'Brandenburg', 1944-1945.

22 With these identity cards the French government could hopefully track down the members of the *Selbstschutzpolizei.*

23 As of 23 July 1941 the separatist group contained about 400 members.

24 Stephan, *A Broken Sword*, p. 6.

25 Von Gebsattel happened to be the cousin of *Oberst* Baron von Stauffenberg.

26 *SS-Dienstalterliste der Schutzstaffel der NSDAP: SS-Obergruppenführer bis SS-Standartenführer. Stand vom 1. Oktober 1944*, ed. SS-Personalhauptamt (Berlin: Reichsdruckerei, 1944), p. 29.

27 Ibid., p. 63

28 Pierre Philippe Lambert and Gérard Le Marec, *Les Français sous le casque allemand* (Paris: Jacques Grancher, 1994), p. 233.

29 Lozowick, *Hitler's Bureaucrats*, p. 219.

30 United States Holocaust Memorial Museum Archive, records (Sygn. 350) RG-15.187M, Files 3-8. *Der Befehlshaber der Sicherheitspolizei und des Sicherheitsdienst in Frankreich*, 1940-1944.

31 Le Marec, *Les Français sous le casque allemand*, p. 224.

32 Archives départementales de la Gironde, Series SC 1020.

33 Lambert and Le Marec, *Vichy 1940-1944*, p. 227.

34 Ministère des Armées, Service historique de la Défense (SHD), La Phalange raciste française: organisation et composition, notes et bulletins de renseignements, 1942-1944, GR 28 P 2 115.

35 Archives Départementales de la Gironde, series W and SC, local collaborationist files, Bordeaux, France.

36 Lozowick, *Hitler's Bureaucrats*, p. 183.

37 Olivier Wieviorka, *The French Resistance* (Cambridge, MA: Harvard University Press, 2016), reviewed by Jeremy Black, *Journal of World History* 30, no. 1/2 (June 2019), pp. 255–6.

38 The *Carlingue* were Frenchmen who worked as police auxiliaries for either the *Gestapo*, the SD, or the German Army's GFP.

39 Lambert and Le Marec, *Vichy 1940-1944*, p. 210.

Chapter 6: The French Resistance

1 Otto Weidinger, *Division Das Reich. Der Weg der 2. SS-Panzer Division 'Das Reich'*. Bd. 5 (Osnabrück, 1982), p. 112.

2 Insa Meinen, *Wehrmacht und Prostitution während des Zweiten Weltkrieges im besetzten Frankreich* (Bremen: Edition Temmen, 2002), pp. 84–90.

3 Peter Lieb, *Konventioneller Krieg oder NS-Weltanschauungskrieg? Kriegführung und Partisanenbekämpfung in Frankreich 1943/44* (München: Oldenbourg, 2007), p. 61.

4   Samuel W. Mitcham Jr., *Panzer Legions: A Guide to the German Army Tank Divisions of WWII and Their Commanders* (Mechanicsburg, PA: Stackpole Books, 2007), p. 208.

5   Yves Cayre, *Histoire de la Manufacture d'armes de Tulle, de 1690 à 1970* (Tulle: Manufacture d'Armes de Tulle, 1973), pp. 139–44.

6   *SS Officers' Service Records*, Series 6400, Roll 219-A: Korten, Friedrich, Bundesarchiv Berlin-Lichterfelde (formerly Berlin Document Center).

7   Philippe Aziz, *Tu trahiras sans vergogne: histoire de deux "collabos", Bonny et Lafont* (Paris: Fayard, 1970), pp. 121–3.

8   Many second-line and rear-area infantry units, as well as occupation troops, *Luftwaffe* ground formations, and especially *Volkssturm* units formed in 1944–5 were regularly issued French rifles (e.g. MAS-36, Lebel, Berthier), FM 24/29 machine guns, and artillery pieces such as the famous French 75mm guns, often re-designated with an (f) suffix. In 1944, *Panzer-Abteilung 100* (a training and replacement tank battalion), along with the *91. Luftlande-Infanterie-Division*, were equipped with French arms and R-35 tanks captured in 1940. The famed *21. Panzer-Division*, stationed in Normandy on D-Day, was heavily equipped with captured French vehicles converted for combat – Marder I tank destroyers using Lorraine and Hotchkiss chassis – and older tanks like the Somua S-35 and Char B-1 in combat and occupation roles. The chassis of these older French vehicles were outfitted with German artillery pieces – making them mobile. As for Czech weaponry, we know that the German *6. Panzer-Division* and *7. Panzer-Division* employed Czech tanks. The *88. Infanterie-Division*, which was part of the German 6th Mobilisation Wave (created in late 1939), upon formation lacked sufficient German weapons and instead was outfitted with Czech arms – small arms, infantry guns, and anti-tank weapons from Czechoslovakia. Several infantry divisions from the 5th (and later) wave formations, raised after the invasion of Poland (e.g. late 1939), were outfitted with Czechoslovak small arms and guns because German domestic supplies lagged. These 'Wave-5' divisions contained Czech infantry weapons and anti-tank platoons which relied heavily on captured Czech arms.

9   Martial Faucon, *Francs-Tireurs et Partisans Français en Dordogne* (Tulle: Éditions Maugein, 1990), pp. 341–3.

10   Stephan, *A Broken Sword*, pp. 55–60.

11   Faucon, *Francs-Tireurs et Partisans Français en Dordogne*, pp. 341–3.

12   *Volontaire. Francs-tireurs et partisans français. Région de la Corrèze et du Lot*, np., nd., pp. 75–80.

13   Leib, *Konventioneller Krieg oder NS-Weltanschauungskrieg*, pp. 365–6.

14   Faucon, *Francs-Tireurs et Partisans Français en Dordogne*, pp. 341–3.

15   Bruno Kartheuser, *Die Erhängungen von Tulle. Der 9. Juni 1944, Walter, SD in Tulle*, Band III (Neundorf [Belgien]: Edition Krautgarten Orte, 2004), pp. 451–7.

16   Lieb, *Konventioneller Krieg oder NS-Weltanschauungskrieg*, pp. 323–6.

17 Jacqueline Duhem, *Ascq 1944: Un massacre dans le Nord. Une affaire franco-allemande* (Lille: Presses Universitaires du Septentrion, 2014); Fabrice Grenard, *Tulle: Enquête sur un massacre. 9 juin 1944* (Paris: Tallandier, 2014); Jean-Jacques Fouché, *Oradour* (Paris: Éditions Liana Lévi, 2001); Sébastien Chevereau, *25 août 1944, Maillé… Du crime à la mémoire* (Turquant: Éditions Hélène Jacob, 2012).

18 Kartheuser, *Die Erhängungen von Tulle*, Vol. 3, pp. 459–63.

19 Antoine Soulier, *Le drame de Tulle. 9 juin 1944* (Naves: [Publisher], 2002; originally published 1954), pp. 109–15.

20 US National Archives and Records Administration (NARA), *T-314, Records of German Field Commands: LVIII Panzer Corps War Diary, roll 1496: France, March–September 1944*, including reports on anti-partisan operations in the Toulouse area and preparations for countering the Allied invasion of southern France.

21 Lieb, *Konventioneller Krieg oder NS-Weltanschauungskrieg*, pp. 366–70.

Chapter 7: The German Police in France

1 Georg Tessin and Norbert Kannapin, *Waffen-SS und Ordnungspolizei 1939-1945* (Osnabrück: Biblio Verlag, 2000), p. 611.

2 Benoist-Méchin, *Sixty Days That Shook the West*, p. 337.

3 Telford Taylor, *The March of Conquest: The German Victories in Western Europe, 1940* (New York: Simon & Schuster, 1958), p. 427.

4 The principal German attack against France and the Low Countries would be launched on 10 May 1940, and involved German armoured units crossing into neutral Belgium, before breaking out of the Ardennes Forest and into open country. By this maneuver, the Germans avoided the strong French defences of the Maginot Line.

5 Taylor, *The March of Conquest*, p. 279.

6 Ibid., p. 282

7 Georges Jerome, 'L'Ordnungspolizei en 1940: L'exemple de la Lorraine annexée', *39/45 Magazine*, no. 162 (December 1999): 15. Bayeux: Editions Heimdal.

8 Stefan Klemp, *'Nicht ermittelt': Polizeibataillone und die Nachkriegsjustiz. Ein Handbuch* (Berlin: Metropol Verlag, 2022), p. 147.

9 *Reserve-Polizei-Bataillon 63* had recently arrived from occupation duty in Rzeszow, Poland. It had temporarily been a part of *Polizei-Regiment 'Krakau'*. In January 1940 it returned to German to reform and redeploy to France. Several commanders led this battalion. From July to September 1939, it was commanded by *Major der Polizei* Robert Wieprecht. Then from September 1939 until February 1940, it was Major Willing. In February 1940, one of the company commanders in the battalion, *Hauptmann der Polizei* Willi Greschuchna, assumed temporary command until April. The new battalion commander arrived in April 1940 to take command. This was *Major der Polizei* Bolte, who left two months later, in June 1940. The next commander was *Major der Polizei*

Hans Scherenberg, who led the battalion from June 1940 to June 1941. On 19 August 1942 *Major der Polizei* Hutter assumed command of the battalion.

10   D. B. Lankenau, *Polizei im Einsatz während des Krieges 1939-1945 in Rheinland-Westfalen* (Bremen: H. M. Hauschild, 1957), p. 15.

11   Massimo Arico, *Ordnungspolizei Vol. 1: Encyclopedia of the German Police Battalions* (Stockholm: Leandoer & Ekholm Publishing, 2011), p. 191.

12   Tessin and Kannapin, *Waffen-SS und Ordnungspolizei*, p. 631.

13   Harald Buhlan and Werner Jung, eds., *Wessen Freund und wessen Helfer? Die Kölner Polizei im Nationalsozialismus* (Köln: Emos Verlag, 2000), pp. 264–76.

14   Ian Ousby, *Occupation*, p. 104.

15   Antonio J. Muñoz, *Hitler's Green Army: The German Order Police and Their European Auxiliaries, Volume 1, Western Europe and Scandinavia* (New York: Europa Books, 2005), pp. 179–81.

16   Stationed in Amsterdam from June to December 1940, then returned to the Reich.

17   Stationed in Eindhoven, Holland beginning August 1941. Sent to north Russia in July 1942.

18   Stationed in Mulhouse in June 1940. This battalion was recalled to *Wehrkreis V* (5th Military District) in October 1940 and then disbanded. While in Alsace, it took part in the expulsion of unwanted French citizens, given that Alsace was now to be German territory.

19   Like *Polizei-Bataillon 54*, this police battalion was used in the expulsion of unwanted French citizens from Alsace. It returned to *Wehrkreis V* the following autumn and then disbanded.

20   Left France in August 1943 as part of *Polizei-Regiment 29 'Todt'*.

21   This battalion first served in Poland, then was withdrawn to Germany to refit as a motorised unit. On 1 October 1940 *Polizei-Bataillon 62 (motorisiert)*, now under the command of *Major der Polizei* Franz Keller, was sent to France. In November 1940 it was located in La Madeleine (near Lille). In March 1941 it was transferred to the Brittany region and placed under the control of the *Militärbefehlshaber Frankreich*. There it remained deployed between Brittany and Normandy. In August 1942 the battalion was designated as the *III. Bataillon* of the forming *Polizei-Regiment 4*, but in November 1942 it became the *I. Bataillon der Polizei-Regiment 28 'Todt'* and performed police duties in Brest (Brittany).

22   In March 1941 the battalion was sent to Brittany. The battalion was supposedly disbanded in the summer of 1941 and its personnel were sent to *Reserve-Polizei-Bataillon 64*.

23   Left France for Upper Carnolia in February 1944 as part of *Polizei-Regiment 28 'Todt'*.

24   *Reserve-Polizei-Bataillon 63* arrived in Luxemburg during the middle of September 1940 to replace *Polizei-Bataillon 66*.

25   *Reserve-Polizei-Bataillon 63* remained in Luxemburg until October 1941, when it returned to the Reich.

26   Transferred to The Netherlands in July 1942 where it became *III. Bataillon der Polizei-Regiment 14*. However, in November 1942 it was

redesignated as *III. Bataillon der Polizei-Regiment 4* thus replacing *Polizei-Bataillon 62* which was acting as the current *III. Bataillon der Polizei-Regiment 4*. At that time *Reserve-Polizei-Bataillon 63* was shifted to the region of Paris, France to join *Polizei-Regiment 4*.

27 Stationed in Marseilles as *III. Bataillon der Polizei-Regiment 4* from the autumn of 1942 until June 1943, when it was transferred (as part of *Polizei-Regiment 4*) to the *Generalgouvernement* (Poland).

28 The battalion was transferred to Flanders in Belgium, then in July 1940 it was shifted to Lille.

29 Transferred to Metz, in Lorraine in March 1941, but sent to Essen in August 1941.

30 The battalion was sent to Walsdorf, near The Hague. In July 1942 it became *III. Bataillon* of *Polizei-Regiment 14*, but was later redesignated as *III. Bataillon* of *Polizei-Regiment 4*.

31 Arrived in May 1940 and remained in The Netherlands until December 1940. Most of its personnel were transferred to *Polizei-Bataillon 66*.

32 This battalion entered Luxemburg in late June or early July 1940. It remained there until October 1940.

33 The battalion was sent to Tilburg, The Netherlands on 19 May 1942. In July it was in Den Haag (The Hague). There it became *I. Bataillon der Polizei-Regiment 3*. The *I. Bataillon* (ex-*Polizei-Bataillon 66*) left for Germany in December 1942. In January 1943 it arrived in Serbia to become *III. Bataillon / Polizei-Regiment 5*.

34 Arrived in May 1940.

35 Left for the Reich in February 1942. It was sent to Poland in May 1942.

36 Stationed in Assen, Holland in December 1940, but transferred to Rotterdam beginning April 1941. It remained in Rotterdam until July 1941 when it was transferred to Amsterdam. Became the *II. Bataillon der Polizei-Regiment 3* in July 1942.

37 Arrived from Riga, Latvia in August 1943. Joined with the regiment's *I. Bataillon* (ex-*Polizei-Bataillon 62*) in France, where the *III. Bataillon* also joined the regiment. Left for Upper Carnolia in February 1944.

38 Initially stationed in Strasbourg, in Alsace in June 1940. It remained there until it was relieved by *Polizei-Bataillon 51*. It then left for the Reich and on its way to Poland.

39 Stationed in The Netherlands from June to November 1940, then sent to the Reich. In July 1942 it was located in Upper Carnolia.

40 Beginning in May 1942 it was stationed in The Netherlands. Initially earmarked as the *III. Bataillon der Polizei-Regiment 12*, in early 1943 it was redesignated as *III. Bataillon / Polizei-Regiment 3*.

41 Sent to Tilburg, in The Netherlands in March 1941. In October it was in Den Haag.

42 Sent to northern Russia in June 1942 to serve under *207. Sicherungs-Division*.

43 Sent in January 1941 to Thionville, in the region of the annexed territory of Lorraine.

44 Transferred by air to northern Russia on 24 January 1942, where it was assigned to *Kampfgruppe Jeckeln*.

45   Transferred to the newly-annexed province of Lorraine in late June 1940
     and stationed in Metz. It was recalled to its home base in Mannheim in
     November 1940.

46   Returned to Lorraine on 20 March 1941 and stationed in Pelters and
     Metz.

47   Arrived in Russia in June 1942, in the region of *Heeresgruppe Mitte*, and
     used to create *II. Bataillon der Polizei-Regiment 14*.

48   The battalion was sent to Luxembourg City in October 1940.

49   In June 1941 it was listed as performing frontier guard duty between
     Luxembourg and the Reich. In October 1941 it was sent to Hallendorf, a
     district of the city of Salzgitter in Lower Saxony, Germany.

50   Ordered to Norway in June 1942 to become *III. Bataillon der Polizei-
     Regiment 7*.

51   The battalion, like *Polizei-Bataillon 123*, was sent to Luxembourg City in
     October 1940.

52   Officially designated as *Reserve-Polizei-Bataillon 124* on 5 January 1941.
     Transferred to Slovenia in the spring (likely between April and May).

53   Arrived in Amsterdam on 16 December 1940.

54   Left for Russia in June 1941.

55   Arrived in Paris in late July 1942 and formed into *I. Bataillon der Polizei-
     Regiment 4*.

56   Sent to Paris, France in July 1942 to become *II. Bataillon der Polizei-
     Regiment 4*.

57   Created in July 1942 using *Polizei-Bataillon 66*, *Polizei-Bataillon 68*, and
     the *III. Bataillon der Polizei-Regiment 12* (i.e.- the ex-*Polizei-Bataillon
     105*). The regiment was assigned the police battalions 66, 68 and 105.
     After its formation, the regiment was transferred to the *Höhere-SS und
     Polizeiführer Nederland*. The staff and the *I. Bataillon* were stationed
     in Tilburg, the *II. Bataillon* in Amsterdam and the *III. Bataillon* in The
     Hague. There, the regiment carried out general police tasks (property
     protection and patrol duty). The *I. Bataillon* was transferred to Serbia
     as *III. Bataillon / Polizei-Regiment 5*. The *I. Bataillon* was first sent to
     Hamburg, Germany in mid-December 1942, then on to Serbia in
     January 1943. A new *I. Bataillon* was not formed until the autumn of
     1944. At which time the regiment was renamed as *SS-Polizei-Regiment
     'Nordost' 1*.

58   Initially created and stationed in the region of Paris, France using
     Polizei-Bataillon 316 and *Polizei-Bataillon 323* as the *I. Bataillon and II.
     Bataillon* of the regiment. Later, *Reserve-Polizei-Bataillon 63* joined the
     regiment as the *III. Bataillon*. The regiment was transferred to Marseilles
     in November 1942 and remained there until June 1943 when it left for
     Poland.

59   At this time, *Polizei-Regiment 14* was rebuilt in France after its
     destruction in Russia.

60   Sent to Upper Carnolia (Slovenia) in March 1944.

61   Sent to the Paris region in France in June 1944. By September 1944
     the regiment was located by Langres (north of Dijon) in the Grand

Est region of northeastern France. It was part of the province of
Champagne, though sometimes Langres is associated with Burgundy.

62 Formed in November 1942 in France, but only the *I. Bataillon* (*Polizei-
Bataillon 62*) was available until August 1943, when the regiment finally
came together.

63 Sent to Upper Carnolia, Slovenia in February 1944.

64 Lankenau, *Polizei im Einsatz*, p. 17.

65 Georg Tessin, *Verbände und Truppen der Deutschen Wehrmacht und
Waffen-SS, 1939–1945*, 18 vols. (Osnabrück: Biblio Verlag, 1974–1991),
Vol. 9, p. 74.

66 Walter Scott Dunn, *Second Front Now 1943* (Mobile: The University of
Alabama Press, 1980), p. 194.

67 Lankenau, *Polizei im Einsatz*, p. 17.

68 US National Archives and Records Administration (NARA), *T-78,
Records of the German Army High Command (OKH), Roll 531: Field Forces
Organisation, Supply, and Manpower Problems, August–December 1943.*

69 Ronald Tarnstrom, *French Arms* (Lindsborg: Trogen Books, 2001), p. 649.

70 In April 1943, Himmler decreed that all German police regiments were
to be prefixed with the title 'SS' in order to honor them for their service
both behind and on the front lines. It was also in keeping with his pre-
war plans to amalgamate the SS and police organisations.

71 Alain Chazette, 'Le SS-Polizei-Regiment 28 "Todt" à Marseille
(1942–1943)', *39/45 Magazine*, no. 132 (June 1997), p. 29.

72 BA MA, RH 20-19, *Anlage C27, Armeeoberkommando 19, Formations
Abteilung, Stand 25.1.43.*

73 US National Archives and Records Administration (NARA), *T-501,
Records of the German Military Command in Belgium and Northern France,
roll 108: Reports of the Field Police Director (Leitender Feldpolizeidirektor beim
Militärbefehlshaber in Belgien und Nordfrankreich) concerning espionage,
underground activities, and crimes, October 1940 – April 1943; with monthly
reports, April-July 1944.*

74 Jacques Delarue, *Histoire de la Gestapo* (Paris: Fayard, 1963), p. 302.

75 Kurt Mehner, *Die geheimen Tagesberichte der Deutschen Wehrmachtführung
im Zweiten Weltkrieg 1939–1945*, vol. 9 (Osnabrück: Biblio Verlag, 1987),
7p. 5.

76 Tessin and Kannapin, *Waffen-SS und Ordnungspolizei*, p. 620.

77 Werner Regenberg, *Armoured Vehicles and Units of the German Order
Police (Ordnungspolizei) 1936-1945* (Atglen: Schiffer Military History,
2002), p. 137.

78 Ibid., p.138.

79 Tessin and Kannapin, *Waffen-SS und Ordnungspolizei*, p. 621.

80 Supreme Headquarters, Allied Expeditionary Force (SHAEF), *The
German Police*, SHAEF G-2 Report No. 121, Section E, 3.

81 Ibid., Section A, 7

82 In July 1944 *Polizei-Freiwilligen-Regiment 3 'Serbien'* was officered
and stationed as follows. The commander was *Oberstleutnant der
Schutzpolizei* Friedrich Graf. The regimental headquarters was in

Kraljevo. The *I. Bataillon* was in Krusevac, and was led by *Major der Schutzpolizei* Sprenglewski. The *II. Bataillon* was in Raska and was led by *Major der Schutzpolizei* Witt. The *III. Bataillon* was in Uzice and was commanded by *Hauptmann der Schutzpolizei* Ernst Buchelt. The IV. Bataillon was located in Kos. Mitrovica, and was under the command of *Major der Schutzpolizei* Henning Scharrenberg.

83   John Mendelsohn, ed., *Covert Warfare: Intelligence, Counterintelligence, and Military Deception During the World War II Era*, vol. 13, *The Final Solution of the Abwehr* (New York: Garland Publishing, 1989), Section 13 – "Excerpts from a Report on the German Sabotage System," 23 July 1945, USFET Interrogation Center, CIR/4.

84   Jeffrey J. Clarke and Robert R. Smith, *United States Army in World War II: The European Theater of Operations: Riviera to the Rhine* (Washington, D.C.: Center of Military History, United States Army, 1993), p. 185.

85   Tessin, *Verbände und Truppen*, Vol. 7, p. 295.

86   Wolf Keilig, *Rangliste des Deutschen Heeres, 1944/45* (Friedberg: Podzun-Pallas Verlag, n.d.), p. 20.

87   US National Archives and Records Administration (NARA), *T-78, Records of the German Army High Command (OKH), Roll 526: Operations Section War Diary, April–December 1944, with annexes concerning order of battle, activation, and deployment.*

88   Clarke and Smith, *United States Army in World War II: The European Theater of Operations: Riviera to the Rhine*, p. 235.

89   Tessin, *Verbände und Truppen*, Vol. 13, p. 206.

90   Friedrich Bruns, *Die Brücke von Neuenburg: Eine Dokumentation über den Endkampf der 19. Armee im Elsaß 1945* (Celle: self-pub., 1990), p. 552.

Chapter 8: The *Sicherheitsdienst* in France: Origins, Structure, and Operations in Occupied and Vichy Territories

1   USHMM, RG-15.187M.

2   Died in a motor vehicle accident in September 1940.

3   The *Kommandeur der Sicherheitspolizei und des SD Paris* served as the command authority overseeing the operations of the *Sicherheitspolizei* (Security Police) and the *Sicherheitsdienst* (Security Service) in the Paris metropolitan area. This office exercised operational control over the various *Einsatzkommandos* active in the region, directing efforts related to intelligence gathering, counterinsurgency, and the systematic enforcement of Nazi occupation policy.

4   *SS-Sturmbannführer* Friedrich Mußgay was drafted into the *Heer* on 21 June 1941.

5   Julian Jackson, *France: The Dark Years, 1940–1944* (Oxford: Oxford University Press, 2001), pp. 75–7.

Chapter 9: The Holocaust in France

1   Ahlrich Meyer, *Die deutsche Besatzung in Frankreich 1940–1944: Widerstandbekämpfung und Judenverfolgung* (Darmstadt: Wissenschaftliche Buchgesellschaft, 2000), pp. 51–4.

2   Robert O. Paxton, *Vichy France: Old Guard and New Order, 1940-1944* (New York: Alfred A. Knopf, 1972), pp. 56–60.

3   Michael R. Marrus and Robert O. Paxton, *Vichy France and the Jews* (New York: Basic Books, 1981), pp. 40–3.

4   Serge Klarsfeld, *Vichy-Auschwitz: The Role of Vichy in the Final Solution* (New York: Beate Klarsfeld Foundation, 1983), vol. 1, pp. 78–90.

5   Richard J. Golsan, ed., *The Vichy Past in France Today: Corrupting the Republic* (Lanham: Lexington Books, 2000), pp. 22–6.

6   Marrus and Paxton, *Vichy France and the Jews*, pp. 211–14.

7   Klarsfeld, *Vichy-Auschwitz*, vol. 2, pp. 145–8.

8   Paxton, *Vichy France*, esp. ch. 6.

9   Henry Rousso, *The Vichy Syndrome: History and Memory in France Since 1944*, trans. Arthur Goldhammer (Cambridge, MA: Harvard University Press, 1991), pp. 10–14.

10 Serge Klarsfeld, *Le mémorial de la déportation des Juifs de France* (Paris: Beate Klarsfeld Foundation, 1978), Introduction.

11 Robert Gildea, *Fighters in the Shadows: A New History of the French Resistance* (Cambridge, MA: Harvard University Press, 2015), especially chapters on Jewish rescue efforts.

12 Dan Michman, *Belgian Jewry and the Holocaust: Survivors, Victims, Perpetrators* (New York: Yad Vashem, 2001), pp. 251–6.

13 Herman Van Goethem, *The Antwerp School: Jewish and Catholic Collaboration and Resistance in Belgium* (New York: Berghahn Books, 2008), pp. 55–72.

14 Dan Michman, *Belgian Jewry and the Holocaust: Survivors, Victims, Perpetrators* (New York: Yad Vashem, 2001), pp. 120–50.

15 Martin Conway, *The Nazi Persecution of the Gypsies* (Oxford: Oxford University Press, 2012), pp. 143–60, also covers the Rexist movement's collaboration.

16 Mark Van den Wijngaert, *The Belgian Resistance during World War II* (Brussels: Royal Library of Belgium, 2010), pp. 85–105.

17 Bob Moore, *Victims and Survivors: The Nazi Persecution of the Jews in the Netherlands 1940–1945* (Amsterdam: Amsterdam University Press, 1997), pp. 90–115.

Chapter 10: Major German Anti-Partisan Operations

1   Stephan, A *Broken Sword*, p. 64.

2   This was a second anti-partisan drive that was named *Frühling*, and was distinct from the operation launched in April 1943 by the same name.

3   Peter Lieb, *Vercors 1944: Resistance in the French Alps* (London: Osprey Publishing, 2012), p. 24.

4   The German soldiers and airmen affectionately referred to this transport plane as '*Tante Ju*' (Auntie-Ju).

Conclusions

1   Rousso, *The Vichy Syndrome*, pp. 315–23.

Appendix II: The German Military Administrative Districts in France

1 Bundesarchiv-Militärarchiv, Freiburg, RW35 – *Militärbefehlshaber Frankreich und nachgeordnete Dienststellen*
2 Bundesarchiv-Militärarchiv, Freiburg, RH-36, *Kommandanturen der Militärverwaltungen der Wehrmacht.*
3 Disbanded 20 June 1942. Used to form *Feldkommandantur 622* (which itself was disbanded on 25 October 1944).
4 Transferred to Dijon in 1943.
5 NARA, T-501 Roll 209.
6 This regional defence battalion was detached from the army and place under the control of the *Kriegsmarine*.

BIBLIOGRAPHY

Primary Sources
Bundesarchiv

Bundesarchiv, *Archivaliensignatur, Akte -Alexander Johann Ostrowski / I. HA Rep. 77, Tit. 354a Nr. O Nr. 4.*

Bundesarchiv - *Hans Keller / Rep. 057-01 Nr. P 1600 k 022 Registratursignatur: B Rep. 057-01 Nr. 1 AR (RSHA) 22/65.*

Bundesarchiv-Militärarchiv (Freiburg). *RH 20-19, Anlage C27. Armeeoberkommando 19, Formationsabteilung, Stand 25. Januar 1943.*

Bundesarchiv-Militärarchiv (Freiburg). *RH 26-1002: Verband 803, Regiment 3 Brandenburg, Panzergrenadier-Division 'Brandenburg', 1944-1945.*

Bundesarchiv Berlin-Lichterfelde (formerly Berlin Document Centre), *Series 6400: SS Officers' Service Records.* Roll 219-A: Korten, Friedrich.

Bundesarchiv Berlin-Lichterfelde (formerly Berlin Document Centre), *Series 6400: SS Officers' Service Records,* Roll 219-A: Krueger, Hans.

Bundesarchiv Berlin-Lichterfelde (formerly Berlin Document Centre), *Series 6400: SS Officers' Service Records,* Roll 219-A: Knochen, Helmut.

Bundesarchiv Berlin-Lichterfelde (formerly Berlin Document Center), *Series 6400: SS Officers' Service Records,* Roll 219-B: Röthke, Heinz.

Archives nationales de France

Archives nationales (France). AJ 40/865, Folder 13. *Letter from the Chairman of the Reich Defence Ministerial Council, Hermann Göring, to the Military Commander of France, February 3, 1941.*

Archives nationales (Pierrefitte-sur-Seine). *AJ/41/1563 à 2131: Délégation française auprès de la commission allemande d'armistice (D.F.C.A.A. ou D.F.A.) et délégation économique (D.E.).*

Archives nationales (France). *La France et la Belgique sous l'occupation allemande, 1940-1944: Les fonds allemands conservés au Centre historique des Archives nationales. Inventaire de la sous-série AJ 40.* Paris: Archives nationales, 2002.

Archives nationales (Pierrefitte-sur-Seine). *AJ/41/1101 à 1343: Section militaire de liaison de Vichy (S.M.L.), groupes de liaison, détachements de liaison et sections françaises de liaison (S.F.L.) (zone sud).*

Archives départementales de la Gironde. *Series W and SC, Local Collaborationist Files.* Bordeaux, France.

Archives nationales (France). AJ 40/865, Folder 13. *Letter from the Chairman of the Reich Defence Ministerial Council, Hermann Göring, to the Military Commander of France, February 3, 1941.*

Archives Nationales (France). Ministère des Armées. Service historique de la Défense (SHD). *La Phalange raciste française: organisation et composition. Notes et bulletins de renseignements, 1942–1944. GR 28 P 2 115*

National Archives Records Administration

CIA - Ci-iir No. 57. *Intermediate Interrogation Report (CI-IIR) No 57 Prisoner: Obst/Lt DERNBACH, Friedrich Leiter III-F Ast ANGERS, S France.*

US National Archives and Records Administration (NARA). *Microfilm Publication T-78. Roll 250, frame 000039. Militär Verwaltungs Bezirk in Frankreich.*

US National Archives and Records Administration (NARA). *T-78, Records of the German Army High Command (OKH), Roll 516: Personnel Documents, 1943-1944.* Personnel file of *General der Artillerie* Oskar Vogl.

US National Archives and Records Administration (NARA). *T-78, Records of the German Army High Command (OKH), Roll 520: Organisational records of the Army High Command and field units from army groups to infantry and mountain divisions, 15 September 1940.*

US National Archives and Records Administration (NARA). *T-78, Records of the German Army High Command (OKH), Roll 526: Operations Section War Diary, April-December 1944, with annexes concerning order of battle, activation, and deployment.*

US National Archives and Records Administration (NARA). *T-78, Records of the German Army High Command (OKH), Roll 531: Field Forces Organisation, Supply, and Manpower Problems, August-December 1943.*

US National Archives and Records Administration (NARA). *T-314, Records of German Field Commands: LVIII Panzer Corps War Diary, Roll 1496: France, March-September 1944.* Includes reports on anti-partisan operations in the Toulouse area and preparations for countering the Allied invasion of southern France.

US National Archives and Records Administration (NARA). *T-501, Records of the German Military Command in Belgium and Northern France.* Roll 108.

US National Archives and Records Administration (NARA). *T-501, Records of the German Military Command in Belgium and Northern France, roll 108: Reports of the Field Police Director (Leitender Feldpolizeidirektor beim Militärbefehlshaber in Belgien und Nordfrankreich) concerning espionage, underground activities, and crimes, October 1940-April 1943; with monthly reports, April-July 1944.*

US National Archives and Records Administration (NARA). *T-501, Roll 209.*

US National Archives and Records Administration (NARA). *T-501, Roll 266. Befehlshaber des Rückwärtigen Heeresgebietes, 1940-1942.*

United States Holocaust Memorial Museum Archive

United States Holocaust Memorial Museum Archives. *Records (Sygn. 350) RG-15.187M, Files 3-8. Der Befehlshaber der Sicherheitspolizei und des Sicherheitsdienst in Frankreich, 1940-1944.*

Supreme Headquarters, Allied Expeditionary Force (SHAEF). *The German Police.* SHAEF G-2 Report No. 121. March 1945.

International Military Tribunal. *Trial of the Major War Criminals before the International Military Tribunal, Nuremberg, 14 November 1945 – 1 October 1946*. NARA, PS-2343, 'Directives on Counterintelligence Organisation in France', April 1941.

Deutsche Digitale Bibliothek. *Personenheft: Wilhelm Schneider (1887–1947)*. Landesarchiv Berlin, B-Rep 057-01, Nr. 2901. Registratursignatur: B Rep. 057-01, Nr. 1 AR (RSHA) 552 / 65. Accessed [date].

SS-Personalhauptamt, ed. *SS-Dienstalterliste der Schutzstaffel der NSDAP: SS-Obergruppenführer bis SS-Standartenführer. Stand vom 30. Januar 1942*. Berlin: Reichsdruckerei, 1942.

SS-Dienstalterliste der Schutzstaffel der NSDAP: SS-Obergruppenführer bis SS-Standartenführer. Stand vom 1. Oktober 1944. Edited by SS-Personalhauptamt. Berlin: Reichsdruckerei, 1944.

Secondary Sources

Magazine Articles

Chazette, Alain, 'Le SS-Polizei-Regiment 28 "Todt" à Marseille (1942–1943)', *39/45 Magazine*, no. 132 (June 1997): p. 29.

Jerome, Georges, 'L'Ordnungspolizei en 1940: L'exemple de la Lorraine annexée', *39/45 Magazine*, no. 162 (December 1999): p. 15.

Mallmann, Klaus-Michael, and Gerhard Paul, 'Die *Gestapo* im besetzten Frankreich: Terror, Kontrolle und Zusammenarbeit', *Zeitschrift für Geschichtswissenschaft* 47, no. 1 (1999): pp. 28–46.

Dissertations

MacGalloway, Niall, *The Italian Occupation of South-Eastern France, 1940–1943*, PhD diss., University of St Andrews, 2015.

Published Works

Arico, Massimo, *Ordnungspolizei. Vol. 1: Encyclopedia of the German Police Battalions*, Stockholm: Leandoer & Ekholm Publishing, 2011.

Aziz, Philippe, *Tu trahiras sans vergogne: histoire de deux 'collabos' Bonny et Lafont*, Paris: Fayard, 1970.

Bade, Claudia, 'Deutsche Militärjuristen in Frankreich: Das Gericht des Kommandanten von Groß-Paris', in *NS-Militärjustiz im Zweiten Weltkrieg. Disziplinierungs- und Repressionsinstrument in europäischer Dimension*, edited by Claudia Bade, Lars Skowronski, and Michael Viebig,. Göttingen: Wallstein Verlag, 2015, pp. 213–28.

Bargatzky, Walter, *Hotel Majestic: Ein Deutscher im besetzten Frankreich*, Freiburg: Herder, 1987.

Benoist-Méchin, Jacques, *Sixty Days That Shook the West: The Fall of France, 1940*, Edited and with a preface by Cyril Falls. Translated by Peter Wiles. New York: G. P. Putnam's Sons, 1963.

Benz, Wolfgang, Gerhard Otto, and Johannes Houwink ten Cate, eds., *Die Bürokratie der Okkupation: Strukturen der Herrschaft und Verwaltung im besetzten Europa*, Berlin: Metropol, 1998.

Bories-Sawala, Helga, Franzosen im "Reichseinsatz": Deportation, *Zwangsarbeit, Alltag. Erfahrungen und Erinnerungen von Kriegsgefangenen und Zivilarbeitern.* Vol. 1, Frankfurt am Main, 1996.

Bruns, Friedrich, *Die Brücke von Neuenburg: Eine Dokumentation über den Endkampf der 19. Armee im Elsaß 1945*, Celle: Selbstverlag, 1990.

Buhlan, Harald, and Werner Jung, eds., *Wessen Freund und wessen Helfer? Die Kölner Polizei im Nationalsozialismus*, Köln: Emos Verlag, 2000.

Burrin, Philippe, *France Under the Germans: Collaboration and Compromise*, New York: The New Press, 1996.

Cayre, Yves, *Histoire de la Manufacture d'armes de Tulle, de 1690 à 1970*, Tulle: Manufacture d'Armes de Tulle, 1973.

Chevereau, Sébastien, *25 août 1944, Maillé… Du crime à la mémoire,* Turquant: Éditions Hélène Jacob, 2012.

Clarke, Jeffrey J., and Robert R. Smith, *United States Army in World War II: The European Theatre of Operations: Riviera to the Rhine*, Washington, D.C.: Center of Military History, United States Army, 1993.

Conway, Martin, *The Nazi Persecution of the Gypsies*, Oxford: Oxford University Press, 2012.

De Jonghe, Albert, *La Belgique sous l'Occupation*, Brussels: Meddens, 1974.

Delarue, Jacques, *Histoire de la Gestapo*, Paris: Fayard, 1963.

Duhem, Jacqueline, *Ascq 1944: Un massacre dans le Nord. Une affaire franco-allemande,* Lille: Presses Universitaires du Septentrion, 2014.

Dunn, Walter Scott, *Second Front Now 1943*, Mobile: The University of Alabama Press, 1980.

Eismann, Gaël. *Hôtel Majestic: Ordre et sécurité en France occupée 1940–1944*, Paris: CNRS Éditions, 2010.

Faucon, Martial, *Francs-Tireurs et Partisans Français en Dordogne*, Tulle: Éditions Maugein, 1990.

Fouché, Jean-Jacques, *Oradour*, Paris: Éditions Liana Lévi, 2001.

Gellately, Robert, *Backing Hitler: Consent and Coercion in Nazi Germany*, Oxford: Oxford University Press, 2001.

Gildea, Robert, *Fighters in the Shadows: A New History of the French Resistance,* Cambridge, MA: Harvard University Press, 2015.

Golsan, Richard J., ed., *The Vichy Past in France Today: Corrupting the Republic,* Lanham, MD: Lexington Books, 2000.

Grenard, Fabrice, *Tulle: Enquête sur un massacre. 9 juin 1944*, Paris: Tallandier, 2014.

Höhne, Heinz, *The Order of the Death's Head: The Story of the SS*, New York: Coward-McCann, 1970.

Jackson, Julian, *France: The Dark Years, 1940–1944*, Oxford: Oxford University Press, 2001.

Jacquemard, Serge, *La bande Bonny-Lafont*, Paris: Fleuve Noir, 1992.

Kartheuser, Bruno, *Die Erhängungen von Tulle. Der 9. Juni 1944. Walter, SD in Tulle,* Band III, Neundorf (Belgien): Edition Krautgarten Orte, 2004.

Kedward, H. R., *In Search of the Maquis: Rural Resistance in Southern France, 1942-1944*, Oxford: Clarendon Press, 1993.

Keilig, Wolf, *Rangliste des Deutschen Heeres, 1944/45*, Friedberg: Podzun-Pallas Verlag, n.d.

Klarsfeld, Serge, *Le mémorial de la déportation des Juifs de France*, Paris: Beate Klarsfeld Foundation, 1978.

——, *Vichy-Auschwitz: The Role of Vichy in the Final Solution*, 2 vols. New York: Beate Klarsfeld Foundation, 1983.

Klemp, Stefan, *'Nicht ermittelt': Polizeibataillone und die Nachkriegsjustiz. Ein Handbuch*, Berlin: Metropol Verlag, 2022.

Lambert, Pierre Philippe, and Gérard Le Marec, *Vichy 1940–1944: Organisations, Mouvements et Unités de l'État Français*, Paris: Jacques Grancher, 1992.

Lambert, Pierre Philippe, and Gérard Le Marec, *Les Français sous le casque allemand*, Paris: Jacques Grancher, 1994.

Lankenau, D. B., *Polizei im Einsatz während des Krieges 1939-1945 in Rheinland-Westfalen*, Bremen: H. M. Hauschild, 1957.

Leide, Henry, *NS-Verbrecher und Staatssicherheit: Die geheime Vergangenheitspolitik der DDR*, Göttingen: Vandenhoeck & Ruprecht, 2007.

Lieb, Peter, *Konventioneller Krieg oder NS-Weltanschauungskrieg? Kriegführung und Partisanenbekämpfung in Frankreich 1943/44*, München: Oldenbourg, 2007.

——, *Vercors 1944: Resistance in the French Alps*, London: Osprey Publishing, 2012.

Littlejohn, David, *Foreign Legions of the Third Reich*. Vol. 1, *Norway, Denmark, France*, San Jose, CA: R. James Bender Publishing, 1979.

Lozowick, Yaacov, *Hitler's Bureaucrats: The Nazi Security Police and the Banality of Evil*, New York: Continuum Press, 2000.

Marrus, Michael R., and Robert O. Paxton, *Vichy France and the Jews*, New York: Basic Books, 1981.

Martens, Stefan, ed., *Frankreich und Belgien unter deutscher Besatzung 1940–1944: Die Bestände des Bundesarchiv-Militärarchivs Freiburg*, Stuttgart: Franz Steiner Verlag, 2002.

Mehner, Kurt, *Die geheimen Tagesberichte der Deutschen Wehrmachtführung im Zweiten Weltkrieg 1939-1945*, 12 vols. Osnabrück: Biblio Verlag, 1983-1992.

Meinen, Insa, *Wehrmacht und Prostitution während des Zweiten Weltkrieges im besetzten Frankreich*, Bremen: Edition Temmen, 2002.

Mendelsohn, John, ed., *Covert Warfare: Intelligence, Counterintelligence, and Military Deception During the World War II Era*. Vol. 13, *The Final Solution of the Abwehr*, New York: Garland Publishing, 1989.

Meyer, Ahlrich, *Die deutsche Besatzung in Frankreich 1940-1944: Widerstandbekämpfung und Judenverfolgung*, Darmstadt: Wissenschaftliche Buchgesellschaft, 2000.

Michman, Dan, *Belgian Jewry and the Holocaust: Survivors, Victims, Perpetrators*, New York: Yad Vashem, 2001.

Mitcham, Samuel W., Jr., *Panzer Legions: A Guide to the German Army Tank Divisions of WWII and Their Commanders*, Mechanicsburg: Stackpole Books, 2007.

Moore, Bob, *Victims and Survivors: The Nazi Persecution of the Jews in the Netherlands 1940-1945*, Amsterdam: Amsterdam University Press, 1997.

Muñoz, Antonio J., *The German Secret Field Police in Greece, 1941-1944*, Jefferson: McFarland & Co., Inc., 2018.

——, *Hitler's Green Army: The German Orpo and Their European Auxiliaries, Volume 1, Western Europe and Scandinavia*, New York: Europa Books, 2005.

Ousby, Ian, *Occupation: The Ordeal of France 1940-1944*, London: Jonathan Cape, 1997.

Overy, Richard, Gerhard Otto, and Johannes Houwink ten Cate, eds., *Die 'Neuordnung' Europas: NS-Wirtschaftspolitik in den besetzten Gebieten*, Berlin: Metropol, 1997.

Paxton, Robert O., *Vichy France: Old Guard and New Order, 1940-1944*, New York: Alfred A. Knopf, 1972.

——, *Vichy France and the Jews*, New York: Basic Books, 1981.

Ready, J. Lee, *The Forgotten Axis: Germany's Partners and Foreign Volunteers in World War Two.* Vol. 1, Jefferson, NC: McFarland Publishing, 1987.

Regenberg, Werner, *Armoured Vehicles and Units of the German Orpo (Ordnungspolizei) 1936-1945*, Atglen, PA: Schiffer Military History, 2002.

Rémond, René, *Frankreich im 20. Jahrhundert: 1918 bis 1958*, Stuttgart: Kohlhammer, 1994.

Rousso, Henry. *The Vichy Syndrome: History and Memory in France Since 1944*, translated by Arthur Goldhammer. Cambridge, MA: Harvard University Press, 1991.

Sajer, Guy, The Forgotten Soldier, New York: Harper & Row, 1971.

Schumann, Wolfgang, and Ludwig Nestler, eds, *Europa unterm Hakenkreuz: Dokumentenedition. Frankreich (1940-1944)*, Berlin: Dietz Verlag, 1990.

Sellier, André, A *History of the Gestapo*, translated by Jessica Spengler, Oxford: Polity Press, 2003.

Soulier, Antoine, *Le drame de Tulle. 9 juin 1944*, reprint, Naves: [Publisher], 2002. Originally published 1954.

Sourd, Jean-Pierre, *True Believers: Spanish Volunteers in the Heer and Waffen-SS, 1944–1945*, New York: Europa Books, 2004.

Stephan, Yann, *A Broken Sword: Policing France During the German Occupation*, Chicago: University of Illinois Press, 1992.

Taylor, Telford, *The March of Conquest: The German Victories in Western Europe, 1940*, New York: Simon & Schuster, 1958.

Tessin, Georg, *Verbände und Truppen der Deutschen Wehrmacht und Waffen-SS, 1939–1945*, 18 vols, Osnabrück: Biblio Verlag, 1974–1991.

Tessin, Georg, and Norbert Kannapin, *Waffen-SS und Ordnungspolizei im Kriegseinsatz 1939-1945: Ein Überblick anhand der Feldpostübersicht*, Osnabrück: Biblio Verlag, 2000.

Tewes, Ludger, *Frankreich in der Besatzungszeit 1940-1943: Die Sicht deutscher Augenzeugen*, Bonn: Bouvier, 1998.

Umbreit, Hans, *Der Militärbefehlshaber in Frankreich 1940-1944, Wehrwissenschaftliche Forschungen*, Boppard am Rhein: Harald Boldt Verlag, 1968.

Umbreit, Hans, 'The Role of the Wehrmacht in the Occupied Territories', in *Germany and the Second World War*, Vol. 5/2, edited by Bernhard R. Kroener, Rolf-Dieter Müller, and Hans Umbreit, Oxford: Clarendon Press, 2000, pp. 935–65.

Van den Wijngaert, Mark, *The Belgian Resistance during World War II*, Brussels: Royal Library of Belgium, 2010.

Van Goethem, Herman, *The Antwerp School: Jewish and Catholic Collaboration and Resistance in Belgium*, New York: Berghahn Books, 2008.

Volontaire. Francs-tireurs et partisans français. Région de la Corrèze et du Lot. n.p., n.d.

Weidinger, Otto, *Division Das Reich. Der Weg der 2. SS-Panzer Division 'Das Reich'.* Bd. 5. Osnabrück, 1982. Quoted in Lieb, Peter, *Krieg in der Ukraine: Der deutsche Kampf gegen die Sowjetunion 1941-1944*, p. 112.

Wieviorka, Olivier, *The French Resistance*, translated by Jane Marie Todd, Cambridge, MA: Harvard University Press, 2016.

Yonque, Marcel, *La guerre 1939-1945. Saint-Mihiel et la Meuse. Les combats. L'occupation. La liberation*, Saint-Mihiel: Éditions Sphères, 2000.

Zielinski, Bernd, *Staatskollaboration: Vichy und der Arbeitskräfteeinsatz im Dritten Reich*, Theorie und Geschichte der Bürgerlichen Gesellschaft 11. Münster: Westfälisches Dampfboot, 1995.

NAME INDEX

FORMATION INDEX

Reconnaissance Units
Sicherungs Aufklärungs-Abteilung 1000,
    ix, 109, 111, 140, 173

Regional Defence Units
Landesschützenregiment 22, 206–07
Landesschützenregiment 34, 202
Landesschützenregiment 35, 207
Landesschützenregiment 44, 198
Landesschützenregiment 64, 200
Landesschützenregiment 65, 200
Landesschützenregiment 66, 198
Landesschützenregiment 94, 197
Landesschützenregiment 95, 202
Landesschützen-Regiment 115, 206
Landesschützenbataillon 279, 200
Landesschützenbataillon 385, 202
Landesschützenbataillon 388, 200
Landesschützenbataillon 389, 200
Landesschützenbataillon 418, 203
Landesschützenbataillon 425, 197
Landesschützenbataillon 452, 200
Landesschützenbataillon 453, 200
Landesschützenbataillon 454, 200
Landesschützenbataillon 455, 200
Landesschützenbataillon 459, 200
Landesschützenbataillon 480, 200
Landesschützenbataillon 484, 205
Landesschützenbataillon 485, 206
Landesschützenbataillon 525, 205–06
Landesschützenbataillon 526, 206
Landesschützenbataillon 541, 197
Landesschützenbataillon 550, 207
Landesschützenbataillon 579, 200
Landesschützenbataillon 582, 200
Landesschützenbataillon 605, 200
Landesschützenbataillon 625, 206
Landesschützenbataillon 626, 207
Landesschützenbataillon 627, 206
Landesschützenbataillon 641, 200
Landesschützenbataillon 651, 205
Landesschützenbataillon 654, 203
Landesschützenbataillon 657, 206
Landesschützenbataillon 658, 200
Landesschützenbataillon 677, 200
Landesschützenbataillon 678, 200
Landesschützenbataillon 691, 200
Landesschützenbataillon 712, 207
Landesschützenbataillon 733, 200
Landesschützenbataillon 737, 206
Landesschützenbataillon 745, 200
Landesschützenbataillon 746, 200

Landesschützenbataillon 768, 202
Landesschützenbataillon 770, 205
Landesschützenbataillon 771, 205
Landesschützenbataillon 773, 205
Landesschützenbataillon 774, 205–06
Landesschützenbataillon 775, 206
Landesschützenbataillon 785, 205
Landesschützenbataillon 835, 207
Landesschützenbataillon 837, 207
Landesschützenbataillon 845, 200
Landesschützenbataillon 863, 207
Landesschützenbataillon 889, 202
Landesschützenbataillon 903, 200
Landesschützenbataillon 904, 200
Landesschützenbataillon 908, 207

Frontier Guard Units
Grenzwach-Regiment Clüver, 205

Kampfgruppen
Kampfgruppe Hellmuth Abel, 173
Kampfgruppe Rittmeister Coelle, 173
Kampfgruppe Johann Enss, 173
Kampfgruppe Schäfer, 188
Kampfgruppe Zabel, 180

**Field Police and Secret Field Police
  Units**
Feldgendarmerie-Bataillon 3 (motorisiert),
    142
3. Feldgendarmerie-Ersatz-Kompanie, 198
1. Feldgendarmerie-Ersatz-Kompanie, 205
2. Feldgendarmerie-Ersatz-Kompanie, 205
Feldgendarmerie-Trupp 64, 171
Feldgendarmerie-Trupp 584, 197
Feldgendarmerie-Trupp 757, 197
Feldgendarmerie-Trupp 785, 197
Feldgendarmerie-Trupp 796, 197
Feldgendarmerie-Trupp 896, 197
Feldgendarmerie-Trupp 903, 197
Feldgendarmerie-Trupp 923, 197
Feldgendarmerie-Trupp 933, 197
Abwehrstelle GFP Gruppe Angers, 200
Abwehrstelle GFP Gruppe Brest, 201
Abwehrstelle GFP Gruppe Rennes, 201
Geheimfeldpolizei-Gruppe 1, 35
Geheimfeldpolizei-Gruppe 2, 28, 30, 34
Geheimfeldpolizei-Gruppe 3, 29, 32, 35–6
Geheimfeldpolizei-Gruppe 7, 28, 30, 35, 202
Geheimfeldpolizei-Gruppe 8, 29, 35–6
Geheimfeldpolizei-Gruppe 9, 29
Geheimfeldpolizei-Gruppe 10, 32